MW01265341

PRESENTS

REPERCUSSIONS

A novel written by

SHAWN STARR

ACKNOWLEDGEMENTS

My heart is indicting a good matter: I speak of the things which I have made touching the King: My tongue is the pen of a ready writer.

THANK YOU FOR BUYING AND READING THIS BOOK.

First and foremost, I would like to say thank you to the Almighty. Without you Lord, I would be a hopeless cause with hopeless intentions. **Thank you.**

I would also like to scream Thank you to all of those who have supported me by purchasing and reading my debut novel DARK INFIDELITY. Thank you all. You all have made my dream a reality, and I'm forever grateful.

To Authoress Redd, my Publisher/mentor; thank you Boss lady. Not only have you given me an opportunity, you've also extended my skills and knowledge. . . And to my extended family at Gutta Publication$; Kim Kaye, Authoress Coco Amoure, Mizz Butterfly, and Mizz Kiki, much love ladies, you all have helped and guided me through another journey.

Thanks also to my sisters Andrea, Allison, and Arlene. The support you all have shown is the kind of support that can only be shown out of love. To Sid, my older brother; here is one more to add to your collection, Bruh. And to my nieces, Shawna, Tiffany, and Shanika, much love.

I would also like to say thanks to Theresa, for always being kind, caring and loving. And to Kimiesha, Nikki Chin, Marsha, Keisha, Cassie, Stephanie, Tameka, Fiona Mcvie, Georgia, Ingrid, Nicola, Yolonda, Tamika, Tricia, Kizzy, Keda, and Annie, thank you all. Also thank you to all of those who I haven't mentioned, thanks for being supportive of me and what I do.

And to Trimane, Rookie, Nutsy, Buju, Carloydė, Ipie, Stulu, Gary and Tokey, we've proven to the world that there is no price on true friendship.

Thanks also to the millions of readers across the globe. Without the support and dedication of you all, my fellow writers and I would have no reason, aim, or drive to do what we do; so much thanks.
I would also like to say thanks and much love to my parents. And to my three beautiful daughters, Toriann, Tamiann, and Dashay, an abundance of love to the three of you.
And finally, I'd like to turn my eyes up above and say, "I miss you my brother, Oliver 'Mojo' Kerr, you're gone but you'll never be forgotten. . . RIP Bruh."

*May God bless you all, and I hope you all enjoy this book and the others that I have coming. And feel free to reach out to me via email at **shawn.kerr01@gmail.com**, or inbox me (Shawn Starr) on facebook.*

PROLOGUE

"Oh God, help me," mumbled a scared Scott Rosenberg, as he loosened the knot of his pink silk tie and swallowed the lump inside of his throat. Fear was emanating from his pores like steam, and the worry lines etched across his forehead were wide and deep.

Even though the small visiting room was frigid cold; the stocky, gray headed Jew was sweating profusely. He had already pissed on himself twice. And the fearful twist inside of his gut had him squirming in his seat, and wishing that he was a Kindergarten school teacher and not one of the most acclaimed criminal defense attorneys in the state.

Tall, extremely black and built like a linebacker, Mike Simms, AKA Blood, turned to face his fear-filled lawyer. "Listen here, you piece 'f shit," he snarled angrily, with his teeth gritted and his face twisted. His big, bald head was glistening. His blood red eyes were huge. And the orange jumpsuit that he had on, seemed to be a couple of sizes too small for his muscular frame.

"I don't give a fuck what you've got to do to get me outta here," he continued harshly. "But get me the fuck out and get me out fast, befo' I kill somebody in this shit."

Scott Rosenberg stiffened and stuttered, "You ha-have to be patient, Mr. Simms. These things t-take ti—"

"Don't tell me to be fucking patient!" Blood leaned across the table and barked in the lawyer's face. "I've been in jail for three fuckin' days now! How much more patience do you want me to have?"

"I'm doing my best to get you a bond."

With his nose flaring, Blood glared angrily at the petrified lawyer. His red abysmal eyes had him looking monstrous, vile, and wicked, just like the murderous drug dealer that he was known as.

After close to a decade of flooding the streets of South Florida with drugs and committing several murders, Blood was finally indicted and arrested; and then hit with a murder charge that had him in a firm strangle hold, with a life sentence dangling above his head.

It wasn't his first time being arrested; however it was by far his longest stay inside of the county jail.

As the driving force behind a multi-million dollar drug empire, Blood had the hands of quite a few cops, prosecutors, and lawyers inside of his pocket. Usually he would've bonded out hours after his arrest. Then like magic, the charges would suddenly disappear. But when the case file for his most recent murder, accidentally landed on the desk of a prosecutor who wasn't on his payroll; a warrant was immediately issued for his arrest and he was quickly arrested and charged.

"What the fuck you mean by you trying your best to get me a bond?" Blood fumed, with his jaws twitching. "I'm not paying you to try, mothafucka! I'm paying you and every cock-sucking cop and prosecutor around town, to keep me outta shit like this."

"But it's not in our hands."

"Fuck whose hands it's in!" Blood raged, as he pounded a fist down on the table. He paused for air and then stated violently, "With all of the fuckin' money that I gave you, you've still got me in this shit. Asshole, you need to get me the fuck out."

The lawyer dropped his head. He then removed his wire-rimmed specs, as he wiped his teary eyes. He knew that Blood was guilty. His finger prints and DNA were all over the machete that was used to hack the victim to pieces.

The newspaper had described the killing as barbaric; an act of savagery that could've only been done by a monster. The victim's mother, who was forced to watch the killing, was left traumatized and demented. Several psychiatrists had deemed her mentally ill and unbalanced. They made it clear that she wasn't capable of testifying against Blood, who she had fingered out as her son's killer.

After a brief pause, to gather his thoughts, the lawyer pinched the bridge of his nose and then muttered, "Getting your case out of this prosecutor's hands won't be easy, Mr. Simms. It's not like I haven't been trying."

"Then you need to try harder!" Blood roared, with clenched fists and bulging eyes. "Did you even offer the bitch any money?"

"Wha-what?" The lawyer asked, shakily.

"You heard me!" Blood barked. "Did you offer her any fuckin' money?"

"No... Not as—"

"What the fuck are you waiting on?"

"Sh-she's not the type." Rosenberg stuttered quietly. "She's not gonna t-take it."

Blood snatched up the metal chair and flung it into the wall, across the room. "Fuck what she'll take!" He barked, behind darts of spittle. "I don't give a fuck what you've got to do to make her drop this charge, but you had better have her do it. You hear me?! I want this charge gone! Gone mothafucka! GONE!"

The lawyer sucked in a deep breath. He then wiped his sweaty forehead and muffled quietly, "She's not gonna do it, because she knows that you're guilty."

"I know that I'm guilty!" Blood raged, as he reached across the table and grabbed the lawyer by the front of his jacket. "Let me tell you something you cock-sucking Jew," he snarled in the lawyer's face. "I'm not gonna do time because of you or this ho. I want you to find out everything about the bitch. I want her name, her phone number, her address, even the name of her fucking dog if she has one."

The lawyer's eyes got wide. "Wha-what?" He asked, with his lips quivering and tears rolling down his cheeks. "What are you gonna do?"

Blood twisted his lips and his nose flared. "Since all you mothafuckas that I'm paying can't get her to drop my fucking charge, then I'm gonna have a couple of my boys pay her a visit. I bet that she'll drop my charges then."

"You can't threaten a prosecutor, Mr. Simms. That's illegal." With a sudden move that the lawyer wasn't expecting, Blood grabbed him by the back of his head and then he slammed his face down on the desk.

"How's that for illegal, mothafucka? Now get your puss-ass outta here, before I break yo' fuckin' jaw!"

CH-1

A late afternoon cloudburst had left a light mist over Broward County. The heavy downpour had gone on for about twenty minutes. But it was twenty minutes of clapping lightening, roaring thunder, and more rain than the county had seen in months.

Despite the feel of a miserable day, the walkway that led up to the main entrance of the Broward County courthouse was a bit more crowded than usual. There were a handful of police officers sprinkled about; along with at least four different media crews that were standing by with microphones, tape recorders, and video cameras in hand.

A well-known reporter from the Miami Herald was the first to spot the prosecutor and her assistant, who were both hurrying towards the courthouse, with determination in their strides. Without even informing his cohorts, the reporter with a small tape recorder in his hand rushed the prosecutor.

"Miss Clarke! Miss Clarke!" He shouted, with the tape recorder outstretched. "Will Mr. Simms be convicted this time? Or will he just walk away, like he always does?"

"That's for the judge and a jury to decide," the feisty prosecutor answered in a cool, yet flat tone.

Another reporter who saw the prosecutor rushed over and shoved a microphone in her face. "What about the charges that were brought up against him in the past?" The female reporter asked. "Will any of them be brought up against him again?"

Still walking, the prosecutor replied, "Those charges are not in his files, so I doubt it."

"Is it true that a couple of your co-workers are on Mr. Simms' payroll?"

The prosecutor stopped to look at the reporter who asked the question. She glared at him angrily, and then stated in a firm, harsh tone, "Mr. Simms may have a lot of pull and clout around town. But I'm certain that he has no influence inside of the State Attorney's office."

With a slow cut of her eyes, the prosecutor turned away. Then with her assistant by her side, she bored her way through the crowd and away from the media chaos.

At thirty three, Amelia Clarke was seated at the number two position inside of the State Attorney's office. She was bold, bright and intelligent, a feisty prosecutor with a witty attitude and an impressive one hundred percent conviction record. Well known for her no-nonsense disposition, Amelia wasn't one of those prosecutors who were always quick to back down and settle for absurd plea deals. She was a force to be reckoned with inside of the courtroom. However, those who knew her away from work knew that she was a sweetheart, and one of the most caring human beings there is.

Saying that she was beautiful was an understatement. Because many tagged her as drop dead gorgeous with her quiet elegance, wickedly sexy eyes, and radiant smile.

Dressed in a navy blue, curve-hugging skirt suit and sky high stilettos, Amelia had her jet black hair flowing freely and loose, in an array of soft, shiny curls, which stopped above her shoulders. Her dark-brown, doe-like eyes were bright behind her Chanel framed specs. And her toffee colored skin seemed flawless.

Her full pouted lips was one of her many erotic assets, but her perfectly shaped ass was what drew the attention of men from every ethnicity. She had curves to die for. And her body was well toned because of the many hours that she spent inside of the gym each week.

As soon as she got away from the crowd and stepped into the courthouse, Amelia ripped off her specs. "I just hate these damn high profile cases," she complained agitatedly.

"So why don't you just leave it alone?"

Amelia stopped and turned her head to face the familiar voice, which echoed from her right. Her lips then curled into a warm, graceful smile when she saw Rick Montgomery walking towards her.

Just seeing him warmed her from the inside out. And she had to take a deep breath, just to ease her tightening pelvis and the light churning inside of her gut.

"Hey there Handsome, what's up?" She beamed pleasantly, when he got up-close.

He embraced her, and then kissed her gently on the lips. "What happened to you last night?" He asked, looking her in the face. "I called you like ten times."

"I was at home," Amelia replied. "But I was going over the police report for the Simms case, so I had the ringer on my phone turned off."

He locked eyes with her, and then he shook his head slowly. "I just wish that you'd leave that case alone, 'Melia. I'm worried for you," he protested in a very concerned tone.

She placed a graceful hand to his chest, and then she flashed him a reassuring smile. "There's no need for you to worry, Rick. Mike Simms ain't getting outta jail," she told him.

"Mike Simms ain't got to be free to get things done, 'Melia. The man is rich, powerful and ruthless."

"I know everything about Mike Simms," Amelia revealed, not daunted. "I also know what he's capable of doing, however I'm not intimidated."

"I know you're not."

"Then stop worrying. I'm a big girl. I know how to take care of myself."

Rick sighed heavily. He then dropped his head as he pinched the bridge of his nose.

Rick Montgomery was the closest thing Amelia had to a boyfriend. He was perceived as a sweetheart, a well poised and intelligent black man who had his affairs in life well intact. He too was a prosecutor. He wasn't as successful as Amelia, but his conviction record was almost just as impressive.

Standing at six-two, Rick was very handsome and well built at thirty five years old. He wasn't the most outspoken, but with bold confidence he carried himself like a GQ model.

The entire State Attorney's office knew about the crush that Rick had on Amelia. He was actually doing everything in his power to make her his wife. But Amelia was clearly in no rush to commit herself to marriage. She felt comfortable with what they had going on, so she didn't see the need to change anything.

After a brief pause, Rick raised his head and said, "I don't know what I would do if anything was to happen to you." Amelia handed her briefcase to her assistant. She then reached up to straighten Rick's black tie. "There's no need for you to worry," she grinned with a playful wink. "Mike Simms may be heartless, but he ain't dumb. Even he knows that harming a state prosecutor is a federal offense." She winked again. "So what's up? What you got going on today?"

Rick studied her face for several beats, and then he checked the time on his TAG Heuer. "Damn," he muttered, when he saw 3:57 pm. "Hey, I've got a four o'clock inside of Judge Felder's courtroom..." he stated reluctantly. "Do you feel like going out tonight?"

Amelia pursed her lips thoughtfully. "I'm not sure about tonight," she told him. "But once I'm through with Mike Simms' arraignment, I'll give you a call."

Something flickered in Rick's eyes and a toothy smile broke out across his face. "Please do," he said, as he stepped off.

"I definitely will," Amelia assured, as she stood and watched him hurry away.

A few quiet seconds ticked by before Amelia's assistant cleared her throat and pulled Amelia out of her lustful trance. "You're so in love," she teased, while staring suggestively at Amelia.

Amelia rolled her eyes at her playfully. "You don't know what I'm in," she giggled lightly. "But if we don't get our asses inside of Judge Horne's courtroom, we're going to be in a whole lot of shit."

$$\$$$

Danielle stepped out of the hotel's bathroom, with a large white towel in her hand and no clothes on. Her naked body was dripping wet and glowing as she walked on by the TV, which was sitting on the table across the room.

At five-six, Danielle was known as a daring provocateur, that wasn't shy or hesitant when it came to showing off her curvaceous body. Her beauty was average, but her smile was beautiful and she had the most erotic eyes that a woman could be blessed with.

As she strode over to where her clothes were laid out on the armchair, she smiled down at the naked man on the bed. She had met him earlier at the Sawgrass Mills mall. He wasn't as handsome as she liked for her men to be. However, the platinum Rolex on his wrist, along with the blood red Mercedes that he was driving was enough to tell her that he was ballin'; ballin' so much that he offered to pay the $2000 shopping bill that she had racked up inside of the Gucci store. Danielle, without even thinking things through, quickly accepted his offer. She even told him "yes" when he invited her back to his hotel room.

"Are you gonna take me back to my car? Or should I call a cab?" She asked him, as she tried her best not to look at the ugly two inch scar below his left eye.

He kept his eyes on the TV. "I'll drop you off," he mumbled. "But I'm waiting on a phone call. I can't leave before I get that call, so just chill out for a minute."

"You know that I can't afford to miss work for the entire day, right?"

"You can afford it," he said, while shifting his head towards the wad of twenty dollar bills on the night stand.

As soon as Danielle saw the money, her eyes lit up.

"Is that fo' me?" She turned and asked animatedly.

He nodded.

She then dropped the towel and leaped onto the bed. "In that case, we can stay and fuck all day if you want to."

He looked her dead in the face, as she straddled him. "I thought you said you had enough?" He asked easily.

"I did. But now I feel like going again," she chortled lightly, before leaning over and nibbling kisses on his neck. She took her time trailing kisses across his shoulder, down his chest, and then over his stomach.

He watched her for a while, before putting a hand at the top of her head to urge her down. "Put it in your mouth," he told her, as she took a hold of his expanding manhood.

She looked up in his face and caught sight of the ugly two inch scar below his eye. It caused her to shudder lightly, but she hid her disgust.

"I'm not into sucking dick," she lied with a playful smirk. "But I'll do it if it's worth it."

He took hold of her upper arm and pulled her up to his chest. "In my world, money's not an issue," he told her. "So if you're worried about it, don't."

She raised an eyebrow and then she smiled at him delightfully.

"By the way," he continued, as he palmed her ass. "Ain't you good friends with that prosecutor chick, Amelia?"

Danielle's reaction was placid. "We're good friends... Why?" She asked, after a thoughtful moment.

"You down fo' making some serious cash?"

Danielle sat up with a puzzled look on her face. She folded her arms across her enhanced double D's, and then she pouted as if she was upset. "I'm always down fo' making money," she pointed out clearly. "However, if you're trying to have a threesome with me and my friend, that shit ain't gonna happen." She cut her eyes at him and sucked her teeth. "Besides, Amelia ain't even like that."

"This ain't got nothing to do with no threesome," he said, as he pulled her back down to his chest.

"So what is it about? And what does me making this money, have to do with Amelia?"

He ran a finger up her crack, and then let his hand settle at the small of her back. "I'll let you know, just as soon as I get this phone call that I'm waiting on."

$$\$$$

The courtroom was in full swing, when Amelia stepped inside. Police officers and courthouse employees were up and about busily, trying to get things in order; and a handful of prosecutors were seated to the right, talking quietly amongst themselves.

There were about a dozen defendants waiting to be arraigned. But there was over twice that amount downstairs, inside of the holding cell, waiting to face the Judge.

Judge Horne, in his usual snail pace manner was the one presiding over the arraignments. He was looking cool, calm, and collected, as he dawdled over each case, as if he was in no hurry at all. Other Judges usually took four to six minutes with an arraignment, but Judge Horne always took ten to fifteen.

"How many arraignments you got?"

Marching down the busy aisle, Amelia turned her head to look at her assistant. "I think it's like four," she answered. "But my number one priority is to keep that murderer, Mike Simms, in jail."

Amelia got to where the prosecutors were seated and found her co-worker, Selena Estefan, reading a case file. "Any luck on getting Judge Horne to go any faster?" She asked jokingly.

"Are you serious?" Selena answered, with an agitated roll of her eyes. "He wouldn't go any faster even if someone held a gun to his head."

Amelia cupped a hand over her mouth and chuckled quietly. "In that case, I might as well get comfortable," she said, as she looked over in the stands at the defendants, who were all wearing orange jumpsuits.

It didn't take her long to spot Blood in the front row. He was glaring viciously at her, with his lips twisted and his jaws twitching. She locked eyes with him and they stared steadily at each other—neither wanting to be the first to blink, or the first to look away.

A single bang of the Judge's gavel was what pulled Amelia out of the deadlock. But just as she was about to take a seat next to Selena, the court clerk called the case, "State of Florida versus Mike Simms."

Quickly retrieving Blood's case file, Amelia's assistant turned to Amelia and said, "It's got to be your lucky day, 'cause we were right on time."

Amelia took the case file and asked quietly, "Did you see how that bastard was looking at me?"

"I saw him... Are you scared?"

"Never that," Amelia replied brazenly, as she turned away and then hurried up to the prosecutor's table.

Blood was cuffed by one of the officers and escorted to the defense table. Scott Rosenberg was there waiting. He was wearing a grey pinstripe suit, with a band aid across the bridge of his broken nose.

"Mr. Simms, you are being arraigned at this time," Judge Horne mumbled into the microphone, without even looking up from the papers on his desk. In a very slow, boring manner, he then went on to explain that Blood was being charged with first degree murder, a charge that carried a sentence of life imprisonment or death.

After about three additional minutes of reading quietly to himself, the old beady eyed Judge raised his head and looked at Amelia. "Where are we on bail?" He asked her.

Amelia glanced over at Scott Rosenberg, who had a very worried look on his face. "The state is asking that the defendant be held without bail, your honor."

"Bitch, you trippin'!" Blood interrupted loudly.

"Excuse me?" Judge Horne spat surprisingly, with his eyes narrowed on Blood.

Scott Rosenberg held onto Blood's arm and then he addressed the Judge, "Please forgive my client, your honor. He's been locked up for a while now. And as you can see, he's clearly frustrated."

"I don't care if they had him locked up for a hundred years. The next outburst I get from him, we'll be doing this arraignment with him downstairs in a holding cell... Are we clear, counselor?"

"Yes your Honor," Rosenberg answered respectfully.

The Judge turned his eyes on Blood. "What about you Mr. Simms, do you understand what I just said?"

Blood sucked his teeth.

"I'll take that as a yes," the Judge declared, and then he brought his attention back to Amelia. "Miss Clarke, what is your reason for wanting the defendant to be held without bail?"

Amelia ignored Blood's fiery stare. "The defendant has a very violent history, your Honor. And this is not his first time being arrested and charged with murder."

"All of those charges were dropped," Scott Rosenberg chipped in. "And there is no documented proof of this violent history that Miss Clarke is talking about."

Amelia rolled her eyes at the lawyer. "What happened to your nose, Mr. Rosenberg?" She asked, with a wry grin. A jailhouse guard had tipped her off, about what had happened inside of the visiting room. She was expecting Rosenberg to deny it all, but it didn't matter because her only aim was to let him know that she knew what had happened.

While feeling on his broken nose, Rosenberg asked, "What does my broken nose have to do with my client being granted a bond?"

"Nothing," Amelia smirked, with an easy shrug. "It's just that I was told that he's the one who did it."

Rosenberg looked at Blood.

Blood glared back at him angrily, but kept his mouth shut.

"Mr. Rosenberg, is this true?" The Judge asked.

Rosenberg looked over at Amelia, who was looking steadily at him and awaiting his response. He knew that the judge could easily find out the truth, by asking for the tape from the visiting room. And because he didn't want to get caught up in a lie and end up in a cell on a perjury charge, he dropped his head.

"I'll take your silence as a yes," the judge said. He paused for a moment to once again read over the papers on the desk in front of him. When he was through, he raised his head to look at Amelia. "I don't see anything on these papers about Mr. Simms' violent history."

"That's because there's none," Rosenberg quipped, with his voice quivering. "My client may not be the most outstanding citizen in the world, but he's definitely not a violent person, your honor."

"Humph," Amelia huffed and then she brought her attention back to the Judge. "Your honor, the complaint form will show that the victim's mother —"

"She's been deemed incompetent," Rosenberg interrupted loudly.

"Incompetent or not, we can't afford to put her in harm's way." Amelia paused to look down at her notes. "There's no question that Mr. Simms should be held without bail. Allowing him to return to the streets will not only endanger the life of our witness. There's also a possibility that he'll try to use his money and his connections to infringe on the outcome of the case."

"That's pure assumption." Rosenberg announced.

"Mr. Rosenberg," The judge said calmly. "There's no reason for us to be going back and forth about this. I'm setting a preliminary hearing for two weeks from today."

"Two weeks?" Rosenberg questioned, as if he was stunned. "Why so long?"

"Two weeks is fine with me, your Honor," Amelia replied.

Rosenberg shot Amelia a nasty look, and then he set his eyes back on the judge. "Two weeks is definitely too long for my client to be sitting around waiting; and what about his bond?" He questioned nervously.

The Judge peered angrily at Rosenberg, and then he continued as if he wasn't rudely interrupted. "It's my duty as the judge, to weigh the facts and render a decision," he explained clearly. "And based on what I've seen and heard, I have no choice but to keep Mr. Simms locked up." He slammed his gavel down on the desk and then announced, "Bail for the defendant is denied."

CH-2

The arraignments were now over with, and Amelia, her assistant, and a couple of co-workers were now gathered inside of the main corridor of the courthouse, just to chit chat.

The corridor was very noisy, with a small crowd making its way to the exit. The media crews were also hurrying away, trying to be the first to get whatever news that they had attained from the courtrooms, out to the public.

Huddled up against the wall, Amelia and her fellow prosecutors were chattering loudly. They were all trying to be heard above the noise, which was coming from the small crowd that was leaving.

Amelia's boss was there. All three hundred and forty five pounds of him were up against the wall, right next to Amelia. To his left was Frank Hibbert, a young but bright prosecutor, who had more gray hair than his age required.

Selena Estefan was the only Hispanic female at the State Attorney's office. She was a good friend of Amelia. However, a lot of the other prosecutors didn't like her because of her cocksure arrogance. She was there standing across from Rick Montgomery, who was staring thoughtfully at Amelia.

"Well, I don't think that he can help it," Selena Estefan was saying. They were talking about Judge Horne and his snail pace arraignments. "I think that he's just senile. After all, he is very old."

"Well I don't think that it has anything to do with old age," Rick turned to Selena and replied. "From what I've heard, he's been that way forever."

"I wonder if he's like that, when he's having sex," Frank Hibbert chipped in jokingly and got everyone to laughing. Amelia slapped him on his shoulder playfully. "Frank, you're such an idiot," she joked. She then hitched a lock of hair behind her ear and was about to say something. Only a sudden shift of the crowd in her peripheral vision caused her to stop and turn her head. That's when she saw who had caused the parting of the crowd, just as Moses had caused the parting of the Red Sea.

He was cuffed and shackled, while walking between two guards and a small entourage of high profile lawyers. Scott Rosenberg was the one leading the charge. The look on his face was pitiful. And he seemed as if he didn't even have the strength to carry the Gucci briefcase in his hand.

Blood, with his face twisted viciously had caused a feel of unease throughout the corridor. If not for the loud chattering of those who had already walked by, the corridor would've been in complete silence.

One could easily tell that the drug dealer wasn't one to be fucked with. The air around him was enough to intimidate others. But Amelia wasn't intimidated at all. She stood with her face scrunched up, staring at him as if he was a piece of rotten meat surrounded by flies.

When he was about four yards away, she pulled off her spectacles and took a deep, settling breath.

Rosenberg was the one who approached her. "Miss Clarke," he said, as he nervously wiped his sweaty forehead. "Do you have a minute? Me and my client would like to have a word with you."

Amelia looked over at her boss. He gave her an approving nod, as he eased away from the wall. He then gathered up the other prosecutors and they all made their way towards the courthouse exit.

"What is this about, Mr. Rosenberg? I thought that we had everything settled inside of the courtroom," Amelia said, as she looked over at the two guards and the other lawyers, who were looking on from a few yards away.

Rosenberg took a quick look around, just to make sure they were out of earshot. He then swallowed hard, before saying at a very low degree, "My client is willing to give you two hundred thousand dollars, if you'll drop his charge, or hand it over to another prosecutor."

A mask of confusion fell over Amelia's face. She cocked her head, and then she looked hard and steadily at Rosenberg. "I don't think that I heard you correctly…" She fumed in a calm, yet composed way. "Did you just offer me two hundred thousand dollars, to drop your client's charge or to give up his case?"

Rosenberg glanced doubtfully over at Blood, and then he whipped his eyes back on Amelia. "Is two hundred thousand not enough?" He asked shakily.

Amelia waited a while, before asking in a crisp, firm tone, "Are you actually trying to bribe me?"

Rosenberg's eyes got wide and his mouth inched open. In a very panicky way, he dabbed his sweaty forehead with his handkerchief and then stuttered quietly, "M-Miss Clarke, this is not a d-demand. We're just asking."

Amelia huffed out an angry breath, and then she glowered at him, "You of all people should know me better, Rosenberg. Are you fucking serious?" She lashed out.

"Let's make it four hundred thousand, in cash."

Amelia turned her head to look at Blood. She cut her eyes at him before saying. "You seem to be taking me for someone else. Mr. Simms, I'm a state prosecutor, do you really think that you can pay me off?"

Rosenberg stepped quickly between them. "Not so loud, please." He begged with a wild look in his eyes. "Miss Clarke, could you at least think about it?"

Amelia took a step back, with her face veiled with rage. "There's nothing for me to think about, Mr. Rosenberg. I can't be bought." She whipped her head back. "Your client is a cold blooded murderer. I have no intention of letting him walk free."

"So you don't want the money?" Blood questioned impatiently.

REPERCUSSIONS by SHAWN STARR

Amelia shoved her head forward and shot him a hard stare. "No, Mr. Simms, I don't," she hissed firmly. "What I want is for you to spend the rest of your life in prison, for what you did." She snapped her head around to face Rosenberg. "As for you," she scrunched up her face at him. "I'm gonna act as if this didn't happen. But if you ever step to me like that again, I promise you, you'll be joining your client in prison."

Ashamed and embarrassed, Rosenberg dropped his head. "Miss Clarke, I'm really sorry about this. I do apologize," he whimpered.

"What the fuck do you mean, you sorry?!" Blood exploded at Rosenberg. "Man, fuck that cock-sucking ho," he scowled at Amelia with murder in his eyes. "Bitch, do you know who the fuck I am?"

Amelia didn't back down.

"I don't care who you are!" She barked in his face. "I'm not afraid of you. Put your hands on me and I'll add another charge to what you already have."

"Bitch, fuck you!" Blood roared.

Cuffed and shackled, he scrambled towards Amelia. Only he was quickly grabbed around the waist and pulled away by the two guards, who were escorting him.

With her pulse racing, her lips tight, and her fists balled up, Amelia stood her ground. She was ready to defend herself if she had to. A small crowd had gathered and several courthouse employees had heard the commotion and ran over.

"Amelia!" Rick shouted, as he came running down the hallway. He was looking worried with his briefcase dangling from his hand. "Are you okay?" He asked, just as soon as he got up to her.

Amelia ignored him. Her eyes were fixed on Blood, who was being hauled away.

"Watch your back, bitch! Watch your fucking back!" He was shouting fiercely. "You wanna fuck with me… Then I'm gonna fuck with yo' stink ass, so watch your fucking back!"

After about an hour of threatening Amelia and his lawyers, Blood was escorted back to his dormitory and relieved of his handcuffs and shackles. Not wanting to talk to anyone, he charged into his cell; after walking by the other inmates, who were seated inside of the dayroom watching TV.
His eight by twelve cell was gloomy and depressing, a horrid step-down from the three mansions that he owned. Its only furniture was the metal commode, which had a face basin attached; a blurred mirror on the wall, and two steel bunk beds.
 As soon as Blood took a seat on his bunk, he was approached by a heavy set C.O who went by the name of Jackson.
 "What the fuck you want?" Blood glared up at him and asked.
Jackson stepped inside of the cell. "Calm down, playa. I've got something for you from Batch'."
 "What?" Blood asked rudely.
 Jackson pulled a cell phone, a large wad of cash, and a Ziploc bag filled with weed from his pants pockets. He gazed at the money greedily, right before handing everything to Blood.
 "Just holler at me, if you need anything; anything at all," he stated willingly.
Blood powered on the phone, and then he looked up at Jackson. "Is this all that he gave you, to give me? What about the information that he was supposed to get from Rosenberg?"
Jackson hesitated, before rushing into his back pocket. "My bad," he apologized, while handing Blood a piece of paper with Amelia's name, phone number, and address on it. "Is that it?" He asked, as Blood gazed at the piece of paper.
 "Yeah, this is it," Blood nodded, with evil dancing in his eyes.

$$$$$$$$$$$$$$$$$$$$$$$$$

Amelia's favorite restaurant was a small and modest Jamaican restaurant, located on Atlantic Blvd. She ate there at least twice a week, and at times she even called in and ordered take-out.

The food there was spicy, but finger licking good. And their jerk chicken was Amelia's favorite. That is what she was there having, with a serving of rice and a small portion of salad on the side.

"So, what are you going to do?" Rick asked, after wiping his mouth and dropping the napkin on his plate of leftovers. Ever since they walked out of the courthouse, he had wanted to ask Amelia about her situation with Blood. But because they drove to the restaurant in separate vehicles, he didn't get the chance to.

"Do about what?" Amelia raised her head and asked.

Rick took a sip from his glass of water before saying, "After what just happened, I really don't think that you should continue with the prosecution against Mike Simms."

Amelia chuckled quietly, as if what Rick had said was a joke. "Do you really think that I'm gonna let him get away with threatening me. Are you fo' real?" She asked quizzically.

Rick took another sip from his water.

"This guy doesn't make empty threats, Amelia. Do you have any idea of who he really is?"

"He's a murderer and he deserves to be in prison." Amelia went back to her jerk chicken, but raised her head, when she heard Rick sigh heavily. She gave her own exasperated sigh. "Is there something else on your mind?" She asked him, sounding a bit agitated.

Rick stared at her, his dark brown eyes glossy and masked with worry. "Why can't you just leave this case alone?" He asked. "Why can't you just give it to someone else? This is not the kind of guy that you should be messing around with, Amelia. I know for a fact that he'll go to the extreme, just to stay out of prison."

"Are you suggesting that I should let him walk free?"

"If it will keep you safe, then yes."

"Rick, are you serious? I'm not gonna let that monster get away with what he did."

"Then let someone else prosecute him."

"No, I won't. Not when there's this continuous buzz that he's got people at the office working for him."

Rick shook his head agitatedly. "Why you got to be so stubborn?"

"I'm not stubborn," Amelia replied firmly. "I just don't like it when people force me to do, what I don't want to do."

Rick sucked in a lung-full of air before saying, "Give the case to me then. Let me prosecute him." He held her eyes with his. "I just can't sit back and let you put yourself in danger. I know Mike Simms is gonna retaliate against whosoever sends him to prison. So let him retaliate against me, if he has to."

"No," Amelia said flatly.

Rick openhandedly slapped the table. "Goddamn Amelia!" He blurted loud and frustratedly. "What are you trying to prove? The entire office knows how good you are at your job. You don't have to risk your damn life, just to prove it to us!"

Amelia suddenly felt infuriated and breathless. She wiped her mouth and flung the napkin down on the plate. "Do you really think that I'm trying to prove shit to my co-workers?" She asked feistily. "This is not about me, Rick. It's about that guy that was chopped to death!"

"He wasn't any better than Mike Simms. He was a drug dealer too."

"So what if he was? Wasn't he still a human being?"

"Yes he was. But are you trying to end up like him?"

Amelia scowled, "No. But it's my job to make sure that nobody else does."

Rick paused with his face muscles twitching. He was clearly upset, but he wanted to take control of the situation. Therefore he swallowed his frustration and asked, "Do you have any idea how much I love you?"

Amelia sighed, and then she licked her lips. "Rick I know that you do. And I also know that you're just trying to protect me. But this is something that I want to do. Mike Simms deserves to be behind bars," she explained.

"And he will end up there," Rick assured. "I just don't want you to be the one to send him."

"I'm not afraid of Mike Simms."

"This has nothing to do with you being afraid. I just don't want you to get hurt."

Amelia got up from her seat and picked up her jacket, from off of the empty chair to her right. She then reached across the table and kissed Rick on the lips. "I don't want to talk about this anymore, because I'm not stepping away from the case."

He watched her, as she gathered her things. "Are you leaving?" He then asked timidly.

"Yes I am," Amelia replied, after a little sigh. "I'm tired, and I'm badly in need of a shower, so I'm going home."

"Can I come over and spend the night?"

She gave him a considering look. Then right before turning away, she said, "Not tonight, Rick. All of this talking about Mike Simms has killed my appetite for sex."

CH-3

It was 8:45 pm and the Mirage was in full swing. The club was at maximum capacity, with about fifty strippers parading around in skimpy outfits and high heels — every single one of them trying to get a few minutes inside of the V.I.P section, which was being occupied by Rebel and his cohorts.

The Mirage was Broward County's most prestigious strip club. It was located in the downtown Ft. Lauderdale area, less than ten minutes away from the Broward County courthouse. To hang out at the Mirage, you had to have it to spend. Idle conversations with the dancers were not tolerated, and security didn't allow for anyone to just sit around and hang out. The most sexually stimulating strippers from across the country danced at the Mirage. And because of this, the club entertained sports figures, wealthy business men, recording artists; and most of all, top tier drug dealers.

Rebel was seated arms wide on the sofa inside of the VIP section. He had a glass of Hennessy in one hand, a large stack of twenty dollar bills in the other, and a Bob Marley sized blunt dangling from his lips.

Smoking wasn't allowed inside of the Mirage, but the entire VIP section was engulfed in smoke reeking from several blunts. There were eight bottles of Hennessy strewn about, and six bottles of Cristal were inside of ice buckets on the floor.

The small table in front of Rebel had about five thousand dollars worth of one dollar bills, which were all piled on top of each other. But that was nothing compared to what was scattered across the floor at his feet — beneath the four butt-ass naked strippers, who were fondling each other for him to see.

Rebel was Blood's younger brother. The two were similar in appearance, but their tendencies weren't the same. Rebel was nowhere as harsh or as violent as Blood, but he played the part well.

Always wanting to be like his brother, he walked around with his chest puffed out and his face screwed up. He wasn't known to be the smartest drug dealer in the streets. But because of his brother, no one ever said it to his face.

With his hands now all over the stripper who had placed herself across his lap, Rebel was smiling arrogantly. He pried her legs apart and then he groped her. "Ain't this too much pussy fo' one ho?" He asked, through a cloud of smoke.

The stripper giggled flirtatiously. "If it's too much, then why don't you just take some?" She suggested. "I know that you can afford it."

He shot her a curious look behind a very arrogant smile. "You say that as if you know who I am?" He questioned. "Everybody knows who you are, Rebel. You're Blood's younger brother," she replied.

His arrogant smile got even wider. He reached for the glass of Cristal that he was sipping on. But just as he brought it up to his lips, he saw Ice walking back from the bathroom with a pensive look on his face.

Ice entered the VIP section and strode up to Rebel. He brought his lips down to Rebel's ear and said, "I just spoke to Blood, and he's pissed. He said that he's been blowing up your cell phone, and you ain't answering."

As Rebel looked up at Ice, his heart gave a little skip. "I left my phone outside in the car," he said, while looking around in a panicky way. "What was he saying?"

Ice glanced around at the strippers surrounding Rebel. "Yo, why don't you ladies give us a minute," he requested calmly. The three who were on the floor got up and walked away, but the one on Rebel's lap turned and asked with a bit of attitude, "Baby, do you want me to leave?"

Rebel cocked his head and shot her a serious look, before shoving her off his lap. "Bitch, you heard the man. Mothafuckin' bounce!" He lashed out.

Stumbling across the VIP, the stripper snatched up her bra. "You didn't have to do that, you know," she cried out, looking embarrassed.

Rebel snatched up his glass of Hennessy and flung it at her. "Get yo' fuck-ass outta here!" He barked, just as Ice's cell phone blared to life.

Ice looked at the screen and then he looked at Rebel. "It's Blood," he told him, in a not so pleased tone.

Rebel hopped up and took the phone. He accepted the call and quickly brought the phone up to his ear. "Big brah, what's up?" He asked, as he hurried out of the VIP.

With a troubled look on his face, Ice took a seat on the sofa and watched Rebel as he made his way to the bathroom. He already knew what the conversation was about. Blood had already told him what he wanted them to do and he was totally against it. But he knew that he'd only be making it bad for himself, if he said that he was. Because with Blood being in jail and badly wanting to get out, there's no telling what he'd have done to those who weren't very supportive of him, and whatever he had to do to evade his charges.

Dark skinned, athletically built and childishly good looking, Ice was mostly known for his calmness and his rationalism. He was hands down, the smartest of all those Blood had around him. The two were by no means good friends, but because of money they stayed connected.

Ice was twenty nine years old. And after close to five years of working with Blood and putting away the majority of what he was making, he was now ready to step away from the drug game and go legit.

With his elbows on his knees and his hands over his neatly done cornrows, Ice leaned forward and sighed heavily. He kept his eyes on the pair of white air forces on his feet, and his mind fixed on what Blood was instructing them to do.

He knew if they were to get caught doing it, that they would all end up in prison. Not even a crew of the best lawyers in the country would be able to stop them all from doing a lengthy bid.

"What you got going on, brah?"

Pulled from his thoughts, Ice raised his head and found Tip standing over him.

"Niggah, you look like you just got word that you're about to die."

Ice smiled and then he shook his head, while reaching over to pour himself a glass of Cristal. "Dying is inevitable," he said easily. "I don't waste my time thinking about it."

"Well, I do," Tip said, as he took a seat on the sofa next to Ice. "With all of the shit that I've done, I just know that my day ain't far away."

"Brah, you sound like my damn grandmother," Ice smirked, as he fell back onto the sofa. He took a sip from his champagne, and then asked, "So what's up? Where the fuck you been?"

"Around the back with Diamond; Niggah, that bitch sure does know how to suck a dick. She was eating me up like cotton candy."

"You say that about every last one of these strippers," Ice chuckled over his liquor.

"Aayyy Ice," three strippers chimed in unison, as they walked by.

Ice waved at them, but his eyes stayed on Tip. "I got a call from Blood, while you were away," he said.

"Fo' real?" Tip sounded excited.

"Yeah...Rebel's inside the bathroom talking to him, right now."

"Is he out?"

"Naw . . . They denied his bond," Ice replied coolly.

Tip looked away from the dancers on stage and then gave Ice his full attention. "Are you fo' real, brah?" He asked, looking disappointed.

Ice settled deeper down onto the leather sofa. "I'm dead serious," he said, as he checked out a big-ass, dark-skinned Amazon that was walking by. *"Damn, that ho fine,"* he thought. "Who is that?" He asked Tip, while still gazing at the stripper. Tip followed his gaze. "That's Honey. She's only been here a couple days now," he said, as he reached over and poured himself a glass of Hennessy. He took a slow thoughtful sip, before asking, "So what's up with all those mothafuckin' cops and prosecutors that Blood has on his payroll? Ain't none of them gonna do shit?"

Ice gave him a questioning look, "What the fuck you mean?"

"Brah, with Blood in jail, how the fuck are we gonna make money?" Tip questioned worriedly. "You know Pedrazza ain't gonna deal with us, if Blood ain't around."

"With all of the money that you've made over the years, you're still stressing to make more?"

"I'm not stressing, but I really ain't got shit saved up."

"That's because you didn't make plans for shit like this. I told you before, brah, you can't live for the drug game like it's a career. It's not a nine to five. The longer we stay doing this shit, the higher our chances of ending up dead or in prison." Ice took a sip from his glass. "I don't know about you, but I'm just about ready to step away from all this shit. After seeing what Blood did to Bam, I ain't gonna lie brah, that shit got me scared as fuck."

"So you're gonna turn your back on Blood, just because he killed a fucking crackhead?"

"That fucking crackhead was a friend of ours," Ice replied, as he shifted his body. "And it's not that I'm turning my back on Blood, either. But the truth is, I wasn't down with him killing Bam, and especially him killing him infront of his mother."

Tip took a quick sip from his glass and then said, "You'd better not say that shit around Rebel or Rev."

Ice deliberately kept his eyes on the naked girls on stage. "I know better," he mumbled and stretched. He looked over at Tip, who he had known since his last year in high school. He then waited a few seconds before saying, "Blood wants us to go by the Prosecutor's house and see if we can get her to drop his charge."

"I'm down fo' that," Tip agreed quickly.

Ice narrowed his eyes on him. "Do you have any idea what would happen to us, if we get caught?"

"Fuck getting caught. I'm down with whatever, to get my dawg outta jail."

"Is it yo' dawg that you're down for, or is it the money that you make when he's around?"

Tip shot Ice a black look. "What the fuck is that supposed to mean?"

"Come on brah, don't try to fuckin' play me," Ice responded, with his brows creased. "I know you long enough, to know you well. And I know that you ain't down with Blood like that. You and I both know that he's an arrogant asshole, who acts as if he's untouchable."

Tip didn't respond. His eyes were focused on a petite Hispanic stripper, who was walking by. He waited until she disappeared into the crowd to ask, "So what, you not down with what he wants us to do?"

Ice took a deep breath. "I'm down," he said reluctantly. "But whether he gets outta jail or not, I'm through with all of this shit."

"Through with what?"

"Through with the game and with selling drugs. I'm through with running the streets, as if I'm still in my fuckin' teens."

"I hear you," Tip replied, as he caught sight of a wide smiling Shanequa, who was making her way through the crowd. "Here comes Shanequa's crazy ass," he pointed out. He got up and picked up a bottle of Cristal from off of the floor. "I'm gonna go and see what's up with Rebel," he said, as he stepped off.

Dressed in a pair of skin tight, leather jeans and knee high Burberry boots; Shanequa who claimed Ice as her man, stepped by the two bouncers, who were standing by the entrance of the VIP.

She ran over to Ice, looking happy and excited. "Baby, why didn't you call me?" She asked, as she embraced him. She then sat her five-three frame across his lap, in order to show ownership.

Ice looked at her seriously. "Who told you that I was here?" He asked aggressively, clearly not liking how she had tracked him down.

"I called Patrice and she told me."

Ice made a quick visual sweep of the club's interior. "Do you have that ho watching me?" He asked, after failing to find Patrice.

"Baby, why would you even think that?"

"Because, she's been watching me ever since I pulled into the fucking parking lot."

Because of her money-hungry ways and her constant need to be seen, Ice was now ready to shove Shanequa aside. He always knew she wasn't the type of chick that he wanted to settle down with. Not that they were seriously involved, because to Ice she was just another trick.

They did share some good times together. Only what Ice thought was going to be a hit and quit, was now shaping them out to be a couple. He did have feelings for her, but they were mostly sexual. That's because she had a body that was worth staring at, and he found her head game to be a notch above all of the other females that he had been with.

Her chinky eyes and luscious lips gave her a very erotic look. But she was by no means, the prettiest that Ice had ever been with. However, Shanequa felt as if her position by Ice's side made her the prettiest, sexiest, and baddest chick in the streets of Ft. Lauderdale.

Eyeing her angrily, Ice snarled, "Why the fuck are you here, Shanequa? I haven't seen or heard from you, all damn day."

She snuggled up to him and placed her head on his shoulder. "I was on the road with my gurl, Candace. We went shopping."

Ice sucked his teeth. "For a person who doesn't have a job, you sure do spend a whole lot of time shopping."

After hearing the coldness in his voice, Shanequa crossed her legs in his lap and then she wrapped her arms tightly around his mid-section. She forced her face inside the crook of his neck, and then she murmured in a sad tone, "Baby, you sound as if you're not happy to see me."

Ice pried her arms from around his waist. "I'm not," he stated firmly. "I'm in the middle of taking care of something. If you had called, then I would've told you that."

"I'm sorry," She muttered dolefully.

"Yow Ice, let's go!"

Ice turned his eyes towards Rebel's gravelly voice and saw him and Tip hurrying towards the VIP.

"Yow let's go!" Rebel repeated firmly.

Ice eased Shanequa off of his lap and then he got up. "What's up? Where are we going?" He asked.

"We're gonna go to take care of this shit for the Boss," Rebel replied. He then turned to Tip. "Yow, go get Rev," he ordered.

Tip took off without complaint.

There was a sudden sour feeling in Ice's gut that had him not wanting to go. But with Rebel, Tip, and Rev going, he knew if he wasn't there, that the situation would only get worse; probably get out of control.

"Where are you guys going?" Shanequa inquired inquisitively.

 Ice glared at her through slits. "Go home Shanequa. This shit has nothing to do with you."

She crossed her arms across her breasts and then shifted her hip to the side. "I'm not going home without you, Ice. I'm not sleeping by myself tonight," she huffed.

Ice sucked his teeth, while looking at her thoughtfully. He knew that he had to play his cards right, if he was going to get rid of her. He had no intention of spending the night with her. So when he saw Tip hurrying back with Rev, he told her, "Go to your house and wait fo' me. I'll be there when I'm through."

She pursed her lips and rolled her eyes in a feisty manner. "You better not play with me, Ice," she uttered, with her head snaking. "If I don't see you by twelve o'clock, then I'm calling you and you had better answer your fucking phone."

With a bit of attitude, she swiped a lock of weave from in front of her face, and then she turned around and pranced away.

Ice watched her for awhile, before pulling his keys from his pocket. He then turned to Rebel who was standing between Tip and Rev. "So, where are we going?" He asked.

Rebel smirked viciously. "Pembroke Pines," he replied. "That's where the prosecutor bitch lives."

 "You got her address?"

"Got it in your phone," Rebel replied, as he turned and stepped off.

With his pulse now racing, his stomach in knots and a voice in his head telling him not to go; Ice swallowed the lump in his throat, then he stepped after his cohorts.

CH-4

It was almost 10:15 pm when Amelia pulled into the driveway of her recently renovated two bedroom townhouse. The streets of her east Pembroke Pines community were lifeless, and the majority of the houses were engulfed in darkness.

Other than the neighbor's dogs that were barking persistently, Beyonce's song, *Drunk in Love,* that was playing inside of Amelia's brand new, silver RX 350, was the only other sound piercing the night.

Still bothered by the heated conversation that she had with Rick over dinner, Amelia killed the truck's engine and cut off Beyonce's melodious voice. She sat back inside of her seat thinking; and trying to figure out if she was doing the right thing, by going against Rick's wishes and pursuing the prosecution against Blood.

She knew that Rick was only looking out for her and her safety. But sending Blood to prison was something that she really wanted to do. And it wasn't just because of whom he was or what he had done. It was also because he had threatened her.

Amelia knew that she had co-workers working for Blood. And because she didn't know exactly who they were, she was very hesitant to step away from the case or to pass it on to someone else. As far as she was concerned, her Boss and Rick were the only straight shooters at the State Attorney's office. They were the only ones that she knew well enough, and trusted to stay away from Blood and his drug money. However, she didn't want to put Rick in harm's way, by giving him the case. And because she didn't know who else she could trust to get Blood convicted, she was adamant about doing it herself.

After pulling the keys from the steering column, Amelia grabbed her briefcase and handbag, and then she stepped down from the Lexus. She was walking up the driveway towards her front door, when her cell phone suddenly blared to life. After pulling it from her handbag, she checked the caller ID. It was her best friend, Danielle.

"What's up, Gurl?" She answered blissfully.

"Bitch! What the fuck were you waiting on to call me?"

Amelia tossed her head back and laughed, as she unlocked and pulled her front door open. "I just got home," she replied loudly. "I was gonna call you just as soon as I changed out of my work clothes. What's going on?" She asked, as she flicked on the lights and placed her handbag, briefcase, and keys on top of the lamp stand by the door.

"I really-really need to talk to you."

"About what?"

"We'll talk about it when you call me back. I'm giving you thirty minutes."

Amelia chortled, "Bye Danielle," then she hung up, as she walked into her bedroom.

Amelia's rented apartment was sparsely furnished, but very neat and clean. It had two large bedrooms, a small and seldomly used kitchen, and a living room that showed off her love for peach.

As soon as she flicked on the lights inside of the bedroom, she started to remove her clothes. She kicked off her stilettos, pulled off her jacket and tossed it onto the bed, then fumbled with the buttons of her white satin blouse before she finally got it off.

She placed her watch and earrings inside of a heart-shaped jewelry box on the dresser, just before she shimmied her way out of her skirt, and then left it in a pile, on the floor by the bed.

Left in a red frilled thong and matching bra, Amelia strolled across the bedroom and turned the stereo on. She skipped through a couple album titles, before she finally settled for Alicia Keys', *As I am*, her favorite album from the very talented female vocalist.

Feeling good to be home, she turned up the volume on the stereo. Then as she tied her hair into a bun, she danced and sang her way into the bathroom.

$$\$$$

"Let's just pry the window open and go in."

"Go in and do what?" Ice turned to Rev and asked quietly. He huffed out a breath and then he sucked his teeth. "I don't know why we're here, because we don't even have a fucking plan," he complained.

"Blood said to do whatever it takes to get her to drop his fucking charge. He just doesn't want us to kill her… As yet," Rebel interjected. "Which means if we have to beat the shit outta her, then we go in and beat the shit outta her."

"I say we all take turns fucking the bitch," Tip implied, while groping his erection that failed to go down, even after Amelia had disappeared inside of the bathroom.

They were all gathered outside at the back of Amelia's house, by her bedroom window. The curtains were drawn, but through the cracks they were still able to get a clear view of inside. The overcast night had them camouflaged in darkness. And the floodlight that usually shone across the backyard was taken out.

Glaring at Tip angrily, Ice asked, "So now you're into raping?"

"I wasn't," Tip giggled freakishly. "But after seeing that bitch with her clothes off, I'm definitely into it now."

"I'm down fo' that," Rebel added. "The bitch got a body that's banging, and it doesn't help that she's fucking beautiful."

Ice shot Rebel an angry look, before looking in at the bathroom door. He too was having a hard time controlling his sexual urge, after seeing Amelia with her clothes off. He felt as if it was his first time ever seeing a woman so flawlessly beautiful. He had surged to hardness the very moment that she stepped inside the bedroom and flicked the lights on. Seeing her with her clothes off, had caused him to completely change his mind about doing what Blood wanted them to do. It just wasn't in him to hurt someone so beautiful. What he now wanted to do was to keep her safe. He wanted to follow the strange sensation that had overtaken him and protect her with his life, if he had to.

"We don't even have a plan," he said, as he tried to formulate a strategy to protect Amelia. "We can't just go in on her, without knowing what to do… We need to put together a plan before confronting her."

"Fuck a plan," Rev muttered bitterly. "All we got to do is go in on her and slap her into dropping Blood's charge."

"Or fuck her into doing it," Tip laughed quietly.

Ice shot him a fiery stare, before turning back to Rev. "First of all," he pointed out seriously. "If we go in on her and slap her around, how are we gonna know fo' sure that she'll drop Blood's charge. She may say that she's gonna do it, just to have us to leave; then call the police and have them to hunt us down, the minute that we leave her alone."

"Then let's just kill the bitch," Rev suggested, in a cold and serious tone. He was the most violent of the four and they all knew it.

"Are you crazy?" Ice looked at him and whispered hotly. "Killing her won't get Blood outta jail. All it would do is make matters worse for him. Besides, Blood made it clear that he doesn't want her killed."

"As yet," Rev mumbled viciously.

"You're always trying to kill somebody," Ice thought, while looking at Rev. He didn't like Rev and he knew that Rev knew it.

After a moment of silence and then a frustrated sigh, Ice bit into his lip and then whispered, "Killing her should *never* be an option. If she gets murdered right now, all fingers will be pointing at Blood. Everyone knows that he's got the money and the power to get a state prosecutor killed. And believe me, the Feds will get involved. Therefore if they don't catch us and have us killed for doing it, they'll find a way to stick Blood with the death penalty."

This got all of them to thinking. Ice realized this and decided to press a bit more.

"Listen," he continued. "We can't get crazy about this. If we fuck up, then Blood will have all of our asses killed."

"So what are you suggesting?" Rebel asked thoughtfully.

"I'm suggesting that we cover our tracks," Ice explained. "We also have to make sure that there won't be any repercussions behind whatever we do. We just can't go in on her, right now."

"I don't see why we can't," Rev voiced flatly, clearly not agreeing with what Ice was saying. "I say that we go in right now, and beat the bitch until she decides to drop Blood's charge."

"Then that's what we should do," Rebel agreed.

"I say that we rape her first."

Ice turned his angry eyes on Tip. "What's up with you and all of this raping shit, brah? You acting as if you're desperately trying to go to prison fo' rape."

Tip's dark eyes matched Ice's coldness. "I wouldn't mind doing a bid fo' that ho," he declared grimly.

Ice's temper was rising. Only he knew that it wasn't the time or the place to argue with Tip, so he turned his eyes on Rebel and asked, "So what you want us to do, brah? You want us to go in? Because if we're not careful; then we'll all be in the county jail, right next to Blood. If we want to get him out, then we have to find a safe way to scare her into dropping his charge. We can't just go in on her right now and act stupid."

"So you're saying that if we go in and slap the bitch around, that won't scare her off?"

"It probably will," Ice answered hastily. "But what's gonna stop her from calling the police, after we leave? And what's gonna stop them from hitting Blood with a conspiracy charge?" Ice locked eyes with Rebel. "Us coming here tonight was dumb from the get go. We should've stayed at the Mirage and put a plan together; one that will get Blood outta jail and not put him deeper in."

"I ain't into all of this complicated shit," Rev lashed out. "If we're gonna scare the bitch, then let's just go in and do it." Thinking quickly, Ice stepped away from the window. "Go ahead, brah. Get us in," he said quietly. "You really think that a state prosecutor is gonna live by herself, with no alarm system on her house? This shit is probably just as secured as the federal reserve."

Indecision fell down on Rev like night dew. He took a look around the outskirts of the window. Then he looked up over his head, in search of security cameras. "So what do you want us to do?" He asked after a couple thoughtful, silent seconds. Ice said, "I've got a plan, which I'm almost certain will scare her into dropping Blood's charge. And it doesn't include slapping her around or raping her," he snipped at Tip. "And we don't have to..." Ice trailed off, after seeing Amelia step out of the bathroom with a large pink towel wrapped around her body and another in her hand, blotting her hair.

Captivated, he stood and stared, unable to take his eyes off of the woman he thought was the most beautiful woman he had ever laid eyes on.

"Damn, that ho fine," Tip said, while groping himself.

Ice started to voice his approval. Only he choked up when Amelia pulled the towel from around her body and tossed it on the bed, giving them an eyeful of her stunning body. Her perky breasts were firm with dark erect nipples, and there was only a shadow of pubic hair around the fist sized mound in between her legs.

Just like Rebel, Tip, and Rev, Ice's mouth fell open, but nothing came out. He was too enthralled to say a word. In his mind, what he was looking at was perfection — all five feet and six inches of it. He took deep settling breaths, in order to ease his sudden lust attack. Then he bit into his lip, to calm down his nerves. He was already hard and throbbing. But thanks to the darkness, he wasn't worried about his cohorts seeing the tent at the front of his pants.

"Damn, she sexy," Rebel echoed, as he inched closer to the window.

Ice turned his head and caught his colleagues all gawking at Amelia, with pure lust swirling around inside of their eyes. He knew the best thing was for him to get them away from her, before they decided to go against his reasoning; so he ignored his surging hormones, took one last look at Amelia and then turned to Rebel and said, "Let's get the fuck outta here, before somebody sees us."

"Wait up, brah," Tip mumbled, while gazing at Amelia and groping himself.

Fighting off the urge to grab Tip by his shirt and punch him in his face, Ice stepped off. "I'm out, yow," he said, in a forced and controlled tone. "I'm not gonna stand here until we get caught. Plus we need to all sit down and go over what we've got to do, to get her to drop Blood's charge."

"He's right," Rebel agreed, still staring at Amelia with a throbbing hard-on of his own. "Let's bounce before somebody sees us."

$$$$$$$$$$$$$$$$$$$$$$

"Every time you kiss me, kiss me like you'll never kiss me again..." Amelia sang along quietly with Alicia Keys, as she sat on her bed with her legs parted, applying lotion to her thighs. She was feeling fresh and rejuvenated, and ready to spend the rest of her night curled up in bed with Authoress Redd's, *PROMISCUOUS*—her new favorite novel.

Squirting a second measure of lotion inside of her palm, Amelia took a look around her bedroom. It was clean, neat, and well put together. The dark brown furnishings were all arranged methodically, while the walls were decorated with not-so-expensive paintings and a small collection of books. After putting away the bottle of lotion, Amelia went back to massaging her legs. She was applying lotion to her inner thighs, when a shadowy movement caught her eyes. She stopped and turned her head. Then for about five long seconds, she stared steadily at her bedroom window.

The curtains were drawn and the window itself was dark, so she couldn't see anything on the outside. But a sudden tingling feeling at the back of her neck sent her pulse and her heart into a frenzied gallop, and had her breathing heavier than normal with her stomach was fluttering.

Feeling as if she was being watched, Amelia clamped her legs together and leaped up off of the bed. She then ran over to her closet and grabbed an over-sized t-shirt and pulled it on. The tingling feeling was now a gut wrenching uneasiness. And it had her standing far across the room, away from the window and not wanting to move.

Alicia Keys was now singing about her prelude to a kiss. But kissing was the last thing on Amelia's mind. She was too busy trying to figure out if someone was on the outside of her house, looking in on her.

After a few deep breaths that didn't do much to calm her nerves, Amelia started towards the window, making slow quiet steps and hoping that it was just paranoia getting the better of her.

She was about three steps away from the window, when a prickly feeling skittered up her spine. Her heart flipped and her breathing started to get heavier. But when she got up to the window and pulled away the curtains, all that she saw was her dark, empty backyard and whatever garbage that she had laying around.

"Idiot!" She laughed at herself, as she flung the curtains back into place.

She was so relieved to find the back yard empty, that she didn't even take notice of the flood lights that were taken out. *"I really need some time off from work,"* she thought, as she turned away from the window.

CH-5

Amelia always started her Saturday mornings inside of her neighborhood gym. She was by no means a gym-rat, but she spent just enough time on the treadmill to keep herself fit and sexily toned.

Just like each and every Saturday morning, the gym was packed and buzzing with an early morning crowd. Those who were dedicated to their workouts were there getting it done. They were literally putting on a show for the undedicated few, who were only there to parade around and body watch.

With her thighs burning and her chest ablaze, Amelia who was on the butt and thigh shaper machine was sweating profusely. She had the ear buds from her iPod jammed inside of her ears, listening to Kelly Rowland's song, *Motivation*, as she forced her way through the sets of reps, which she had set for herself.

Dressed in a gray Nike sweatpants and black Nike sports bra, Amelia was looking sexy as hell. She had her hair tied back into a tight ponytail, showing off her high cheekbones and chiseled beauty. The expensive diamond knobs in her earlobes were glittering beautifully, but they were still a notch below her glistening toffee-colored skin.

She had started her two hour workout with sets of squats and lunges, and she was now unable to ignore the pain that they had left behind. So with her pulse galloping and her teeth gritted fiercely, she grimaced her way through the last six reps; then afterwards, she stepped down from the machine on aching rubbery legs.

After yanking the ear buds from her ears, Amelia bent over at the waist and rested her hands on her knees. "That's it fo' me," she gasped heavily, while trying to slow down her pulse, which was galloping away.

"I don't know how you do it," Danielle, who was seated on the stationary bike, said coolly. "Gurl, I refuse to push myself that hard."

"I have to," Amelia replied, panting. "I'm not trying to look forty, when I get to forty."

Stepping down from the bike in some skimpy work-out shorts that rode high above her ass cheeks, Danielle joked, "Ain't no greater workout than sex. One night of raging, turbulent fucking is equivalent to ten trips to the gym."

Amelia chuckled, as she stepped over to the bench by the wall and picked up her towel and her bottle of Zephyrhills. "I'm getting just enough sex to keep me content," she said in a light tone. "So until I find someone who knows how to keep me happy, yet is smart enough to keep us both financially secured; I won't change a thing."

Danielle wrinkled her nose conflictingly. "I thought Rick was that someone?" She grilled.

"Maybe he is," Amelia replied, as she wiped her sweaty face with the towel. "I do like Rick," she admitted. "He's kind, he's caring, and he's smart. He's a good guy. But honestly, I'm not sure if I'm ready to get into a serious relationship with him."

"Do you really think that you'll find someone better?" Danielle asked, with a hand propped on her backside. "I'm willing to bet my last dime that you won't."

"I probably won't, that is why I'm not gonna take that bet," Amelia chuckled, as she brought the water bottle to her lips. Danielle and Amelia were best friends. The two had met seven years ago at a hair show in Atlanta, and had been close ever since.

Danielle, who was known as a sassy and vivacious individual, was a party animal who was sold on the idea, that she would eventually find a rich balla; one who would willingly seat her in the lap of luxury. Because of her wild and free spirit, she stayed with her pearl white teeth showing. And even though her job as a hairstylist paid her well, to her it just wasn't enough to keep her in the glitz and glam of the streets. Therefore at times, she conned and cajoled her way into the pockets of whatever men allowed her to do it.

"So are you coming by the shop today?" Danielle asked, as she snatched up her bottle of Gatorade from off the bench. "You know how much I hate seeing you walking around with a pony tail."

She was referring to the beauty salon in Lauderhill, where she worked.

"I'll probably just wait until Monday," Amelia replied. "I've got this big case that I'm working on, so I'll be spending my weekend going over it."

"Who are you're trying to send to prison now?"

Amelia frowned and then stated, "A drug dealing murderer named Mike Simms."

"Who?" Danielle asked, with a puzzled look on her face.

"Mike Simms," Amelia repeated flatly. "You probably don't know him. But from what I've heard, he's just about the biggest and the most vicious drug dealer in Fort Lauderdale."

Danielle studied Amelia for a moment. "Hold on," she then muttered, behind her wagging pointer finger. "Are you talking about Blood?"

With her lips pursed, Amelia shrugged, "I think that's his AKA. You know him?

"Amelia, everybody and their momma knows Blood," Danielle blurted out, with her eyes wide and wild. "Whosoever doesn't know this man personally, knows him by reputation. He's fucking crazy!"

"Well, his streak of craziness is just about over," Amelia said firm and clear. "Because I'm going to make sure that he spends the rest of his life in prison."

Danielle gawked at her best friend. "Do you even know who Blood really is?" She asked emphatically. "Do you have any idea of the things that he'll do just to walk outta jail?"

Amelia rolled her eyes at Danielle's dramatic expression. "Let him do whatever it is that he has to," she announced, then swallowed a mouthful from her water bottle. "He's where he's supposed to be. And I'll be doing what I have to, just to keep him there."

Shaking her head slowly, Danielle said, "Blood isn't someone that you should be messing with, 'Melia. As a friend to a friend, I think you should just leave that case alone."

"Not you too?" Amelia cocked her head at Danielle. "Why is everybody trying so hard to push me away from this case?"

"Probably because everybody knows of the things that Blood is capable of doing."

"Well, I don't care. My job is to send his ass to prison for what he did; and that's what I'm gonna do."

"Do you really think that Blood is just gonna sit back and let you have your way with him. Knowing him, he's probably already put a hit out on you."

Amelia giggled, "I really think that you've been watching way too much TV."

"And I really think that you don't know who Blood really is," Danielle shot back seriously. "The man is a monster, Amelia. And he's got a bunch of monsters working for him. Do you think that they won't hurt you, just to get him outta jail?"

"They can do whatever they want, I'm not gonna drop the charges against him."

"Goddamn, Amelia! Why you got to be so hard headed? I'm telling you, these people won't hesitate to hurt you."

"And I'm telling you, I'm not walking away from the case," Amelia said, as she punched a fist into her hip. "Mike Simms can hire an assassin if he wants to. But it will make no difference to me, because I will not let him or anyone else intimidate me."

Danielle grabbed Amelia's arm. "Don't you know that these people will kill you," she advised. "I'm telling you, Blood is not the type of person that you should be fucking with!"

Amelia cocked her head and then she gave Danielle a questioning look. "Sure sounds as if you know this Blood guy, very well."

"I don't know him like that," Danielle replied hastily. She then turned her eyes away from Amelia, and then said, "But I've heard enough about him to know that he's a monster, and that he's feared by just about everyone who knows him."

Amelia sucked her teeth, undeterred. "Well, he won't be the first feared and dangerous person that I send to prison," she said, as she picked up her vibrating cell phone from off of the bench. She looked at the screen, to see who was calling. "Will you at least think about it?"

Amelia glared at Danielle, and sighed agitatedly. "There's nothing for me to think about, Danielle. Mike Simms' ass is going to prison," she stated confidently, as she brought her iPhone up to her ear.

$$$$$$$$$$$$$$$$$$$$$$$$

Ice pressed his palms down against the marble on both sides of the white porcelain sink, inside his bathroom, while gazing at his reflection in the mirror. He was butt-ass naked, and sweating as if he had just completed an hour long sprint.

He could hear the moans and groans of the whimpering female, coming from the TV inside of his bedroom—her carnal cries getting louder, as she forced her way to an orgasm. He wasn't a lover of porn. But because Honey had brought it with her and asked to play it while they had sex, he obliged.

Even though it was his first time having sex with Honey, Ice had already considered it his last. Not that he didn't enjoy having sex with her—because he actually did. He actually enjoyed seeing her naked and having her to please him, in whatever way he paid her for. But something about having sex with her, just didn't feel right. It was as if he couldn't focus on her stunning body and the sexual pleasures that she gave. Even during his orgasms, his mind was flitting about wildly.

After seeing Amelia with her clothes off, Ice just couldn't get her off of his mind. He couldn't figure out what had spurred the driving need that he had for her, but it was there. And as far as he could remember, he had never wanted a woman as bad as he wanted Amelia.

In a desperate attempt to get Amelia off his mind, Ice forced his palms against the marble and pressed his forehead into the glass. He had his eyes closed, and his teeth gritted, as her beautiful face bounced around inside of his head.

A sudden image of her naked body sent his pulse into a frenzied gallop, and had his heart thumping heavily. He got lost in his musings of her. And it wasn't until he felt a hand on his sweaty back, did he killed his thoughts and snapped his eyes open.

Breathing unevenly, he looked in the mirror and saw Honey standing behind him. She was naked and staring at his reflection in the mirror, while gently rubbing his back.

"Baby, you okay?" She asked. Her voice came out at a whisper, but was dripping with lust.

Ice turned to face her, while resting his bare ass against the edge of the sink. He wanted for her to go, but he just didn't know how to tell her to leave.

"What time are you leaving?" He finally asked her.

She took hold of his manhood and stroked him lightly. "Right after I get some more of this," she replied, smiling as he expanded.

Ice didn't reply. Instead he placed a hand at the top of her head, and then he eased her down to her knees.

She knew exactly what he wanted, and she was more than ready to give it to him.

She wrapped her hand around the base of his manhood. Then with her eyes open and her lips pursed and parted, she took him inside of her mouth and down her throat.

Ice gripped onto the sink and moaned. Then as Honey expertly slurped on his hard, veined nine inches, he closed his eyes and went back to thinking about Amelia.

$$\$$

"— well just think about it," Rick said into his cell phone, after another failed attempt at getting Amelia to give up on the pursuit of convicting Blood.

After a loud, heavy sigh, Rick then tossed the phone onto the passenger seat of his spanking new Barolo red Benz, as he wondered what he could do to force Amelia into giving him the case, or get her to drop the charge.

He knew her well enough to know that once her mind was made up about doing something, it was almost impossible to get her to do otherwise. But he was bent on getting her to step away from the case, because he knew that there would be a whole lot of repercussions if she didn't. And by Blood being the way that he was, she wouldn't be the only one affected. After another loud and heavy sigh, Rick killed the engine of the Benz, and then dry washed his face. He glanced at his Ulysse Nardin and saw 8:57am; twenty seven minutes past his scheduled session of golf with his father. It was so unlike the old man to be late. He was a very punctual individual, with a scheduled lifestyle. So this out of the blue tardiness had Rick a bit worried.

Being the son of a retired college professor and having the top veterinarian in the state as his mother, Rick was well raised and educated. He was known to be a hard working prosecutor, who constantly chased after perfection. But in truth, his life was nowhere close to being perfect. He had a secret that only a few people knew about. A secret that would surely be exposed, if Amelia didn't drop or step away from the case against Blood.

Relieved to see his father's Cadillac STS pulling into the parking lot, Rick picked up his cellphone, and then he popped his door open. He was at the Weston Hills country club in Royal Palm. It was a beautiful and upscale country club with a large and immaculately kept golf course, and the most prestigious homes around it.

The sun was out and shining beautifully. And a gentle breeze was blowing across the many acres of green grass.

Rick stuffed his hands into the pockets of his slacks, and then he leaned back against the Benz as the Cadillac cruised to a stop, just a few yards across from him. Because of the dark tinted windows, he couldn't see inside. So when the driver's side window rolled down and he saw who was behind the steering wheel, his heart slammed against his chest and his knees buckled.

"Yo, what's the deal?" The driver of the STS smirked dryly. He had a Bob Marley sized blunt dangling between the fingers of his left hand; and the pair of dark sunglasses that he had on just weren't big enough to hide the ugly two inch scar below his left eye.

With a queasy feeling inside of his gut, Rick stepped towards the Cadillac. "What the fuck are you doin' in my father's car? And where is he?" He asked firmly.

The driver of the Cadillac took a pull from his blunt. Then he coolly blew a cloud of smoke up into Rick's face. "Your old man is straight... Fo' now," he grinned.

"Where is he?!" Rick barked.

The driver gave him a hard stare, right before he snickered, "He's probably still standing in the middle of his garage, wondering what the fuck happened to his Cadillac."

Rick shot him a hard stare of his own. "You'd better leave my parents outta this!" He warned. "They have nothing to do with what we've got going on!"

"Blood is still in jail, mothafucka. So they've got everything to do with it."

Rick huffed out an angry breath. "Don't you think that I'm trying to get him out?" He asked, a bit louder than he really wanted to. "It's not like I can just take the case away from Amelia and get rid of it."

"A Niggah ain't trying to hear all that shit. You're the one who fucked up by letting her get her hands on it. So you'd better do something, and do it quick, or else."

"Or else what?" Rick asked, behind a fiery glare.

With a devilish grin, the driver looked around inside of the Cadillac, and then passed his hand over the dash. "Or else..." he paused. "My next visit to your parents' house won't be to take their car."

Rick charged towards the Cadillac, with his fists tight and his eyes wide. "If you ever lay a finger on my parents I'll—"

"You'll what, mothafucka?" The driver snarled as he pulled a 9mm pistol from inside of his jacket, and stopped Rick dead in his track. He aimed the gun at Rick's head, and warned bitterly. "If I was you I wouldn't be out here trying to play golf. I'd be spending my time trying to get Blood outta jail. Because the longer that he stays in there, the closer it gets to a whole lot of people getting hurt."

Rick swallowed the heavy lump inside of his throat. "Is that a threat?" He asked timidly.

"That's exactly what it is," the driver of the STS announced. He glanced over at Rick's Benz. "Nice car," he smirked. "I wonder how many of your friends knows that Blood is the one who bought it fo' you."

"Fuck you!"

The driver tossed his head back and laughed. "There's no reason for you to be so upset, Ricardo. You were gladly taking Blood's money when he was giving it to you. And I know that once he's outta jail you'll be gladly asking for more."

"After this, I'm through."

"No you're not. You're through whenever we say that you're through," the driver grinned, as he removed his sunglasses. He narrowed his eyes on Rick, giving him a clear view of the two inch scar below his left eye. "This is what I got from Blood for wanting out. I'm sure that you don't want an ugly scar like this on your pretty little face." He slid the sunglasses back over his eyes and then shifted the car into drive. "If it was in my hands, I wouldn't be chasing behind you, Rick. I did what I was supposed to. You're the one who fucked up. So get this shit fixed, before we all end up in prison."

Rick hurried towards the Cadillac, as it started to creep way. "What about my father's car?" He asked loudly.

The driver poked his head out through the window and said, "You want it back, get Blood outta jail."

CH-6

Ice was having a hard time getting rid of Honey, until at about 1:30 in the afternoon she grabbed her belongings, kissed him on the cheek and told him, "bye."

As soon as she was out of the apartment with the door closed behind her, Ice snatched up his cell phone. He then called Tip, who had been blowing him up all morning.

"Where the fuck you at, Niggah?" Tip came on and asked after two rings.

"I'm still at my crib. What's up?"

"We're about to do that thing, brah. I tried to call you, but you wouldn't pick up."

Ice closed his eyes and then he sighed heavily, "Are you niggahs fo' real?" He asked, clearly frustrated. "I thought that the plan was to stake out her crib for a while, and then do it when she's not there."

"The bitch ain't there, brah. She's at the Pembroke Lakes mall."

"Who told you she's at the mall?" Ice asked, taking a seat on the bed.

"I've been following her around all damn day. I followed her to the gym earlier this morning. Then I followed her to the mall, just now. I even got another look at her walking out of her bathroom with all her clothes off," Tip giggled.

Ice huffed out an angry breath, as he got up. He then started pacing. "I think that we should wait until tonight," he said, trying to put a stop to what they had planned. "It's too much of a risk for us to do that shit in the middle of the day."

"It's much too late for you to be saying that shit now, brah, because Rebel and Rev are already inside."

Ice stopped his pacing and started gazing at the blank TV screen across the room. "They're already inside of her house?" He asked, as if he hadn't understood what Tip had just said.

"They just got in," Tip answered. "I don't know how long they're gonna be in there. But I'll tell Rebel to give you a call, just as soon as they get out."

"Make sure you do that," Ice retorted. But Tip didn't hear him, because he had already hung up.

Agitated, Ice flung his cell phone down onto the bed. Hearing that Rebel and Rev were inside of Amelia's house had left him unsettled and pissed. He knew what they were in there to do. But he also knew what would happen to Amelia, if she were to walk in on them. So instead of spending his day inside of his apartment doing nothing, as he had planned; he took a quick shower, got dressed, and then hurried out of his apartment.

$$\$$$

Rebel stood over Amelia's queen-sized bed with a can of red spray paint in his hand, and a Cheshire cat smile plastered across his face. He was steadily gazing down at his artwork, wondering what he could add to it to make it a bit more intimidating.

"What you think?" He turned to Rev, who was walking out of Amelia's bathroom. "You think that this is enough to scare her off?"

Rev walked over to the bed and looked down at what Rebel had done. After about two seconds, he sucked his teeth and turned away. "I already told you, brah, that suckah-ass shit that Ice suggested ain't gonna intimidate that bitch. She'll probably just laugh at us when she sees the shit."
"So you don't think that this will scare her off?"
"Fuck no," Rev replied, pulling Amelia's closet door open. "We could stay here all damn day and spray paint this whole fucking house, and that bitch still wouldn't let Blood go."
"So you got a better idea?" Rebel asked, shaking the can of spray paint.
"Damn right I do," Rev replied, as he stepped inside of the closet. He picked up one of the two baseball bats that were on the floor. "Here, you're gonna need this," he said, tossing the bat to Rebel.
Rebel caught it.
"Need this for what?" He asked, while examining the bat.
Rev stepped out of the closet, with the other bat inside of his hand. "Come on and I'll show you," he said, as he started towards the dresser.

$$\$$

As it usually is on a Saturday afternoon, the Pembroke Lakes mall was crowded when Ice got there. It seemed as if window shopping was the event of the day, because the majority of those at the mall were walking around with empty hands and wide eyes.
With a black and yellow Yankees fitted hat pulled down firmly over his eyes, Ice scoured the mall looking for Amelia. He had already been in and through every single store that was at the mall. He had searched Victoria's Secret twice, and he was now walking out of Macy's for the third time.

Sighing heavily, Ice ran a frustrated hand down over his face. *"Wild fucking goose chase!"* He thought, as he once again scanned the busy hallway. He was hot, he was exhausted, and he was agitated. He was on the verge of going home, but just as he was walking by JC Penney for the fourth time, he caught sight of her in his peripheral vision—and almost broke his neck doing a double take.

She had her back turned, but he was certain that it was her. He was positive that the dime strutting through JC Penney, with her head held high and her jeans painted on was the very same person that he had been thinking about for the past sixteen hours. The same person that Blood was trying to hurt and he had vowed to protect.

After watching her for a few minutes; just to make sure that she was by herself, Ice hurried into the store. Finally finding Amelia was the best thing that could ever happen to him. He considered it to be a gift from heaven—nothing short of divine intervention.

For about ten minutes, he wandered through JC Penney with his eyes on her. He trailed her through the cosmetics section, where she purchased a couple bottles of lotion. Then afterwards, he followed her over to the perfume counter. That's where he decided to make his move.

With Amelia fixed in his peripheral vision, Ice approached the lady standing behind the perfume counter. She greeted him with a warm, "Good afternoon. Do you see anything that you like?"

Ice glanced over at Amelia. She was only a couple of yards away, over at the far end of the counter, sampling a bottle of Burberry body perfume. "May I see a couple bottles of your most frequently sold perfumes?" He asked the sales lady.

"Perfume or cologne?" She asked.

"Perfume," Ice confirmed.

The older woman turned away. And then a few moments later, she came back with four bottles of perfume. She placed them all on the showcase in front of Ice, and then said, "You can't go wrong with any of these."

Ice smiled at her, but turned to Amelia, who was walking by. "Umm, excuse me," he stopped her. "If it's possible, can I please have one minute of your time?"

Amelia gave him a brief once over, then with a pleasant smile she said, "If it's only a minute, sure."

Ice slid the four bottles of perfume across the showcase towards her. "If a guy was to give you any one of these as a gift, which one would excite you the most?"

Amelia cocked her head slightly, and then she threw a smile at Ice that sent desire surging throughout his veins. She scrunched up her nose, and then she looked down at the perfumes and said, "That depends. Who is the guy?" She asked easily. "Is he a friend, a boyfriend, or family?"

Ice looked her dead in the eyes. "He's a total stranger," he said, behind the most charming smile that he could muster. "But he's trying to be your friend, hopefully your boyfriend."

Amelia looked perplexed. "Well if that's the case," she stated. "It would be the Coco Chanel for me. But that doesn't mean that whosoever you're getting it for will like it."

"She will," Ice replied smoothly.

"Well I hope that she does," Amelia said and then she started off.

Ice watched her as she sauntered away with her handbag draped over her shoulder. She also had two logo'd shopping bags, dangling from her hands. "Hey! Thanks for your help!" He shouted at her, when she was about ten yards away.

She didn't answer, but she looked back at him and smiled.

As soon as she walked out through the door, Ice turned to the saleslady. "How much fo' this?" He held up the bottle of Coco Chanel and asked.

"One hundred and eighty dollars," the saleslady replied.

Ice pulled a stack of bills from out of his pocket. He quickly peeled off four fifties; dropped them on top of the counter, and then ran off.

"Wait for your change and receipt!" The saleslady shouted at him.

"I'm good!" He shouted back at her, as he ran out of the store. As soon as he stepped out into the hallway, he saw Amelia stepping into Victoria's Secret. He didn't hesitate; he hurried in after her and then he walked up to her and asked, "Do you always shop by yourself?"

A bit startled, Amelia turned her head. Instinctively, her face lit up when she saw him. "Oh, hi," she smiled. "I guess now you need my help to choose a set of sexy lingerie for your girlfriend?"

Ice snickered and gave her a slow once over before saying, "I wouldn't need your help for that. Because just by looking at her, I can tell that she's into thongs."

Amelia cackled, "You said that, as if you were referring to me."

"I was."

"Excuse me?"

"Please don't get defensive," Ice implored, when he saw the surprised look on her face. "But I saw you and just had to tell you."

"Tell me what?"

"Tell you that you're just about the most beautiful woman that I've ever laid eyes on."

Amelia smiled and shook her head. She pulled the straps of her Louis Vuitton handbag up on her shoulder and then she turned away. "Thanks for the compliment," she said. "But I don't get flattered by duplicity."

He walked after her. "Why would you think that I'm lying?" He questioned. "I'm sure that you've heard that many times before."

She stopped and turned to face him. "I hear it every day from my boyfriend," she said, trying to nudge Ice away. "When he tells me, I believe. But when I'm approached in the mall by a total stranger, who just bought a bottle of expensive perfume for his girlfriend; it goes in one ear and leaves out through the next."

"I didn't say that the perfume is for my girlfriend."

Amelia rolled her eyes, "So who did you buy it for, the chick on the side?"

Ice smiled and then he offered her the bottle of Coco Chanel. "I actually bought it for you," he said boldly.

She looked at him puzzled, and then she looked at the bottle of perfume inside of his hand. "You really expect me to believe that you bought that fo' me?"

"You may not believe me, but it's the truth. If you weren't so busy shopping, you would've noticed that I've been following you around for the past thirty minutes."

"Is that so?" She said, with a slight tilt of her head. "So did you know that stalking is illegal in Florida?"

"I do. But I also believe that it should be illegal for someone to be as beautiful as you are."

Amelia actually blushed. She subconsciously licked her suddenly parched lips and tried to catch her breath that was hitching. She couldn't help but to notice how thuggishly handsome that Ice was. And without the least bit of warning, she felt her pelvis churn.

Feeling a bit embarrassed because of her surging hormones, Amelia dropped her eyes on the perfume and asked, "Do you always go out your way to buy perfumes for strangers?"

"It's my first time. And if it wasn't for you being so beautiful, I don't think that I would've done it."

She smiled, "Well I really wished you hadn't, because it's not in me to accept a two hundred dollar bottle of perfume from a total stranger."

"So, let's put an end to me being a stranger."

She arched her brows. "And how are we gonna do that?" She asked with a tiny grin.

He offered his hand, and said, "Hi, my name is Ice."

Amelia laughed a beautiful quiet laugh. "Me knowing your name doesn't change a thing," she told him. "And don't tell me that your mother actually named you Ice."

Seeing her laugh was enough to have Ice knowing that he had her fully engaged. So without dropping his hand, he said, "She actually named me Travis. But all of my friends call me Ice."

Seeing that he still had his hand extended, she took it, shook it, and said, "Hi Travis. My name is Amelia. It was so nice of you to buy me that bottle of perfume, but I don't think that I should take it."

"Well, I think that you should. And if it will make you feel any better, I'm not expecting anything in return."

"You know that's not true. If I was to take that perfume and leave without giving you my number, I know you'd be pissed."

"If you let me take you out to lunch, I wouldn't be."

She narrowed her eyes and then she shot him a questioning look. She could tell that he was a bit younger than she was. Therefore she couldn't understand why she was still standing there, forcing herself not to blush like a little school girl.

The way that he was staring at her had her feeling sexy as hell. She found him to be bold but laid back. He was clearly a thug—but not the wild and rowdy kind.

But as far as Amelia knew, bad boys weren't her type. So why she was still there with her eyes locked on his lips was puzzling to her. She tried to tell herself that what she was feeling would pass and pass quickly. But each time that he looked her in the eyes, her breath hitched and her body throbbed.

After a long moment of silence between them, Amelia decided to walk away and put a stop to her childlike infatuation.

"Anyway, Travis, it was nice meeting you. But I have to go. I've got to get back home to do some work."

Her saying this sent regret surging throughout Ice's body. He immediately remembered what Rebel and Rev were at her house doing. And even though he was only trying to protect her by suggesting that they do damage to her home and not hurt her; anguish still pulled at his gut and had him grimacing.

"You okay?" She asked, once she saw the slight change of his facial expression.

He swallowed his compunction and forced out a smile.

"Hey, do you really have to go home, right now?" He asked, not wanting her to get there, only to stumble into Rebel and Rev. He knew that they would hurt her if she did. And her getting hurt was the last thing that he wanted to happen.

"Please let me take you out to lunch," he suggested, hopefully.

"I really don't—"

"Please," he held her arm and cut her off. "I promise, I'll be a perfect gentleman the entire time."

Twenty minutes after leaving Victoria's Secret, Ice and Amelia were seated inside of the food court. They were at a table that was up against the back wall, and away from the crowd. The food court was buzzing and loud. But Ice was so captivated by Amelia's beauty, sexiness, and elegance that he seemed not to notice.

"So Amelia, other than shopping; what else do you do?" Ice asked, after taking a sip from his Pepsi.

Amelia looked up from her fries. "Other than work, I really don't do much," she shrugged.

"Are you a model?" He joked.

She rolled her eyes at him playfully. "No Travis, I'm not a model. I work with the State Attorney's office."

"So you're a prosecutor?" He asked looking a bit surprised, as if he didn't already know.

She smiled and then nodded, while leaning back in her seat. "What about you? What do you do?"

Ice took another sip from his Pepsi. "Presently, I don't have a job," he said. "But I'm in the process of opening up my own business."

"Which will be?"

"Selling cars… I've always wanted to own and manage a car dealership, and now I'm very close to doing so."

She scrunched up her nose and then looked at him skeptically. "So you're not trying to be a rapper, a producer, or the next Nino Brown?"

"No," Ice shook his head and chuckled. "I wanna sell cars. I wanna own a couple of the biggest and the best car dealerships in the state."

"I see," she said behind a fascinated smirk. There was something about him that had her attracted. Something had her throbbing all over, each and every time that their eyes met. Smiling up at him, she asked, "How old are you, Travis?"

He reached for a couple fries. "I'm twenty nine. Why?"

She snickered, "Do you know that I'm four years older than you are?"

He smirked slightly. "If I was the one four years older, would it have been an issue?" He asked, locking eyes with her.

She looked away timidly. "I didn't say it's an issue," she responded with a sexy frown.

He sat back in his seat and studied her for several seconds, then tried to change the subject by asking, "Can I take you out to dinner sometime? I'd really like to see you again."

She didn't look at him. Instead, she kept her eyes on the tip of her straw, which was up close to her pursed lips. "I don't think that's a good idea," she said quietly. "After all, you do have a girlfriend and I'm seeing somebody."

"I don't have a girlfriend," Ice declared.

She leaned back in her seat and looked him over. "I find that very hard to believe. Because I think that you're a very handsome guy, and you don't seem to be financially disabled."

"I'm only single, because I choose to be."

"Then if that's the case us going out is a waste-a-time. I'm not looking for a fling.

"I don't do flings."

"So what is it that you do? Sleep around?"

"I do it when I have to," Ice admitted.

Amelia gazed at him, looking surprised.

Smiling, he gazed back at her. He loved the look of her pearly white teeth, up against her plum-moist lips that were flanked by the two dimples in her cheeks.

"So, can I take you out to dinner sometime? Please don't say no," he just about begged.

She took a deep, settling breath, as she sat a little straighter inside of her seat. "I don't know about dinner. I told you that I'm seeing somebody."

"Okay then, let me get your phone number."

"I don't know about that either. But I will take yours, under one condition."

"Anything," Ice replied quickly.

She leaned forward and locked eyes with him. "I need my perfume," she whispered with a smirk.

He cracked a pleased grin. "It's already inside your shopping bag," he whispered back at her.

CH-7

Amelia had a delightful smile plastered across her face, as she drove home from the mall. She had Rihanna's song, *Unfaithful*, playing inside of the Lexus but she wasn't listening. That's because her mind was on Ice and the wonderful time that she had spent at the mall with him.

Even though she would never admit it, she was looking forward to seeing him again. She actually enjoyed being around him. She liked the way that he carried himself with a calm, yet bold confidence. And the way he made her smile whenever he had to.

Her time with him had turned out to be much better than she had anticipated. He wasn't very talkative, but he did say all of the right things to keep her engrossed. And engrossed she was, because not only was she looking forward to going out with him; she couldn't help but to wonder what he was like inside of the bedroom.

It was almost eight o'clock when Amelia turned the Lexus into her garage. Still smiling broadly, she turned off the ignition, and then grabbed her handbag and the two shopping bags from the back seat, while stepping down from the truck. The quiet crunching of glass beneath her feet caught her attention and made her stop and look down.

"What happened here?" She wondered, as she tried to sidestep the shards of broken glass, which was scattered all across the garage.

Not thinking much of it, she walked around the truck and towards the door which led into the kitchen. That's when she saw the source of the broken glass and she jerked to a stop. "Oh my God!" She gasped, as cold sweat sprung from her pores.

The single pane of frosted glass that was inside of the door that led into the kitchen was smashed out and the door was left wide open.

Ignoring the painful twist inside her gut and the sound of crunching glass beneath her feet, Amelia dropped the bags and ran into the kitchen. She looked around in a panicky way—searching to see if anything was out of place or missing. As far as she could see, everything inside of the kitchen was intact. But when she stepped into the living room a cloak of heat engulfed her and sent her heart slamming against her chest.

She looked around through blurred eyes. Her once immaculately kept living room was looking like a tornado had hit home. Everything was ripped apart, shattered, or thrown out of place. The framed paintings on the walls were all taken down and smashed to pieces. And the sofas were all sliced up and tossed across the room.

Nothing was left untouched. The entertainment center was pulled away from the wall and slammed to the floor. And her glass coffee table was in pieces, right next to the tipped over plants by the front door.

Amelia looked around the room, not even knowing what to do. She didn't want to believe her tear-filled eyes, but the sour feeling in her gut was telling her that it was all real.

On rubbery legs, she moved towards her bedroom. She stepped over books, magazines, CDs and DVDs, which were all scattered throughout the room. She wasn't surprised by what she found. Her bedroom was just as ransacked and dismantled as the living room. And her clothes and shoes were tossed everywhere.

"Oh my God, who could've done this?" She whimpered quietly, as she searched her pockets for her cell phone to call the police.

She found it; but just as she was pulling it from her pocket, she caught sight of the bold red words written across her bed. Instead of pain and fear, anger shot throughout her body, when she stepped over to the bed and read: *Let Blood go, Bitch... Or else it will get fuckin worse!!!!!*

Amelia stood and stared at the bold red words for a long moment, and then she exploded.

"He's never getting out!" She screamed, as pure rage surged throughout her veins.

She snatched up one of the Gucci platforms that were on the floor by her feet and she flung it into the wall across the room. "You'll never get out! I'm gonna make sure that you rot in prison!" She screamed at the wall.

Furious, she grabbed the blanket and ripped it off of the bed, and then she tossed it across the room. She was about to go check out the guest bedroom, but a knocking on the front door stopped her.

Kicking things out of the way, she stormed towards the front door and yanked it open.

"Hey you, what's up?" Rick greeted her with a smile.

Without saying a word, Amelia huffed out a breath and then she spun away.

Rick stepped inside after her, only he stopped when he saw the ravaged living room. "What the fuck happened here?" He asked, with his eyes wide and unbelieving.

Amelia turned to face him. "Mike Simms happened, Rick. Mike Simms sent his people to my house and they did this." She took a look around the room, before picking up an unbroken vase. "If he thinks that this is enough to make me back off, then he's got it so fucking wrong!"

Rick stepped over a pile of books. "How do you know that Mike Simms' people were the ones who did this?" He asked.

Amelia spun away and charged inside of the bedroom. "Because-of -this! Because-of -fucking-this!" She came back yelling, with the white blanket outstretched. "You see why I know that it's him?"

Rick read what was written across the blanket and then he dropped his head. "Oh shit," he mumbled, as he wiped his perspiring forehead.

Amelia flung the blanket down onto the floor. "If there was any chance of me stepping away from this case, now it's all gone," she raged. "Now I'm gonna work my ass off to send him to prison, for the rest of his life."

"Amelia, you're letting your anger get the best of you," Rick said, while picking up the TV's remote. "You need to calm down and think things through, before you do anything stupid."

"There's nothing for me to think through, Rick. Look around you. Look at what the bastard did to my house."

"And it could've been worse. I told you that this guy doesn't play fair. His next move will probably be to hurt you."

"He already did!" She barked.

Rick wiped his face with the back of his hand. "Amelia I'm begging you. Please leave this case alone."

"No!"

"Amelia."

"I said fucking no, Rick! What part of no don't you understand?!"

Rick flung his hands up in the air, completely frustrated. "What the fuck is wrong with you?" He cursed loudly. "You rather die, than to leave Mike Simms alone?"

"If it cost me my life, then so be it; 'cause I'm not stepping away. I won't stop until Mike Simms is in prison fo' the rest of his life."

"Do you have any idea of how stupid that you sound right now?"

She glared at him. "I'm not stepping away from this case. I don't give a fuck what Mike Simms wants to do to me."

Rick stared angrily at her. "You'll give a fuck when your ass is laid up on a hospital bed, or either inside of a coffin."

She clamped her hands over her ears. "I don't wanna talk about this!" She screamed.

"Well I do!" Rick barked at her. "I told you that this would happen, if you pursued this case. I told you to leave it alone."

"And I told you that I won't!"

Rick spun away angrily. "Then don't you fucking call me, when this shit gets worse!"

With her fists clenched and her teeth gritted, Amelia stepped after Rick, who was storming towards the front door. "I don't have to call you, Rick! It's easier to dial 9-1-1, than dial your damn number!"

He stopped and turned to face her. "It seems as if you really don't know who Mike Simms is. The man has lawyers and judges in his pockets, Amelia. He's even got the damn police working for him."

"What about you, Rick? What about you? Are you working for him too?"

For about five tense, silent seconds, Rick stood and stared at Amelia with his nose flaring and his jaws twitching. "Fuck you!" He then barked suddenly. "Fuck you Amelia! Don't call my fucking phone when this shit gets worse!" He raged, and then he stormed out through the front door.

$$$$$$$$$$$$$$$$$$$$$$$

Ice was trying his best to stay calm as he listened to Rebel and Rev go on and on about what they had done to Amelia's apartment. The animated expressions on their faces had him wanting to snap. But he knew that snapping wouldn't help the situation one bit. The damage had already been done and he was just as responsible as they were.

"I'm telling you, my Niggah, we fucked that shit up real fucking good," Rebel bragged, as he walked in from the patio of his South Beach condo. He walked across the living room and then over to the mini bar. "We were tossing shit everywhere," he continued with a dry cackle, staring at Ice, as he poured himself a shot of Hennessy. "And if it wasn't for the police car that drove by, we would've stayed longer and fucked up the other rooms."

"You niggahs went way beyond what we planned," Ice said, with his eyes narrowed on Rebel. He leaned back on the couch and huffed out a breath. "The plan was to go inside and spray paint threatening messages across her walls. Not to destroy her whole fucking house."

"That shit wouldn't have worked."

"You don't know that," Ice shot back. "Now what's gonna happen when she calls the police?"

Rev sucked his teeth. "Who gives a fuck?" He uttered harshly. "The bitch should be glad that we didn't burn the mothafucka down."

Rebel laughed. "That should be our next move, if Blood ain't out by Monday."

A burn started inside of Ice's gut.

"The bitch ain't dumb. She'll let the boss go," Rev said seriously. He fired up the freshly rolled blunt between his lips and then he took a hard drag. "If she doesn't, then we can visit her mother over in Sunrise. I found her address when I was searching around inside of the dresser."

"Fuck visiting her mother. I say we fuck the bitch," Tip said, from across the room.

Ice shot him a hard stare. "What's up with you and all of this raping shit?" He sneered. "You think that raping her is gonna get Blood outta jail?"

"You never know," Tip giggled.

"Raping her is better than killing her," Rev grumbled seriously.

"Let's hope that we don't have to go that far," Rebel chipped in. "What we did to her house should be more than enough to get her to back off."

"Or just piss her off," Ice hissed.

Rev turned his eyes on Ice. "Sounds like you're pissed off?" He questioned.

"Fo'real," Rebel chimed in, with his glass at his lips and his eyes narrowed suspiciously at Ice.

Ice shifted around on the couch. "There's nothing fo' me to be pissed off about," he defended firmly. "But all of this shit shouldn't be about raping and hurting this prosecutor. It should be about getting Blood outta jail and nothing else."
"It is about getting Blood outta jail," Rev said sharply. "Ain't nobody gives a fuck about that bitch."
"I give a fuck," Tip chuckled, as he groped himself.
Ice glared at him angrily. "Niggah, you need to grow the fuck up," He spat hotly. "You take every mothafuckin' thing for a joke." Ice hopped up from the couch and then he started towards the door. "I'm out, yow," he said to no one in particular. "I'll holler at you niggahs in the A.M."
"So what, you leaving?" Rebel asked.
Ice pulled the door open. "That's what I just said," he replied icily, before stepping out of the room.

$$\$$$

Because Amelia was a prosecutor, the police were at her house within a couple of minutes from her call. It was as if the entire police force had showed up. And they went through and around the house with slow diligence, searching for anything that could lead them to the culprits.
In spite of the interest that was being shown for her safety, Amelia was glad when the last two police officers told her goodnight and walked out through the front door.
Even though it was after midnight, Amelia still managed to re-arrange and clean her bedroom. It was a long way from what it was before, but it was clean enough for her to sleep comfortably.
After checking to make sure that all of the windows and doors were secured, Amelia ventured into the bathroom and took a long hot shower. When she was finished, she spent another ten minutes flossing and brushing her teeth.
It was 2:56am when she finally crawled into bed. But her eventful day just wouldn't let her go to sleep, so she picked up her cell phone and she called Ice.

"Yeah…Who's this?" Ice answered sleepily, after the phone rang six times.

The sound of his voice surprised Amelia with a shiver of pleasure. She took a deep settling breath before saying, "Hi, Travis, I didn't mean to wake you up."

"Who is this?" Ice asked again.

Amelia hesitated before saying, "It's me. Amelia."

There was a long pause before Ice came back on.

"What's up?" He asked. "I thought that you would've called me earlier."

"I wanted to," Amelia said sadly. "But my house was broken into today, so it's been very hectic since I got home from the mall."

There was another long pause — much longer than the one before.

"Hello? Travis, are you still there?" Amelia inquired, after a while.

"I'm still here," Ice answered quietly. "Are you okay?" He asked.

Amelia bit into her lip, and then she closed her eyes. "I'm fine," she muttered softly. "My house is a mess, but I'm gonna spend the day tomorrow putting it back together."

"Mind if I come over and help?"

"I'll be okay. My girlfriend Danielle is coming over to help me out. Then my mom and my cousin will be here too, so I'll be fine."

"Is that a no?"

Amelia chortled lightly. "It's not a no," she said, as she rolled over in bed. "But I just don't know if I should be inviting you over to my house, after just meeting you yesterday."

"I understand," Ice told her. "But if you ever need my help, don't be afraid to ask for it."

"I won't," she smiled, and then she snuggled onto her side, placing a hand in between her thighs.

After a few quiet seconds, Ice said, "You know, I feel as if I'm to be blamed for your house being burglarized."

"And why is that?" Amelia questioned.

"Because if I hadn't forced you out to lunch, then you probably would've been home, and it probably wouldn't have happened."

"Well I'm glad that I wasn't here, because what was done to my house wasn't about stealing. It was about hurting me. So only God knows what they would've done to me, if I was here."

"So what did the police—"

"Trav'," she cut him off. "Can we talk about something else, please? 'Cause I don't wanna talk about what happened today. And I really don't wanna talk about me and my issues."

His heavy sigh caused her to cringe.

"So what do you wanna talk about?" He asked caringly.

She closed her eyes and then rolled onto her back. "We can talk about anything. I just don't wanna talk about me and what I've got going on."

CH-8

"Simms!" The guard yelled from the front of the dorm. "Get ready, you've got an attorney visit."

Blood got up from the table, where he was playing spades with three other inmates. He zipped up the front of his orange jumpsuit and then he walked up to the guard. "I'm not expecting no visit from my attorney," he grumbled.

"So you don't wanna go?" The guard asked.

Blood checked the time on his diamond encrusted Bvlgari. He sucked his teeth. "Let's go man," he then muttered miserably. "This mothafucka better have something good to tell me."

Blood was shackled and cuffed. Then afterwards he was escorted by two other guards towards the visiting room. It was Monday, so the hallways of the jailhouse were practically empty, because the majority of the inmates were at court. The few who were standing behind the doors and windows were staring at Blood as he walked by. They all knew who he was. They also knew that it was best to keep their mouths shut and not to say a word, until he was long gone.

"Try not to do anything crazy while you're in the visiting room, Simms. If you do, then we're gonna have to step in and do our jobs," the shorter of the two guards said.

Blood turned his head and shot him a fiery stare. "What the fuck is that supposed to mean?" He asked, as he stepped onto the elevator.

"It means that we can't stand by and let you put a finger on this person."

"So, it's not that cock-sucking Jew?"

"No, it's not."

As soon as Blood stepped off of the elevator, he saw her through the glass walls of the visiting room. She was seated at the metal table, looking elegant in a brown pin-striped skirt suit and a crème scarf around her neck. She had her briefcase on the table in front of her, and her Chanel specs were sitting pretty on her face.

"Prosecutor Clarke," Blood smiled, as he stepped inside of the room. He took a seat on the chair across from Amelia and then he placed his cuffed hands on top of the table. Amelia coming to see him had him thinking one thing. *"Somebody finally got through to the bitch, and they convinced her into giving me my freedom."*

With a sedate look on her face, Amelia removed her specs and looked up at the two guards. "Could you leave us alone, please?" She asked.

The two guards turned away and walked out of the room. Once the door was closed, Blood, with an arrogant grin on his face, asked, "So what's the deal, yow?"

Amelia leaned back in her seat and looked him dead in the eyes. "Do you really think that you can scare me away from your case?" She asked firmly.

Blood's expression changed from relaxed and cocky, to anxious and confused.

"What?" He asked drearily.

"You heard me, Mr. Simms. You will not scare me off of your case. So having your little boys to wreck my house is not enough to stop you from going to prison."

Blood's jaws twitched and his nostrils flared slightly.

"I don't know who's responsible for doing it," Amelia continued, with her eyes on Blood. "But on everything that I love, I won't stop until they're caught and living in a cell across from you." Her face flamed, but she huffed out a breath to contain her burning rage. "You're going to prison, Mr. Simms. I have no intention of stopping until you're there."

"Is that the reason why you're here?" Blood asked, with his temper rising. "You're here to tell me that somebody ran through your fucking house?"

"It's one of two reasons..." Amelia stated in a business-like tone. "The other is to inform you of the additional charge that I'll be filing against you."

"What fucking additional charge?" Blood flared up, with his teeth gritted.

"Did you really think that I was going to let you get away with thrashing my house? I know that you're the one who gave the order for it to be done. But it didn't scare me, Mr. Simms. All that it did was give me another reason to send your ass to prison."

Blood balled up his hands and poked his head forward. "Bitch, you can't prove shit!" He barked.

Amelia smirked candidly. "It's not for me to prove that you did it," she explained in a conniving tone. "It's for you to prove that you didn't."

Blood leaped to his feet, with his nose flaring. "Do you really think that you can keep me in jail?!" He raged, with his eyes wide. "Bitch, I own Broward County. I can have you and everybody that you know killed!"

A bit shaken, Amelia responded, "Are you threatening me?"

"Fuck a threat! Bitch, you think that I play games. You think that I'm one of those nickel and dimers across the street. Bitch, I'm Blood! I own people like you!"

Amelia reached for her briefcase. But with his hands cuffed, Blood slapped it away.

"I'm just about tired of you and your bullshit!" He barked. "Bitch you wanna see what I'm about? I'll show you what the fuck I'm about."

Amelia got up. "I'm not afraid of you; and I don't care who you own. You don't own me."

"Fuck this shit," Blood growled and then leaped across the table. But before he could get his hands on Amelia, the two guards barged into the room and grabbed him from behind. "Chill out, yow!" The shorter guard pleaded, as they struggled against Blood.

"Get off of me!" Blood fumed, still trying to get to Amelia. "I wanna snap her fucking neck!"

"Get him out of the room!" The other guard screamed at his partner, as they wrestled with Blood. "Drag his ass out the room!"

"Who this fucking bitch think she is!" Blood was raving, as two other guards ran over and helped to pull him out through the door. "Bitch, you can't keep me in jail! You hear me! You ain't big enough! You ain't fucking big enough!"

Clearly ruffled by Blood's outburst, Amelia stood on rubbery legs in the far corner of the room and looked on as Blood was dragged away. Her heart was pounding heavily and her body was shaking.

Yet and still, nothing that Blood had done or said had deterred her from sending him to prison.

$$\$$$

"Take your time, yow," Rebel gritted out, as he tightened his grip on Cristal's blonde weave.

She grimaced and glanced up at him, but did what he asked and slowed the bobbing of her head.

"That's it; just like that," he urged her on, as he leaned back onto the gray sectional, with his legs spread wide, and his solid manhood all the way inside of her mouth.

He took a hard pull from the lit blunt between his fingers, and then he reached for the bottle of Hennessy at his feet.

For fifty dollars, Cristal was always willing to please Rebel, in whatever way that he asked. She didn't care what he did to her, or what he asked to be done to him. For her it was all about getting paid. And for a fourteen year old, fifty dollars was a whole lot of money.

After a mouthful of Hennessy, Rebel grabbed Cristal by the back of her head and forced his erection down her throat. She gagged and gripped his bare legs, but she kept her lips tightly around his veined cock.

He looked down at her and smiled, when he saw the strained look on her face. He knew that she was having a hard time with him down her throat, but he didn't care. He even wanted to go deeper. But just as he stretched out on the sectional to give her more; his cell phone, which was on the end table next to a line of cocaine, blared to life.

He reached for it and then he answered, "Yow, I'm busy."

"Well, you've got one fucking second to get un-busy."

Rebel's heart skipped a couple of beats when he heard Blood's voice. He shoved Cristal away from down between his legs and sat up quickly. "Whassup, big brah. What's the deal?" He asked, in a tense tone.

"The deal is that I'm still in fucking jail. And that prosecutor ho was just here, telling me that I'm not getting out."

$$\$$$

The State Attorney's office was located on first Avenue in the downtown section of Ft. Lauderdale. Amelia's office was on the fifth floor of the massive high rise building. It was a large and lavish corner office with dark brown furnishings, floor-to-ceiling windows behind her desk, and mahogany book shelves mounted onto the clean white walls.

The early morning confrontation with Blood was still fresh in Amelia's mind, when she stepped off the elevator and started towards her office. She tried to tell herself that she wasn't worried about the things that he would try to have done to her. But deep down inside, she was very concerned. Not once in her illustrious career had she ever faced off with someone like Blood. He had money, he had power, and he was crazy with it.

As she approached her office, Amelia thought nothing about the door, which was cracked open. She was thinking that it was just her assistant who also had a key that was the one inside, so she barged straight in.

"You won't believe wha—"

Amelia froze when she found Rick behind her desk on her computer, and detective Scott Batchelor, standing in front of her file cabinet with the two top drawers open.

"What are you two doing here?" She asked angrily, as she stormed over to her desk to look at what Rick was doing on her computer. The screen was blank. "What were you doing on my computer, Rick?"

He got up and then he slid her high-back leather swivel chair back into place. "I was checking out a few state laws."

"So what happened to the computer inside of your office?" She asked hotly. "And how did you get in here?"

"Kyla let us in," Rick answered as he walked over to her. "Where were you?" He then asked, with a smug look on his face. "I was waiting to talk to you."

She cocked her head at him. "What happened to your computer, Rick? Why were you using mine?"

"Sam was waxing the floor inside of my office and I didn't want to disturb him."

Amelia sucked her teeth unbelievingly, and then she stormed over to where the detective was standing. She looked briefly inside of each cabinet drawer, before closing them.

"Detective Batchelor, it's quite odd seeing you here," she hissed.

"I'm just hanging out with my boy, Rick, that's all," the detective replied, with a dry smile. "He told me that your apartment got broken into over the weekend… Any word on who did it?"

"Not as of yet," Amelia replied.

"Well don't be afraid to ask for help, if you need it. You know that we government workers have got to stick together."

"Thanks for offering, but I've got all of the help that I need."

"I kind of figured that. But any good friend of Rick is a good friend of mine. So I had to make the offer… By the way," the detective slid his hands down inside of his pockets. "How are things going with the Mike Simms case? I heard that you've got him by the balls."

Amelia gave the detective a skeptic look while trying her best not to focus too hard on the ugly two inch scar below his left eye. After hearing so much about cops and prosecutors working for Blood, she was now leery about trusting anyone, especially detective Scott Batchelor, a veteran cop who was rumored to be crooked and corrupted.

Rolling her eyes, Amelia turned away. "I can't discuss that case with you, detective. The truth is, you're not known to be very ethical."

Batch threw his head back and laughed, "You shouldn't believe everything that you hear, Miss Clarke. And I only asked because I know how dangerous that this guy is. He's not someone that you should take lightly."

"What you're saying, I've already heard many times before. But I will not be deterred," Amelia announced, as she took the seat behind her desk.

Smirking, Batch pulled his hands from his pockets and then he moved towards the door. "Hey Rick. Gimme a call later on," he grinned. "I'm gonna go drink me a couple of beers and smoke up some weed."

Rick didn't answer. But as soon as Batch stepped out through the door, he stepped towards Amelia.

Amelia stopped him with a raised hand. "Rick, don't . . ." she said, with her face bent up. "How dare you bring that bastard inside of my office? You know that he can't be trusted. And what was he doing inside of my file cabinet. It was locked."

"No one went inside of your file cabinet, Amelia. It was wide open, when we got here."

"You actually expect for me to believe that? I always lock my cabinet."

"So now you're calling me a liar?" He stepped towards her and turned her chair, so that she could face him. "Amelia what's up with you? What's up with us?"

She got up. "I don't like the way that you've been acting, Rick. And I definitely don't like your new friend."

He held her by her arm and then he pulled her up against his chest. "I know I've been a bit on edge lately. But 'Melia, you've got to realize that I'm worried about you." He told her. "I'm really-really worried about you handling the Mike Simms' case. And honestly, I'm worried about us."

"You didn't seem too worried on Saturday. You walked out on me, when I needed you the most."

"I'm sorry," he apologized, as he swept hair from across her face. He kissed her gently on the forehead. "Let's have dinner at your place tonight. We haven't done anything romantic in a very long time."

She dropped her head. "I don't know, Rick. I'm still trying to get my apartment back together." She looked him in the eyes, when he raised her head with a finger below her chin. "I don't even—"

He cut her off by pressing his lips against hers. She was tentative at first. But when he gripped a handful of her ass and pulled her front against his; her longing for intimacy drove her to wrapping her arms around his neck and returning his kiss.

$$\$$$

The Range Rover exited the I-95 on Sunrise Blvd, then it cruised for a few minutes before making a right on 31st Ave. Ice wasn't the type who enjoyed hanging out in the hood, but he did slide through at times just to holler at his cousin, Yogi; or get a shave inside of his barbershop.

Cruising down 31st Ave at about 40 mph, Ice kept his dark tinted windows up, as he gazed out at the many females who were strutting by, in their hood-rat attire. For a brief moment, Amelia flashed through his mind. But that brief moment was all he needed, to react in the groin area.

"Damn, I'm losing it over this chick," Ice thought, as he pictured him and Amelia having sex in the wildest of ways.

Having sex with Amelia was now a constant thought of his. It was as if he had a naked image of her fixated in his mind. It was now almost impossible for him to think about sex, without thinking about Amelia. And whenever he thought about her, he found himself thinking about sex.

In an attempt to ease his on-coming erection, Ice powered up his hi-tech music system and scrolled through his song titles. He settled for Jay Z's, *Hard knock life* — one of his few favorites. Then he turned the volume up a bit and took a deep settling breath, as he tried to get Amelia off of his mind.

After cruising 31st until he got to 41st street, Ice made a left at the green light, and then he made another left inside of the small strip mall. He pulled up next to Yogi's red and white Ducati motorcycle, which was parked in front of his barber shop; that was two doors down from the small crowd that was gathered in front of the liquor store.

After checking to make sure that he had his 357 secured in his waistband, Ice stepped down from his black on black Range Rover, with his hair out in a fro. His eyes were hidden behind dark Gucci sunglasses, and the expression on his face was stern.

Before he could slam his door shut, Yogi was up on him. "What's up fam'?" Yogi greeted him loudly, with a firm dap. Yogi and Ice were not only cousins, they were also best friends. Yogi, who was a retired but still feared drug dealer, was the owner of three barbershops and a couple hair salons across Broward County. He was eight years older than Ice, but he didn't look it. That was because of the toothy grin that he walked around with, which kept him with a childlike glow. Because of his spontaneous attitude and his six-six, two hundred and fifty pound frame, he was given the name Yogi Bear. He was very easy going and friendly. But never say the wrong thing to him or cross him in any way, because then you'd see a side to him that's not very cuddly.

"What's up with the crowd?" Ice asked, once he had the Range Rover's door closed.

Yogi sucked his teeth. "Bullshit," he hissed, as he placed his back up against the Range Rover next to Ice. "So what's up, cuz, what's the word on that fool, Blood?"

"He's still down," Ice answered, as he pulled off his sunglasses and made a second look down at the crowd in front of the liquor store. "He's pulling a lot of strings trying to get out. But they've still got him cased up."

"Well, I hope they keep his ass in jail for a very long time," Yogi retorted. "I ain't down fo' no one going to prison. But sometimes it's the best place for some of us to be. Blood has done a lot of grimy shit that got looked over. But it's hard for me to look over what he did to Bam."

Ice hesitated before saying, "You ain't the only one feeling that way. A lot of people want him gone. But you know dude got a lot of pull. It's hard to keep him down, 'cause he's got the hands of quite a few big people in his pocket. Therefore, him getting a long stretch probably won't happen."

"To what I've been hearing, it probably will. Word on the streets is that the prosecutor on his case ain't backing down."

"So far, she ain't," Ice replied, after a heavy sigh. The mention of Amelia made his gut tighten with pleasure, and had him thinking about sex. He swallowed hard to maintain control. "But knowing Blood," he continued. "He'll eventually get her to back off."

Yogi sucked his teeth, feeling disappointed. "I pray to God that she doesn't," he quipped as he kicked away a Pepsi can that was at his feet. "So what you gonna do if he gets out?" He asked Ice.

Ice looked at him. "Brah, I already told you that I'm through. And now that I've got my dealership license, I'm good to go with the dealership. So I ain't going back to the game."

"That's what's up," Yogi smirked and then gave Ice some dap.

Ice took a look inside of the barbershop before asking, "You had lunch already?"

"Naw. Not yet."

"Then let's go get somethin' to eat."

"You buying?" Yogi asked, joking around.

"Don't I always," Ice snickered, then turned and slid his sunglasses back over his eyes.

But at the very moment that he was about to climb up inside of the range Rover he heard, "Ice, I wanna talk to your ass." Ice turned his eyes in the direction where the voice had echoed from and he saw Shanequa marching towards him. "I ain't got time fo' this shit," he grumbled quietly, when he saw the disgruntled look on her face.

Shanequa strutted towards him, with her eyes blazing and her hands in tight balls at her side. She was dressed daringly in a pink wife beater with no bra underneath, cut-off jeans shorts that rode high on her ass cheeks, and a pair of pink and white Converse.

She got up-close to Ice and propped a hand on her backside. "You and I need to talk," she huffed and pointed.

He gave her a once over, pausing at her firm erect nipples that were boring holes through the thin material of her wife beater. The provocative way that she stood caused his dick to stir, but he shook away his sexual urge and said harshly, "Seems as if you haven't learned shit during our time together."

She saw his hostile reaction and the fire in her eyes dimmed, "What is that supposed to mean?" She droned, as her fists loosened.

"It means, don't walk up on me and try to show out."

"I wasn't even trying to show out," she murmured, with a pitiful look on her face. "It's just that you've been treating me like shit lately."

"Didn't I tell you that it's over between us?"

"Why Ice? What did I do?"

"I ain't got the time to get into all of that," he said, as he turned and popped the door on the Range Rover.

Tears threatened the corners of Shanequa's eyes and her lips started to tremble. "So now you wanna dump me for that bitch that you were in the mall with," she spieled. "Patrice saw you, Ice. She told me about the sadity bitch. Told me how you were all up in her face, like a fucking pimple."

Ice turned and shot Shanequa a fiery stare that sent her two steps back. He saw the frightening look on her face, and knew then that he didn't have to say another word to get his message across. So he turned, climbed up inside his truck, and then slammed the door shut.

"Crazy-ass ho," he muttered, as he fired up the range and slid it into drive.

Yogi snickered. He was slouched back in the passenger's seat, gazing out the window. He waited until Ice made the right out of the parking lot to ask, "So who's this sadity bitch that Shanequa is talking about?"

Ice glanced over at him, "If I told you, then you'd probably think that I'm crazy."

"Niggah you ain't got to tell me that shit fo' me to think that. You are a crazy mothafucka."

Ice gripped the steering wheel and chortled, as he navigated the Rover down 31st Ave.

"So who's this chick, yow?" Yogi pressed. "Do I know her?"

Ice glanced over at him. "Between just me and you," he said in a calm tone. "It's the prosecutor that's prosecuting Blood."

Yogi narrowed his eyes on his younger cousin. "Are you messing with her fo' real? Or you're just fucking with her head to get Blood outta jail?"

Ice bit into his lip, as he hesitated. "I really like her," he confessed, after a while. "And it's not only to get some pussy, brah... I think that I'm falling in love with her."

Yogi snickered and shook his head in disbelief. "Niggah, you are fuckin crazy," he muttered. "You know that Blood will try to have your ass killed, if he finds out?"

"Fuck Blood," Ice cursed.

Yogi looked at him, and then busted out laughing. "Didn't know you had it in you cuz, but I'm with you on that... Fuck Blood."

CH-9

Rick showed up at Amelia's with a bottle of wine and a single red rose. He went casual with blue jeans, a fresh out the packet white Polo tee, and black Prada loafers.

"Am I late?" He asked, as soon as Amelia opened the door to let him in.

She greeted him with a peck on the lips. "Not even close," she said, as she took the wine.

He pulled his hand from his back and surprised her with the rose. "Something to put a smile on your face," he said, smiling charmingly.

Amelia took the rose and then she kissed him much harder than before. "Thank you," she then smiled warmly before prancing away, looking radiant in a simple but sexy yellow sundress.

Rick trailed behind her. "So what's up?" He asked. "I heard about the face-off that you had with Mike Simms today."

"I knew that you would. But I really don't wanna talk about it."

"No problem," he replied smoothly. He waited a few seconds to ask, "So what time did you get home?"

"I got here at about five thirty." Amelia replied, as she glanced over her shoulder at him. "What about you, how did your day go? It had to have been better than mine."

Rick took a look around the almost empty living room, and then he took a seat on the brand new sectional that was still covered with plastic. "I had a good day at work," he smiled. "But I kept thinking about spending the night with you."

Amelia returned from the dining room smiling. "You sure you wanna spend the night here with me, at my raggedy apartment?"

"I really need to," he responded, with a quiet chuckle.

Laughing lightly, Amelia took his hand and helped him up from the sectional. "You say that, as if you're desperate."

"But I am," he replied. "You know how long it's been, since we made love?"

"I was thinking the same thing earlier," Amelia said, with her brows raised. "But just so you know, my bedroom is practically empty."

"Is your bed still there?"

"Hmm-mmm," she nodded, with her lips pursed sexily.

"And it's been a while since we used it."

"It's been too long. I can't wait."

"Me neither. So let's hurry up and eat," she said, as she led him inside of her small dining room.

Amelia had prepared roast beef, coconut rice, and steam vegetables for dinner. Rick found it to be absolutely delicious. And by the time Amelia had finished with her plate, he was putting away his second.

"Was it that good?" Amelia asked smiling at Rick, who was seated across from her, licking his fingers.

"It was superb," he answered, still licking away at his fingers.

"Well, I've got vanilla flavored ice cream for dessert," she grinned. "You want some?"

"Of course I do. Go get it," he replied happily, and then reached for his wine.

Amelia pushed away from the table. "I'll be right back," she said, as she got up.

She stepped away from the table and sashayed into the kitchen, towards the stainless-steel, double-door fridge. She pulled it open; then reached inside and came out with a quart of Ben and Jerry's ice cream—just as her cell phone that was on the counter, next to the sink, blared to life.

She reached over and picked it up. Then she answered, "Hello."

"Hey, what's up?"

Amelia's heart did a tiny flip after hearing Ice's voice. She glanced over her shoulder to see if Rick was still sitting at the dining room table. He was, so she put away the ice cream and asked quietly, "Hey Trav', what's up with you?"

"Ain't shit going on. I called you like four times today and you didn't answer. What's up with that?"

Amelia quickly checked on Rick again, before saying, "It was a very crazy day fo' me. Plus you called me while I was in court, so I couldn't answer. . . I'm sorry about that."

"It's all good. . . So what's up? I miss you. I've been thinking about you all damn day."

"What were you thinking?"

"Do I have to tell you?"

"Not if you don't want to."

"Well, I don't want to."

"Why not?" Amelia asked with a childish chuckle. "Is it because your thoughts were sexual?"

"Yeah, they were . . . and I don't want you to think that I'm a perverted freak, so I rather to keep my thoughts to myself."

Amelia busted out laughing, but then she hurried and clamped a hand over her mouth when she remembered about Rick. She turned her head to check on him, but he wasn't at the dining table.

"Trav,' can I call you back?" She asked, as she made slow steps towards the arched doorway that led into the dining room.

"Can I see you?"

She wet her suddenly dry lips. "Maybe later on, 'cause he's here."

A couple of silent seconds ticked by, before Ice said, "A'ight, just holler at me later on."

"I will," she promised, right before she hung up.

When she stepped into the dining room, she found it empty. Thinking that Rick had opted for a seat inside of the living room, that's where she went next. Only he wasn't there. Surprisingly, her heart started racing and uneasiness started skittering across her skin, like cool breeze. Cold sweat started to slowly emanate from her pores. And the queasy churning inside of her gut was telling her that something was amiss. *"Where is he?"* She wondered, as she moved towards her bedroom. But when she finally got up to the open doorway and saw Rick bent over her bed — going through her wide open briefcase, that churning in her gut quickly transformed into burning rage.

"Rick! What the fuck!" She screamed and then she charged at him.

Startled, Rick spun around and then he backed away quickly. "Amelia, wait. I can explain," he blurted briskly.

"I don't want you to explain shit to me. I want for you to get out of my house. Now!"

"Will you at least let me explain?"

"No! Get out!" She stepped up to him and then she snatched away the file folder that he had inside of his hand. "Get the fuck out!" She exploded in his face.

"Amelia, wait . . ."

She shot him a fiery glare. "Don't tell me to fucking wait! Just leave and don't make me have to call the police."

He stood silently, staring at her with his head shaking. His face was masked with pain and his eyes were red and glossy. He swallowed the dry lump in his throat, "Amelia I—"

"What the fuck are you waiting on?!" She cut him off, and then she glared at him with her right hand in a tight ball by her side. "I don't wanna hear shit that you have to say! I just want you to leave, so leave now!"

"You just don't know what's going on."

Amelia flung her hands up in the air. "I can't believe this shit!" She cursed unbelievingly. "You are the one person, who I actually thought that I could trust."

"Amelia—"

"Why are you still here? And why are you calling my fucking name!" She stepped closer to him. "You think that I don't know what you were doing? I'm not dumb, Rick. I had already figured out what you were about, when I caught you inside of my office on my computer. But I wanted to be wrong about you. I didn't want to believe that you'd stoop so low."

"I wasn't looking fo' anything."

"Liar! You're a fuckin' liar! You were looking for Mike Simms' case file."

He reached out to her.

She stepped back and slapped his hand away. "Don't, fucking touch me!" She barked at him, and then pointed to the door. "You need to leave, now."

He hesitated before saying, "All that I'm trying to do is protect you. You just don't seem to understand what you've gotten yourself into. Mike Simms is not one of those little wanna be kingpins that you're used to prosecuting. The man is dangerous."

"I don't care how dangerous he is. He's not above the law."

"He's not above it, but he knows how to get around it."

"That's because he's got people like you, kissing his ass."

Pausing, Rick bit into his lip to control his burning rage. Her words were like daggers slicing into his gut, and it had him now scowling at her, with his jaws twitching.

"You really do think that you're better than me, don't you?" He growled. "Bitch, you're not even close. If it wasn't for me, you wouldn't be where you are. Remember, I'm the one who got you your job. And bitch, it ain't hard to find ways to have you lose it."

Amelia's mouth dropped open. She then cocked her head slightly, with her brows creased. "Did you just call me a bitch?"

"Yes I called you a bitch. I called you a fuckin' bitch, Amelia." Without hesitating, she pulled her hand all the way back and slapped him hard across the face.

He responded with a backhanded slap, which caught her square on the jaw and sent her sprawling across the bed. "Don't you ever put your fucking hands on me!" He roared at her. Then after glaring at her nastily, he spun on his heel and stormed out of the room, slamming the door behind him.

$$\$\$\$\$\$\$\$\$\$\$\$\$\$\$\$\$\$\$\$$$

Danielle felt her stomach move, when she stepped out of the Jamaican restaurant and saw the blood red Mercedes cruising towards her. Something was telling her to turn around and go back inside. Only that thought quickly dissipated when the Benz sped up, and then screeched to a stop at her feet.

Because of the dark tinted windows, she couldn't see inside. But she knew that Batch was sitting behind the steering wheel, staring out at her. She could feel his eyes on her. And the thought of being around him had her stomach in knots.

Wishing that she could turn back the hands of time and un-meet the corrupted detective, Danielle with her pulse racing, stepped up to the car and pulled the passenger's side door open.

From behind the steering wheel, Batch looked up at her. "Get in," he ordered.

Without saying a word, Danielle ducked down inside. She dropped her bag onto the floor at her feet, and then pulled on her seatbelt.

"What's up?" Batch asked, as the Benz pulled away from in front of the restaurant.

Danielle glanced over at him and felt something trickle down her spine, when she caught sight of the ugly two inch scar below his eye. "I was gonna call you," she said nervously. He glared at her.

She bit into her lip and hesitated before saying, "I already did what you asked me to do."

"You mean what I paid you to do," he said glowering. He pulled up behind the restaurant and then he parked next to two dumpsters. "So what happened?" He asked, in a very unfriendly tone.

Danielle wiped her sweaty palms on her jeans. "I can't get her to change her mind," she sputtered quietly.

The muscles in Batch's jaws twitched. His eyes were already dark and filled with flashing fury, and his nostrils were flaring. He turned his head and looked at Danielle with his lips sneered. "You told me that you could get her to let him go."

Danielle dropped her head and then she cowered in her seat. "I'll try again, if you want me to," she whimpered.

"What the fuck you mean by, if I want you to? Are you forgetting that I paid you twenty thousand dollars to do this?" She raised her head and looked at him. "I haven't touched the money that you gave me, so you can get it back if—"

He slapped her hard across the face, sending her head whipping back against the headrest.

"Bitch, are you fucking with me?" He growled.

She raised a hand to wipe away the blood from her mouth. But before she could even touch her face, he grabbed her by her throat and shoved her head up against the window.

"Seems as if you don't understand the severity of what's going on," he scowled. "Do you want me to explain it to you again?"

With tears gushing from her eyes, Danielle shook her head.

"Good," Batch grinned wickedly.

Danielle sucked in a deep breath to stop herself from sobbing. Her ears were ringing with a pulsing pain that had her flinching, and her mouth was filled with the coppery taste of blood.

Jerking her head fiercely, Batch leaned towards her and asked, "Can you get your friend to drop Blood's charge?"

"I don't—"

Another fierce jerk cut her off.

"Can you get your fucking friend to drop Blood's charge?" He barked in her face.

Reducing her hiccupping sobs, she nodded.

"What? I can't hear you," he snorted and shook her again.

"Yes, I'll get her to drop Blood's charge," Danielle cried.

He let go of her throat and said, "Good girl. That's all I wanted to hear."

Gasping and sobbing, Danielle reached for the door handle. He grabbed her wrist. "Where do you think you're going?" He asked her, with a devilish grin plastered across his face. When she turned her head to look at him, she saw him pulling down his zipper. "Please," she begged and started to sob. "I'm begging you, please don't do this. My mom is at my house waiting fo' me."

"Well, I've been waiting on you fo' days now," Batch smirked, as he pulled out his erection. He placed a hand at the back of her head. "Do it right and I won't take too long," he said, as he forced her mouth over his hard, veined cock.

CH-10

Ice silenced his cell phone, then he stuffed it into his pocket when he saw that it was Shanequa calling.

"Sorry about that," he apologized to Amy Cage, who was seated across from him, going through her briefcase.

"Wasn't a problem," the middle-aged attorney replied. She swiped a lock of hair from in front of her face, before offering Ice a sheet of paper. "As I was saying, I really think that it's a good buy for you. The lots are not huge. But they're big enough to hold at least seventy cars.

"I'm not worried about the lots," Ice replied, as he read over the paper.

"So what are you worried about?"

He glanced up at his lawyer, before setting his eyes back on the sheet of paper inside of his hand. They were both seated around Amy's desk, inside of her office — A large and immaculately kept office with dark brown furnishings and gray marble tiled floor.

"So what are you worried about?" Amy asked, for a second time.

"The price," Ice answered, as he put away the sheet of paper and leaned back in his seat. "I'm going to have to do a lot of work on this place, in order to get it to where I want it. Therefore, I need a better price than this."

"How much better?"

Ice inhaled deeply. "Get them to go down ten percent, and then we'll settle," he said.

The attorney looked at him dubiously. "Ten percent is a lot, Travis. I don't think that I can get them to go down that much."

"At least try."

She gave him a long, considering look, and then shifted her head slightly. "Whatever you say . . . . You're the boss," she told him. She picked up her pen and scribbled something on the notepad in front of her. Then after a quiet moment between them, she asked, "If you do buy this car dealership, will you expand, or will you just keep it as is?"

"I'm already making plans for expansion," he replied."This is a lifelong dream of mine. I'm not gonna keep it bottled up."

"I hope that you don't," she said, with a warm smile. She put the pen away and leaned back in her high-back leather chair. "Travis, can I ask you something?"

He gave her a steady look. "What's up?" He asked.

She hesitated before asking, "Are you really out of the drug game? Or you're just bullshittin'?"

"I'm out, fo' real. . . What? You don't believe me?"

"I want to."

He grinned. "Amy, how long have you been my lawyer?"

She cringed her eyes at him. "About three years... Why?"

"Have I ever lied to you?"

"Not that I can remember. But I've seen so many guys try to get out and they never do."

"That's because they said that they wanted to, but they weren't really trying to."

She laughed a little, then folded her arms below her breasts and asked, "So how are things between you and Shanequa?"

Ice frowned, and then gave the lawyer a long and steady look. Even though she was forty seven years old, her features were that of a woman in her mid thirties. He had always considered her to be beautiful. But what he felt for her was more motherly than sexual.

"Shanequa is nothing but a pain in my past," he said. "She's not a part of my future."

"Is that so?" Amy asked, with her brows going up. "So who is now the new recipient of your affection?"

He smiled at her coyly. "Are we going to talk about buying this car dealership? Or are we going to waste our times talking about shit that's irrelevant?"

"Let's waste our times talking about shit that's irrelevant," the lawyer cackled quietly. She leaned across her desk and fixed Ice with a caring stare. "So tell me," she inquired. "Who am I competing with now? And I hope that she's nothing close to Shanequa's ghetto-ass."

"She's not," Ice answered proudly.

Amy's eyes got wide. "So there is somebody," she said a bit loudly. She sat up a bit straighter, in her seat. "So tell me about her. What's her name?"

Ice allowed himself a few seconds to think about Amelia. He then flashed Amy a devastated grin, glad for the opportunity to talk about the woman that he was quickly falling in love with. "Her name is Amelia," he answered.

"Is she pretty?"

Ice chortled.

"Answer me," Amy giggled at him. "I wanna know if she's pretty, so tell me."

"She's beautiful, and she's a prosecutor," Ice revealed.

Amy's eyes got huge. "Eeeerrrkk . . . . Hold up there Mr. Burke. Pump yo' brakes, right there," she said, showing him her palm. "Are you talking about Amelia Clarke? State Attorney, Amelia Clarke."

Ice nodded. "You know her?" He asked.

Amy narrowed her eyes. "Of course I know Amelia Clarke," she stated. "We're not friends, but I do know her. And honestly, I don't believe you."

"I wonder why?"

"You know why."

"No, I don't," Ice said, shaking his head. Just then his cell phone chirped. "Do you really think that I'd make up such a thing?" He questioned, while pulling his cell phone from his pocket. When he looked at the screen and saw who was calling, he smiled, and then he offered the phone to Amy. "Here, since you don't believe me, go ahead and answer it. It's her."

"Her who?"

"Amelia," Ice replied.

$$\$$$

"Who was that? Was that your mother?" Amelia asked Ice, after talking to Amy for about five minutes.

"No. Amy's my lawyer," Ice answered.

Amelia took a seat on her bed and then she crossed her legs. Due to the fully separated curtains and the wide open windows, the inside of her bedroom was flooded with rays of the mid-day sun. "It sounds like you two are very close," she said.

"We are. Amy's been like a mother to me. She's the one taking care of the paper work for the car dealership that I'm trying to buy."

"So, how's it going?"

"Just as I had expected."

"So, when am I gonna see this car dealership?" Amelia asked playfully.

"As soon as it is officially mine," Ice told her.

"And when will that be?"

"Hopefully, it will be sometime this week."

When Amelia heard how close he was to owning the dealership a pleasant warmth oozed throughout her limbs. She didn't consider Ice to be her man. Didn't even consider them close, as of yet. But it was pleasing to her to see that he had his life going in a lucrative direction.

"So are you at work?" He asked, after a few seconds of silence between them.

Amelia got up from off the bed. "No. I'm at home. They delivered the rest of my furniture this morning, so I took the day off to re-arrange my apartment. But I should be through, within another hour or so."

"That's what's up," Ice said, sounding pleased. "Hey, do you feel like checking out a movie, later on tonight?"

"Are you asking me out to the movies?" Amelia asked, with a wide happy smile.

"Yeah," Ice replied. "I just wanna hang out with you. Take you away from all that you're doing at your house."

She rolled her eyes and pursed her lips. "Only because I really need the break," she said, looking at Danielle who had just stepped into the bathroom with a box of cleaning supplies. "Can you come pick me up at about seven?" She asked Ice.

"Seven o'clock will be fine. . . Okay then, I'll see you later on."

"No problem. Bye," Amelia chirped, before hanging up. Smiling broadly, she stuffed the cell phone into the back pocket of her jeans and then she started over to Danielle. "Are you gonna clean the bathroom?" She asked her.

Danielle shot her a questioning look before nodding. Then scrunched up her nose and asked, "So who was that?"

"Trav'," Amelia replied, with a twisted grin. "He wants to take me out to the movies tonight," she said, as she pranced towards the closet with her ass bouncing around sexily.

"So, are you going?"

"I sure am. I need to do something to take my mind off of all the shit that's been going on in my life."

"So, when am I going to meet this Trav'?" Danielle asked, while pulling on a pair of latex gloves.

"If you're here later on, I'll let you meet him then. He's coming to pick me up at seven."

"I'm probably gonna be gone by then," Danielle said, walking over to join Amelia, who was inside of the closet. She looked around for a while then asked, "So after all of this, are you still gonna continue with the prosecution against Blood?"

Amelia turned her head and looked at Danielle quizzically. "Do you really think that I'm gonna back off now?" She huffed. "A tornado couldn't pull me away from his case right now."

Danielle picked up a pair of jeans from off of the floor and then she tossed it on top of the bed behind her. "'Melia, I know that you're still pissed off about what they did to your apartment. But don't you think that it will only get worse, if you don't back away?"

"I'm not backing off. Mike Simms deserves to be in prison."

"So you're willing to risk your life, just to keep this man off the streets?"

"If you don't stand for something, then you'll fall for anything."

"'Melia, this is your life that we're talking about."

"Trust me, I'll be fine."

"But for how long? Blood is not gonna slow down."

"Neither am I."

Danielle twisted her lips, and then sighed disappointedly. "I just hope that I don't have to come and visit you inside of a hospital," she said dejectedly. "You may not know how dangerous Blood is, but I do. And I know that as long as you're pushing to send him to prison, he's gonna push to hurt you."

Amelia looked back at her friend, with her face scrunched up miserably. "Why are we talkin' about this?" She asked.

"Because you're my best friend, and I don't wanna see you get hurt.

Amelia looked at Danielle through slits. "Is that your only reason?" She asked suspiciously.

Not wanting to look Amelia in the eyes, Danielle stepped out of the closet. "What other reason could there be?" She asked, with a forced grin. "You are my best friend, 'Melia. I don't know how I would take it, if something were to happen to you. And I just feel like something will, if you keep pushing to send Blood to prison."

"How about we just don't talk about this anymore?" Amelia said, while sorting through the pile of clothes that she had on the floor. "It's like I've said, so many times before . . . . I'm not letting Mike Simms go."

$$$$$$$$$$$$$$$$$$$$$

REPERCUSSIONS by SHAWN STARR

"I don't want no part of that shit," Ice protested angrily. He was amongst Rev, Rebel, and Tip. He had met up with them, after leaving Amy's office and now he was wishing that he hadn't. "That lady has nothing to do with what's going on," he continued, with his jaws tight.

"Tell that shit to Blood," Rebel retorted. He fired up the freshly rolled blunt that Tip had given him. "Blood is the one who said that we should go ahead and do it," he continued. "And if Blood said we should do it, then it's gonna get done." Ice shot Rebel a cold look, right before turning away. He was fuming, clearly pissed off by what Blood wanted them to do.

"I say we should go ahead and do it tonight," Tip suggested, as he took a seat on the sectional in front of the Samsung 62" HDTV. They were inside the living room of his Coral Springs condo. "The sooner that we do it, the sooner that Blood gets outta jail," he said. "And we need him outta that shit, 'cause I'm broke."

Ice glared at him.

"Blood did say that we should do it tonight," Rebel announced. "And he made it clear that we shouldn't be easy about it. He's pissed that he's been locked up fo' this long. So he said that we should do whatever to get him out."

"And whatever means killing somebody, if we have to." Ice turned his eyes on Rev. "I don't see how killing this lady is gonna get Blood outta jail," he said. "We all could end up in there with him, if someone sees us and calls the police." Rev eased away from the wall by the door and then stepped towards Ice. "What's up with you, brah?" He grilled Ice up and down. "You've been on some real sucker shit, ever since Blood's been gone. I'm starting to think that you're against him getting out."

Ice returned Rev's menacing stare. "Be careful of how you walk up on me, brah. Say whatever the fuck you want, but stay out my face."

"Niggah you ain't built like that," Rev quipped aggressively.

"Walk up on me again and you'll find out."

"Niggah, you just yapping."

"Yow, Rev. Chill out man," Rebel intervened.

"Then someone else needs to check this bustah-ass Niggah!" Rev snapped, with his face bent up viciously.

Ice matched his stare. "I said what I had to say, so I'm through talking," he announced and then he turned away. A few seconds of tense silence ensued. Tip was the one who broke it by asking, "So what's the deal, yow? We gonna do this shit fo' Blood, or what?"

"You need to ask your fucking home-boy," Rev snarled, with his eyes narrowed on Ice. "He's the only one bitching like a ho. I'm starting to think that his fuck-ass is against Blood getting outta jail."

Tip walked over to Ice and nudged him in the side. "What you wanna do, man? You riding with us or what?"

Ice took a moment to think things through. He knew if he couldn't get them to change their minds about taking the order from Blood, that he would have to go along with them and find a way to stop it from getting out of control. Thinking that he would make another attempt at stopping them, he said, "There's got to be another way to get this prosecutor to drop Blood's charge. Going in on this lady is way too risky. We don't even know shit about her or where she lives."

"I don't give a damn," Tip quipped.

"Me neither," Rebel added, while smirking.

Ice inhaled deeply, and then turned his eyes on Rebel. "I really don't wanna be a part of hurting that lady," he told him. "She has nothing to do with what's going on."

Rebel sucked his teeth, and then he looked at Ice through the haze of smoke from his blunt "If you don't wanna be a part of it, then stay the fuck home," he lashed out.

"Fo' real," Rev added, smirking wickedly.

CH-11

"What time are you going to bed?" Aisha asked, as she entered the living room with a steaming cup of herbal tea.

"Maybe in another thirty minutes, or so," Miranda answered.

"Did you know that it's almost midnight?"

"I know," Miranda replied, as she lowered the pair of wooden knitting needles. She placed them, along with the multi-colored scarf that she was knitting, on the sofa next to the ball of yarn at her side. "Thank you," she told Aisha, as she took the tea.

"I'm going to bed," Aisha announced, as she reached for the text book that she had left on the sofa.

"Are you through studying for the night?" Miranda asked her.

"Mmm-mmm . . . I'm tired."

"As always," Miranda chortled, as she sipped on her tea.

Smiling, Aisha gave her aunt a quick peck on the cheek. "See you in the morning," she said, as she turned and flounced away.

"Sweet dreams, baby girl," Miranda replied lightly.

Miranda Simpson was a kind and caring kindergarten school teacher who spent a lot of her time helping others. She stayed with a warm smile on her face, and her smooth olive complexion and bright doe-like eyes gave her features a youthful glow. At fifty one, Amelia was her only child. But she was also the guardian of her fourteen year old niece, Aisha.

After a few slow sips from her tea, Miranda put the tea cup aside and reached for her knitting needles and scarf. She was about to get back into her knitting, when a quiet knock on the front door stopped her.

A bit startled by the late night interruption, Miranda got up and tied the strings at the front of her housecoat, and then she started towards the door.

"Who is it?" She asked, when she was about an arm's length away.

"Pizza delivery."

"Pizza delivery?" Miranda mumbled, looking confused. She unlocked and pulled the door open. "I didn't order any pi—" A hard shove in her chest cut her off and sent her stumbling back across the room. She landed hard on her ass, knocking over the vintage end table and the lamp in the process.

One of the four masked men who were standing at the door barged inside of the house and grabbed Miranda by the front of her housecoat. He then shoved a .45 special in her face and growled fiercely, "Scream and I'll put a bullet in your fucking head."

"Please don't hurt me," Miranda pleaded, with her hands held high. "If it's money that you want, then I'll give you all that I have."

"Are you alone?" Rev asked. He was the one holding the gun at Miranda's head.

Miranda hesitated.

Rev slapped her across her face with the .45. "I asked you a fucking question!" He barked at her. "Are you alone?"

"Yes!" Miranda cried out loudly, as blood trickled down the side of her face. "Yes, I'm alone! I'm alone! There's nobody here with me!"

"She's lying," Rebel said, stepping next to Rev. He turned to Tip and Ice, who were decked out in full black with ski-masks pulled down over their faces. "Search the house," he ordered.

"I'm alone!" Miranda yelled, and got another skull cracking slap from Rev.

Ice cringed and grimaced.

"Go search the fuckin' house!" Rebel repeated loudly.

REPERCUSSIONS by SHAWN STARR

Tip took off, but Ice hesitated with his fists clenched tightly and his teeth gritted beneath his face-mask. Seeing Rev slapping Miranda across her face had spiked his anger. He didn't want to leave her alone. What he really wanted to do was pull out his Glock and shoot Rev between his eyes.

"What the fuck you standing there waiting on, yow! I said to go and search the fucking house," Rebel barked again.

"I said I'm alone," Miranda repeated, but not as loud or as strong as before.

But even then, Rev slapped her again and growled, "Shut the fuck up, bitch."

Ice started towards Rev, but stopped when it dawned on him that Miranda really wasn't alone inside the house. He remembered Amelia mentioning her younger cousin who stayed with her mother. He knew that if this younger cousin was to be found by Tip, that it would add a whole lot of complications to an already complicated situation. He didn't want to leave Miranda by herself with Rebel and Rev. But he knew that he had to, so he turned and hurried away.

Tip had gone towards the closest bedroom that Ice assumed belonged to Miranda. So he hurried by it and ran down the hallway to search the rooms at the back of the house.

The first door that he got to was painted light pink with an "I'M BUSY STUDYING" sign posted on it.

"*Please God, if she's here let me be the one to find her,*" Ice prayed to silently, as he pushed the door open and stepped inside. He took a quick look around the crammed but well-kept bedroom. The lights were all on, and the faint voice of Keisha Cole was coming from the ear buds of the iPod that was on the bed.

Sensing that someone was inside of the room, Ice closed and locked the door behind him. Then he pulled the Glock 40 from his waistband. He had only taken two steps, when a shadowy movement caught his eyes.

He turned to his right. "I'm not gonna hurt you," he said quietly, as he moved slowly towards the closet. When he got up to the door, he took hold of the handle. "I wanna help you, so please don't scream," he whispered, as he pulled the door open.

"Please d-d-don't hurt me," Aisha whimpered quietly. After hearing the chaos inside of the living room, she had leaped off of her bed and ran inside of the closet to hide. She was now covered down in a dark corner with her arms wrapped tightly around her knees. Her face was matted with tears and she was shaking as if it was twenty below zero.

Ice put a finger to his lips. "I'm not gonna hurt you," he told her quietly.

Aisha didn't budge. Only her fear-filled eyes moved from Ice's masked face, down to the gun inside of his hand.

Ice saw her eyes and shoved the gun back into his waistband. "Do you have a cell phone?" He asked her.

She shook her head fearfully.

"*Shit!*" Ice thought. He took a quick look around the room. "I want you to get out of the house," he said. "Go next door and call the police."

Aisha's eyes got wide with confusion, but she still didn't move.

Ice offered his hand. "Don't be afraid," he pleaded. "If my friends find you, then they'll hurt you. You've got to get out of this house."

Aisha's lips twitched, but she was still wrapped up in fear. "Are they go-gonna kill my auntie?" She asked shakily.

Ice took a quick look back at the door. "I won't let them," he whispered. "But they'll hurt her, if you don't go and call the police."

Still unable to move because of fear, Aisha just stared steadily at Ice.

"Fuck," Ice muttered quietly, then grabbed her by her upper arm. "You've got to get outta here," he told her, as he pulled her up to her feet. He looked around the room frantically, before setting his eyes on the window by the dresser. "I'm gonna help you out through the window. Go next door and call the police."

Aisha hesitated. But when Ice started off, she wiped her teary eyes and then she started out after him.

"Now, this is what's gonna happen," Rebel said, pacing slowly as if he was an army general addressing his troops. "You're gonna call your daughter. And you're gonna convince her to drop whatever charge they've got against Mike Simms."

Miranda looked up at Rebel through riled eyes. She was seated on the sofa, with her hands tied behind her back, and left side of her face was now covered with blood. "You might as well kill me," she snarled. "'Cause I won't do shit fo' you."

Rebel stopped, and then he turned and backhanded Miranda hard across the face. "You think this is a fucking joke!" He barked at her. "You're gonna do what the fuck I say, or I'm gonna put a bullet in yo' fucking head."

"Go ahead and do it!" Miranda uttered, crying. "I'd rather die than to do what you want."

"Fuck this shit," Rev growled and then he charged down on Miranda. He struck her over the head with the butt of the .45, and then he grabbed a handful of her hair and pressed the muzzle of the gun into her jaw. "Listen here, you stubborn bitch. You're gonna get your daughter to drop Blood's charge, you hear me?"

A bit dazed, Miranda looked Rev dead in the eyes. "Do what you have to," she muffled weakly, as blood trickled from her mouth.

"Stubborn bitch!" Rev snarled, as he struck her across the head again. He punched her in the gut with his left fist, and then came up with his right hand and slogged her below the chin with the gun.

Miranda groaned painfully, as she fell back onto the sofa, barely clinging onto consciousness. Blood was gushing from her head, her nose, and her mouth. Her lips were busted and swollen out of shape. And there was a deep bloody hole above her left eye.

"Let's just kill the bitch and get the fuck outta here," Rev suggested irritably. "The bitch is just as stubborn as her fucking daughter."

"She is," Rebel agreed.

"Then let's just kill her and bounce," Rev pressed, with his gun pointed at Miranda's head.

"There's no need to kill her, as of yet," Ice said, as he hurried back into the living room. He stopped and looked steadily at Miranda, before turning to Rebel. "Just look at her," he said, grieving inside. "If this doesn't get her daughter to drop Blood's charge, then nothing will."

"Killing her will only double the pain for that prosecutor bitch," Rebel said. He gave Ice a skeptical look. "And where the fuck have you been?" He asked rudely. "What took you so long?"

Ice turned his head and looked at Miranda. "I thought that I heard someone running through the backyard, so I went outside to check it out."

This caused Miranda to slowly raise her head and look at Ice through her one good eye. The other had swelled into a horrid-looking black and purple baseball sized knot.

"So did you see anybody?"Rebel asked.

Ice shook his head. "Naw . . . The back yard was empty."

"Niggah, you sure?" Rev asked bitterly.

Ice glared at him. "No, I'm not fucking sure," he replied, with his voice as hard as steel.

Rev aimed his gun at Ice's head. "Niggah, you gonna keep going until I have to cap your fuck-ass."

"Make sure that I'm dead, when you do it," Ice fired back, and then he turned to walk away. But he stopped when he saw what Tip was doing.

"Niggah, you fucking serious?" He snapped sharply.

"I ain't gonna let this shit go to waste," Tip giggled. He was standing next to Miranda, with a hand down inside of her housecoat, fondling her breasts. "I say that we all take turns on her. Give her and her daughter a little something to remind them that Blood ain't somebody to be fucked with"

"That's what's up," Rev said, with his eyes fixed steadily on Ice.

Ice was glaring at Tip. "Niggah, you that desperate?"

"This ain't got nothing to do with desperation. This is all about getting my dawg outta jail," Tip replied, as he ripped apart the front of Miranda's housecoat. "Now this is what I'm talking about," he blurted out, when he saw that Miranda was only wearing a pink lacy panty underneath her coat.

Miranda was so weak and disoriented; all she could do was look up into Tip's masked face. "Please," she groaned weakly. But Tip ignored her and grabbed one of her breasts, even though they were both covered with blood. He then looked back at Rebel. "You want me to go first?" He asked anxiously.

"Go ahead. Do your thing," Rebel urged, smiling.

If it wasn't for the ski-mask over his face, everyone would've seen how Tip's face lit up like a Christmas tree. He slid a hand down between Miranda's legs and groped her. "Damn, old woman," he uttered, as he fondled her aggressively. He tried to force her down onto the sofa, but Miranda started to struggle against him. She was desperately trying to hold on to her dignity, with the little bit of strength that she had left.

Ice stood and looked on with a painful pull in his gut. He was trying to come up with a way to help Miranda, but he was having a hard time concentrating. He swallowed hard and grimaced when Tip ripped off Miranda's panties. Then as if he was possessed, he grabbed her by her throat and pried her legs apart.

"Are you niggahs really gonna do this?" Ice questioned angrily. "You niggahs really gonna rape a woman, who's old enough to be our fucking mother?"

"We ain't only gonna rape her. We're gonna kill her ass after," Rev blurted.

"It's whatever to get Blood outta jail," Rebel added.

"Man, what the fuck are you waiting on? Fuck the bitch," Rev jeered. His voice was steady and harsh, but he was smiling beneath his mask.

Even though Miranda was squirming and twisting around on the sofa, Tip still forced his way in between her legs. "Calm the fuck down!" He growled loudly, and then slapped her across the face.

Ice moved towards him.

Rev aimed his gun at Ice's head and stopped him. "Chill the fuck out and let the man do his thing," he threatened.

Ice shot Rev a deathly stare. "Niggah, you bettah kill me!" He barked. "'Cause I ain't gonna let you niggahs rape this woman."

Rebel grabbed onto Ice's arm and pulled him away. "You need to back off, yow. We gonna do this fo' Blood, whether you like it or not."

Ice ripped his arm away. "Raping her ain't gonna help Blood!" He gritted out then looked over at Tip, who had Miranda pinned down.

Tip let go of Miranda's throat, and grabbed a handful of her hair. "You're only making this shit hard on yourself," he said, as he hustled to unbuckle his pants. But just as he got it unbuckled, Miranda rose up on the sofa and sank her teeth into the left side of his face, with the ferocity of a deranged pit bull.

Tip howled in agonizing pain, as Miranda tore into his flesh. When she finally let go of him, he fell back onto the floor with his hands over the left side of his bloody face.

Laughing at Tip, Rev walked over and punched Miranda square in the face. Her head snapped back and she groaned, as she collapsed back down onto the sofa.

Washed with rage, Tip got up with his ski-mask ripped and stained with blood. He snatched the .45 away from Rev and stumbled towards Miranda.

"Fucking slut! I'm gonna fucking kill you!" He cried out loud, as he raised the gun. But just as he was about to aim it at her head, Ice stepped in front of him.

"Hol' up, brah!"

"Get the fuck off of me!" Tip barked and shoved Ice away.

Ice grabbed onto his arm. "Wait the fuck up, man. You niggahs don't hear that?" He asked, hoping that it was the police sirens that he heard and not his ears ringing.

"Get the fuck off of me!" Tip snapped again.

"Shut the fuck up and listen!" Ice barked in his face.

The room went still and silent. Then from in the distance, Rebel heard the sounds of blaring sirens. He looked at Rev.

"That's the fucking police," he blurted like a coward, and then ran towards the front door. "Let's get the fuck outta here," he announced apprehensively.

Rev moved after him, but Tip was still fixed on killing Miranda. He tried to pry his arm away from Ice. "Get off me, yo! I'm gonna kill this bitch before I leave!"

Ice forced him towards the door. "She's fucked up as it is, man. Let's just get the fuck outta here."

"I'm not leaving her alive!"

Ice looked back at Miranda and he felt his heart sputter, when their eyes met. Her nakedness and disfigured face sent remorse surging throughout his veins, like adrenaline. He looked away quickly, unable to stomach the bloody state that she was in.

"Let's get outta here man," he pleaded with Tip.

"Look at what she did to my fucking face!" Tip barked, as he jostled to aim the gun at Miranda's head. But Ice wouldn't let him. He held onto Tip, with every bit of strength that he could conjure and forced him out through the door.

The sirens were now loud and close by.

"Yow, let's go!" Rebel barked from inside of the rented Infiniti Q45.

Tip hesitated, but when a sudden burst of red and blue lights hit the corner at the far end of the street, he snatched his arm away from Ice and they both ran towards the Q45.

CH-12

Dressed in a pair of blue Gap jeans and white Reeboks, Amelia barged through the doors of Broward Medical Hospital and sprinted through the hallway. She raced up to the information desk and shoved the lounging janitor out of the way.

"I'm looking for Miranda Simpson! She was brought in about thirty minutes ago!" She barked at the young, blonde hair representative, who was sitting behind the desk taking sips from a can of Red Bull.

The representative rolled her eyes and pursed her lips, as if she wasn't in the mood to be bothered. "Please have a seat and wait," she said, with a bit of attitude. "I'll be with you in a minute."

Amelia slapped the Red Bull out of her hand. "Don't tell me to fucking wait. I need to see my mother now!"
Startled, the representative turned her full attention towards the computer in front of her. "Wha-what's your mother's n-name?" She asked shakily, as her fingers danced over the computers keyboard.
"Miranda Simpson."
With her eyes fixed on the computer screen, the young blonde said, "Miss Simpson is still inside of the OR, undergoing surgery."
"Where is the OR?"
"Down the hall," the representative pointed.
Amelia took off down the hallway, like a raging bull.
""Hey! You can't be running through here like that!"
Amelia ignored the security guard and kept on running. She made it around the corner, just in time to see a male paramedic leaving the operating room with an empty gurney.
"Excuse me!" She called out to him. "Can you please tell me if Miranda Simpson is in that room?"
The Paramedic stopped and gave Amelia a leery once over. He then wiped his sweaty forehead with his forearm. "Are you family?" He asked, as if he was tired.
"I'm her daughter," Amelia answered quickly.
The paramedic glanced over his shoulder at the OR's door. "Your mother is currently undergoing surgery. So your best bet is to go and wait inside of the waiting room."
"How is she?"
"I'm not a doctor so I—"
"I don't care. Just tell me something. Please."
The paramedic sighed and then he pinched the bridge of his nose. "Your mother was beaten very badly," he said in a sad, quiet tone. "She received a lot of blows to her head. And I really don't want to lie to you, but I think that she's got a fractured skull."

Amelia's shaking hands went up to her mouth. With her lips quivering and her eyes gushing tears she asked, "Will she be okay?"

"I really don't know what to tell you," the paramedic shrugged. "But from what I've seen, I can tell that your mom is a fighter. She's a very strong woman. So I wouldn't be surprised if she made a full recovery." He started off and then he looked back at Amelia, when he was only a few steps away. "I hope that you guys catch whosoever's responsible." Amelia dropped her face into her hands. "I'm starting to think that I should let him go," she muttered, while sobbing.

$$$$$$$$$$$$$$$$$$$

Ice was seated and slouched over at the bar with a bottle of Hennessy and an aiming to get pissy-ass drunk. Normally, he wouldn't go beyond a buzz. But after seeing what happened to Miranda, and knowing that he was a part of it, the only aid that he could find for his remorseful pain was alcohol. As he filled his glass for the sixth time, an image of Miranda's bloodied, bruised, and battered face popped up into his head. He grimaced and tried to hold in his pain, but even a blind person could see that he was clearly hurting. He was devastated by what had gone down.

It was almost three o'clock in the morning, but Sophia's Pub and Lounge was still open for business. The glowing liquor advertisements behind the bar had the place flooded with bright colors. And Lionel Richie's *Stuck on you* was playing on the stereo. Four men were seated to Ice's right, at the far end of the bar. And another was at his left, hunched over a glass of Jamaican white rum mixed with Pepsi.

"You'd better have a good reason to be here drinking your way into fucking oblivion."

Yogi, who had just walked in, fumed as he walked up to Ice. Still hunched over his glass, Ice wiped his sweaty forehead. "How you found out... that I was here?" He muttered.

"I called him," Sophia, the owner of the Pub said, from inside the bar.

Ice gave her a blank glance, and then went back to his liquor. Yogi placed his motorcycle helmet on a nearby stool. "Hey, you a'ight?" He asked, as he pulled off his gloves.

"I'm good," Ice mumbled.

"You don't look good to me. You look like shit."

Ice swallowed a mouthful from his glass, then cringed as the liquor burnt its way down to his gut. He hesitated before saying, "They almost killed her, brah… They almost killed that lady and I would've been involved."

Yogi's jaws got tight, as he slammed his gloves down on the counter. "Brah! I told you to leave that shit alone!" He fumed quietly. "I told you not to go with those mark-ass niggahs. You said that you wouldn't. You said that you were going to the movies with Amelia."

"We did go to the movies."

"So how the hell did you end up around fuck-ass Rebel and Rev?"

"I had to go with them," Ice replied, as he wiped his mouth on his sleeve. "If I wasn't there, then they would've raped and killed her."

Yogi sighed heavily, as he closed his eyes and pinched the bridge of his nose. "So how is she?" He asked, after a few seconds had ticked by.

"I don't know… The police showed up, so chances are, she's at the hospital."

Shaking his head pitifully, Yogi took a seat at the bar. "You've got to pull away from Blood and his bullshit. This whole shit is bound to end up badly."

"That's easier said than done."

"What the fuck you mean?" Yogi was hot.

Ice took a sip from his glass. "You know what happens to those who cross Blood?"

"Fuck that Niggah. Whatever he wanna bring, then let him bring it. We've got guns too."

"But it's not only about me, brah... What's gonna happen to Amelia, if I pull away?"

"The same shit that's happening to her now. . . Niggah, you ain't doing shit to protect her. How do you think she's gonna take it when she sees her mother laid out on a hospital bed, close to death? You could've stopped that shit before it happened and you didn't."

Ice raised his head and glowered at Yogi. "If it wasn't for me shit would've been worse."

"Keep telling yo'self that," Yogi spat bitterly. "Niggah, there's no justification in playing both sides of the fence. It's either you're with Blood or against what he's doing. I've never known you to be a coward. But right about now, you're acting like one. . . Brah, if you're ready to step away from that fuck-ass Niggah, Blood, then tell that Niggah fuck you and step the fuck away. Whatever comes after that then we'll deal with it—guns blazing, if that's the direction that he wants to take it."

"I'm not afraid of Blood," Ice replied, then took another drink from his glass. "But I'm afraid of what he'll do to Amelia, if I'm not there fo' her. I can't let them hurt her."

Yogi huffed out a breath. "Brah, you better open your fucking eyes," he said seriously. "She's already hurting. And until Blood is in prison for good and that fool Rebel is either dead or in prison with him, she's gonna go through more . . . . Probably go through much worse."

"I won't let that happen," Ice muttered.

Yogi raised his hand to Sophia, asking for an empty glass. "You really think that Amelia is gonna wanna be with you, when she finds out that you're neck deep in this shit?"

"I'm neck deep because of her," Ice growled. He took another full-mouthed drink from his Hennessy, and then banged the empty glass down on the counter. "If it wasn't for her, then I would've stayed my ass at home tonight. I wouldn't have been a part of what went down with her mother."

"You don't need to convince me," Yogi replied, as the bartender returned with the empty glass. He took it and poured himself some Hennessy. "You're gonna need to convince her when she finds out that you're involved. And believe me, she will find out."

Ice grunted and winced. Then he reached for the Hennessy bottle.

Yogi snatched it away. "You need to chill out, man. You've already had enough to drink," he said firmly.

Ice sucked his teeth and then he got up. He stumbled a bit, but grabbed onto Yogi's shoulder, before he could fall. "I'm outta here," he grumbled, as he pulled his truck keys from his pocket. "I'm gonna take my ass home and get a nice cold shower."

"Wait up. I'll drop you home."

"I'm good. I can manage," Ice said, as he stumbled.

Yogi turned the glass to his head and emptied it with one drink. He then got up and snatched the keys out of Ice's hand. "I'm not asking you to let me drop you home," he said, reaching for his gloves and helmet. "I'm telling you that I'm taking you home, so come the fuck on; let's go."

$$$$$$$$$$$$$$$$$$$$$$$

Amelia looked up at the big round clock in the hospital's waiting room and saw that it was 3:52am. Her mother was still in surgery and she was worried sick. A few close relatives and friends had shown up and were there waiting patiently, along with three of Miranda's co-workers, who were seated next to each other with sad looks on their faces.

After a heavy sigh Amelia turned to Aisha, who was curled up inside of the chair next to her. "You okay?" She asked her quietly.

Aisha wiped her teary eyes and nodded.

Amelia put an arm around her and then she pulled her close. "Mom's gonna be okay. You'll see," she said, tearing up. "I'm so proud of you. If you hadn't of gotten away and called the police, they probably would have killed her."

A streak of tears rolled down Aisha's cheek. "I just don't understand why that guy let me go and told me to call the police. He was one of them."

"I don't understand it either," Amelia said, stroking the back of Aisha's head. "I'm grateful for what he did. But let's not bust our brains trying to figure out why he did it. He's a part of what happened to mom, so that's still enough for us to hate him."

"But what if he didn't wanna be there? What if he was forced and left without a choice?"

"There's always a choice."

"But what if he wasn't there? Don't you think that his friends would've killed me and auntie?"

Amelia sat motionless, staring at her much younger cousin and not knowing what to say.

"Amelia Clarke?"

The entire room hopped up.

Amelia hurried up to the doctor. "I'm Amelia," she said anxiously. "Please tell me that she's okay."

The doctor hesitated for a moment, and then he curled his lips into a tiny smile. "Your mom is going to be just fine."

The entire waiting room erupted.

Smiling broadly, the doctor waited a while before saying, "Miss Simpson is a very strong woman. She took a hell of a beating. But miraculously she pulled through, without any life threatening injury. She has a fractured skull, but it's not that serious enough for you guys to lose any sleep over it."

REPERCUSSIONS by SHAWN STARR

"What about brain damage?" Miranda's good friend, Cynthia asked.

"Surprisingly, there is none. Her face is a bit disfigured and there are a few lacerations and an ugly contusion on her forehead. But in time, those will all go away."

"When can we see her?"

"You all can go see her right now. She's on her way up to recovery. But . . ." The doctor turned to Amelia, "She asked to have a few alone minutes with you and your cousin."

Ten minutes later, Amelia slowly pushed open the door to her mother's semi-private hospital room and stepped inside behind Aisha. Miranda was lying in bed with her eyes closed. About sixty percent of her head was wrapped in bandage, and she had several wires and tubes attached to her body.

"Mom," Amelia called out quietly, as tears gushed from her eyes.

"Amelia," Miranda croaked. She eased her eyes open and then turned her head. "Hey there," she managed to smile, when she saw Amelia and Aisha.

"Auntie, are you okay?" Aisha asked crying.

"I feel much better than I look," Miranda smiled weakly at her. She patted the bed next to her. "Come here."

Aisha walked over and climbed up on the small bed next to her aunt. She hugged her gently and kissed her on the forehead.

Miranda smiled and said quietly, "I was so worried about you. But all of my worries went away, when I heard that you were safe."

"One of the robbers found me and he helped me to get away."

"They weren't robbers," Miranda said, shaking her head slowly. "And that person that helped you to get away must've been the very same person who saved my life. I would've been dead if he hadn't stepped in front of his friend." Miranda slowly turned her head to look at Amelia. "They did all of this because of their friend that's locked up. They want for you to let him go."

Once again Amelia burst into tears. "Oh mom, I'm so sorry." She dropped her face into her hands and cried, "I'm sorry. I'm so sorry. I could've stopped it from happening. I'm sorry."

"Amelia I don't blame—"

Miranda was interrupted by Amelia's blaring cell phone. As she sobbed and wiped her eyes, Amelia pulled the cell phone from her pocket and answered, "Hello."

"Did I call at a bad time? Sounds as if you're crying?"

"Who is this?" Amelia asked, looking puzzled.

"How is your mother? I heard she got fucked up, real bad." Amelia stiffened. She looked steadily at her mother and then asked again, "Who is this?"

"Stop playing dumb, prosecutor Clarke. You know who the fuck this is. I'm the same niggah that you're trying to send to prison."

Amelia shuddered. "How are you calling me from jail? How did you even get my number?"

"The same way that I got your mother's address," Blood answered. "Money is a powerful thing, prosecutor Clarke. You'd be surprised by the things that you can get done, when you have money. So how is your mom?"

"What do you want from me?" Amelia gripped the phone tightly and cried.

"You know what I want. Drop the fucking charge you've got against me, so that I can get out of this shithole."

"You didn't have to do this to my mother."

"I'm in jail. I didn't do shit," Blood giggled. "But believe me; it can get a whole lot worse."

"Please, stop what you're doing," Amelia cried, as she turned away from her mother's unblinking stare. "I'll drop your charge. Just please stop what you're doing. I'll drop—" He hung up on her. "Hello. Hello."

"Amelia."

"Hello," Amelia cried into the phone.

"Amelia."

Wiping her tear-stained face, Amelia turned to face her mother.

Miranda raised her hand with the intravenous line. "Come here," she called over Amelia.

Amelia hesitated. Then with her head lowered, she walked over and took her mother's hand. "Mom I'm sorry," she whimpered. "I'm so sorry. All of this is because of me being stubborn."

Miranda reached up and she wiped her daughter's tears. "Stop saying that you're sorry," she whispered, too weak to raise her voice. "I don't blame you for what happened. But I'll never forgive you, if you give those bastards what they want."

"Mom I—"

"Shhhh!" Miranda hissed, as she caressed the back of Amelia's hand. "Baby girl, don't be afraid of these people. You've got a job to do, so do it."

"Mom, you just don't understand."

"I understand full well, what's going on," Miranda grimaced. "These bastards are trying to scare you into giving them what they want…Do you think that I'm dumb?"

"You're the smartest person that I know," Amelia muffled out, as she gave her mother's hand a light squeeze. "And the strongest," she added lightly.

"Then listen to me," Miranda said, while hugging Aisha and pulling her close. "I try not to get involved in what you do. But I'll never forget what happened to me last night. I don't hold it against you. But nothing will make me happier, than seeing those responsible behind bars. You're in the position to do that, baby girl. So don't get side-tracked because of what happened to me. Use it as your motivation to rid the streets of all of those responsible."

"But what if they try to hurt you again?"

"Believe me, they won't. They know better. I got one of the bastards real good. Bit out a good piece of his face."

Amelia reacted with wide eyes. "Were you actually fighting back?" She asked, surprised by her mother's actions.

"If I didn't, then I wouldn't be your mother. I'm just as stubborn and persistent as you are. I argue and fight for what I believe in. I know that me being here looking like this is very painful for you. But please, don't give in to these people and what they want."

Amelia actually smiled. She waited a long while before leaning over to kiss Miranda's cheek. "Just for you, I won't," she said with determination.

"That's what I wanna hear," Miranda smiled, grimacing right after. She touched her bandaged forehead and then said, "Make sure that you show those bastards that they fucked with the wrong bitches."

Amelia and Aisha stared wide-eyed at each other, and then busted out laughing.

CH-13

Danielle added another coat of lip gloss to her already glossy lips, and then she looked at herself inside of the dresser's mirror. She was getting ready for work, but she really wasn't in the mood to go.

Because of Batch, she had grown hesitant to even leave her house. She had found out in a painful way that making a deal with him was the biggest mistake that she had ever made. Due to the fact that she couldn't get Amelia to drop the charge against Blood, he had become very aggressive and abusive. It had even gotten to the point where he was now threatening to kill her, if she didn't do what he had paid her for.

On several occasions, she tried to return the money that he gave her. Only, he wouldn't take it back. And the one time that she mentioned going to the police, he punched her in her face a couple times and told her that he'd kill her or have someone to kill her if she did.

Danielle so regretted agreeing to what Batch had asked her to do. She felt as if she had betrayed Amelia, and that wasn't her intent. Not when she considered Amelia her best and dearest friend.

After retrieving her bag, cell phone, and keys, Danielle headed out of the bedroom and towards the front door. When she stepped outside, she closed and locked the door behind her. Then she started towards her car, which was backed into the driveway.

She was only a couple of steps away from opening the car door, when she took notice of Batch, who was leaning against a black Escalade parked across the street. Danielle felt her spine stiffen when he eased away from the SUV and started towards her.

Her vision suddenly got blurred and her breathing got heavy. The bitter taste of fear was now heavy on her tongue. She bit down on her quivering lip and then she pulled the straps of her bag up on her shoulder. "How did you find out where I live?" She asked, in a very fearful way when Batch got up to her.

He smirked. "I followed you home last night."

She watched him fearfully, as he removed his sunglasses. "You can't just show up at my house like this, you know. My neighbors are very nosy and they don't like seeing strangers around," she protested, with worry lines etched across her forehead.

"Let them call the police," Batch giggled disgustedly.

Danielle swallowed the lump inside of her throat and then she inhaled heavily. "I really don't have the time right now; I've got to get to work," she told him, while raising the car's remote to unlock the doors.

He grabbed her wrist and then he started to pull her across the driveway towards the house. "I don't give a fuck about where you've got to go. I wanna know what's up with your friend."

"I already told you that I can't get her to do it."

"And I told you that you'd better get her to do it."

He stopped at the front door and then he glared at her. "Open the door," he ordered.

"Please." Danielle begged. "I've got to go to work."

He dug his thumb into her wrist and grinned, as she grimaced in pain. "Don't let me ask you again," he said icily.

$$$$$$$$$$$$$$$$$$$$

Amelia spent the first half of her Tuesday morning in a meeting with her boss and a few co-workers. The meeting had ended twenty minutes ago, so she was now back inside of her office with Kyla, going over Blood's case.

They were seated across from each other at Amelia's desk, with photos of Bam's hacked body scattered between them.

REPERCUSSIONS by SHAWN STARR

With a sickening look on her face, Amelia dropped one disturbing photo and then she reached for another. "Only a heartless monster could do a human being like this," she said, while staring at a photo of Bam's severed arm,
"Do you think that it's Mike Simms' first time doing something like this?" Kyla asked.
Amelia lowered the photo and then she looked over at her assistant. Kyla had been her assistant for just about three years — and a wonderful three years it had been for them. At five-two, Kyla was very shapely and petite. She had a beautiful oval shaped face, with large doe-like eyes and a smile that was infectious. Amelia liked Kyla a lot. She liked how bright and respectful she was, and she also liked how Kyla took pride in her job as her assistant.
As she picked up another photo, Amelia said, "He's been charged with murder before. But his ass has never been convicted."
"Do you think that he'll be convicted this time?"
"After what he did to my mom, believe me, he will," Amelia lashed out angrily, and then tossed the photo down onto her desk. She sucked in a deep breath. "This monster is going to prison, Kyla, and I'll be asking for him to get the max."
"You know he fired Scott Rosenberg and hired Bill Ferentz, right?"
"I don't care if he hired a dead fucking Johnnie Cochran!" Amelia snapped. "His ass is going to prison. And I won't stop until all of his flunkies are there with him."
After a moment to look over a photo of the machete that was used to kill Bam, Amelia picked up the police report and got up from behind her desk.
"Kyla," she called out to her assistant as she walked barefooted over to the filing cabinet across the room. "I want for you to set up a meeting with the arresting officer," she instructed. "And I also want you to get me a list of Mike Simms' prior charges."

Kyla got up. "You want me to set up a meeting for today?" She asked.

"No. Set it up for tomorrow," Amelia said, just as her cell phone rang. She turned away from the filing cabinet and walked back over to her desk. "Set it for tomorrow morning," she told Kyla, as she picked up her cell phone.

"Tomorrow morning it is," Kyla assured, as she walked out the office.

Amelia checked her cell phone, and then smiled when she saw Ice's number on the screen. "Hello," she answered pleasantly.

"Hey, what's up?" Ice came on and asked.

Amelia felt a surge of tingling pleasure swirl around inside of her stomach. Propping her ass up against the edge of her desk, she cooed, "Hi Travis, what's going on?"

"You tell me... Are you avoiding me?" He asked. "I haven't heard from you in days."

Amelia sighed, "I've just been really busy. And I told you that my mom was in the hospital, so I was spending a whole lot of time there."

A few quiet seconds ticked by before Ice asked, "Is she out? Is she okay?"

"She's back at home and she's a lot better than what she was, so I'm grateful." Amelia closed her eyes and said a quick prayer, then asked. "So why haven't you called me, it's not like you don't have my number?"

"I really wanted to, but I had so much shit on my mind I had to take a few days to think things through. . . So what's up with you? What time are you getting off work?"

"At five...Why?"

"I wanna take you out."

"On a Tuesday? Trav', I can't go out tonight. I've got to be at work early in the morning."

"We don't have to stay out late. We could just get something to eat and call it a night."

She sighed. "Now is not a good time, Trav'. I've got too much shit going on."

"That's why you should let me take you out. I want to take your mind off of things for a while."

She eased away from the desk and then walked over to the window. "I'm really sorry," she apologized. "But now is not a good time for me. I told you, I'm in the middle of a very complicated case."

"I don't think you stepping away for a few hours to enjoy life will make that case any more complicated."

"It probably won't. But time wasted is time lost."

"And too much work will make you dull and gray."

Amelia threw her head back and laughed; something that she hadn't been doing too much of lately. She walked back over to her desk and then she eased down onto her leather swivel chair. "Did you just call me old and boring?" She asked, kicking her feet up on her desk.

"I think that I did," he answered joking around. "But you can prove me wrong, by going out with me tonight."

Amelia smiled and then she took a deep settling breath. "Can I think about it?"

"What is there to think about?"

"You, and if I wanna get caught-up with your young-ass," she giggled.

He sucked his teeth and then said, "Whatever yow, I'll hit you up when I'm on my way to scoop you up."

"Scoop me up from where?" She asked loudly—but he had already hung up.

Amelia looked at the phone and shook her head. There was something about Ice that had her liking him more than she should. She couldn't pin point what it was. But it was enough to pull her mind away from all she had going on around her, and give her an adrenaline rush, that had her feeling bold and radiant.

With a content smile on her face, Amelia leaned all the way back inside of her chair and crossed her legs at the ankles. She then snatched up a file folder off the desk. But just as she pulled it open to read it through, Kyla appeared in the doorway.

"Mr. Ferentz is here to see you."

"Mr. who?" Amelia asked, sitting up.

"Mr. Ferentz... Mike Simms' lawyer."

Amelia got serious. "Send him in," she said, while clearing her desk.

As soon as Kyla turned away, Bill Ferentz stepped inside the office. He was tall and lean, with a full head of gray hair and a heavily lined face.

"Miss Clarke, thank you for taking the time to see me, without any notice," he grumbled, as he approached Amelia's desk.

Amelia stood and reached out to shake his hand. "Not a problem," she replied. "Please have a seat." She pointed at the chair across from her.

Bill Ferentz placed his briefcase on the desk, as he lowered himself down on the chair. "I know that you're probably wondering what this visit is about."

"Not really," Amelia responded, while swiping away a lock of hair from in front of her face. "I was already informed that you were hired by Mike Simms."

"Good, good," the lawyer smirked arrogantly.

"However, I wasn't expecting a visit," Amelia continued. "Especially with you being as busy as you are."

"With the right amount of money, my clients usually get what they want."

Amelia gave the lawyer a curious look. She knew exactly what he meant, but she ignored his sarcasm and asked, "So what can I do for you, Mr. Ferentz? I know that you're not here to chit chat."

"Definitely not."

"So, why are you here?"

The lawyer leaned back in his seat and straightened the front of his navy blue, Armani jacket. "I'm here because my client, Mr. Simms, informed me that you and he had a phone conversation a few nights ago, where you agreed to drop the charge against him. If this is true, I just want to know why it is that he is still in jail?"

"He's still in jail, because that's where he belongs. And I'll be putting my all into keeping him there. I have no intention of dropping that charge against him, so he'd better get comfortable."

"So, you actually lied to my client?"

"Call it what you will," Amelia raised an eyebrow and grinned. "You lawyers lie to your clients all of the time. So why can't prosecutors do it too?"

Ferentz scowled. "Are you trying to insult me?" He asked, with his face muscles twitching.

"Did I?" Amelia fired back, with a wry grin. "I wasn't trying to," she teased, as she displayed a hand down on the desk in front of her and gazed at her manicured fingers. "Please advise your client that he'll be doing life in prison. And if it was up to me, he'd be doing it in one of those shitholes in Mexico."

Ferentz hopped up from his seat. "I had no idea you were so disrespectful and rude—"

"I wasn't always like this," Amelia's voice was as hard as her eyes. "Your client forced me to change," she hissed. "But please let him know that I'm not fazed by what he did to my mother. As a matter of fact, it only fueled my hatred for him." She leaned forward and picked up the file folder that she had from earlier. "Please see yourself out Mr. Ferentz, I've got to get back to work."

Ferentz snatched up his briefcase from off the desk.

"You'll be seeing me in court young lady, so prepare yourself for a battle," he said, red-faced and furious.

"I'm prepared," Amelia replied nodding. "Believe me, I'm prepared."

"Not for what you'll be getting from me," Ferentz said hotly. "Your conviction record means nothing to me, Miss Clarke. You've never battled with the likes of me before."

Amelia rolled her eyes rudely. "Bye, Mr. Ferentz," she waved him off.

He shot her a nasty look and huffed out a breath. Then without saying another word, he turned and stormed away angrily.

$$\$$

Like a mad man, Tip was chain smoking and sipping on a bottle of gin, as he paced the floor of his bedroom. He was barefooted and shirtless, with a .9mm stuffed inside of his waistband, and a stern and riled look upon his face.

"I'm telling you man, somebody's gonna pay fo' this shit!" He grumbled at himself, as he paced. "I'm not gonna let her get away with doing my fucking face like this! Now I've got to walk around with this ugly-ass shit fo' life."

He marched over to the dresser and then he paused to look at the unsightly sore that Miranda's flesh-ripping bite had left behind. "Fuck no!" He barked, when he saw that it was once again leaking puss.

Because he had failed to go out and get proper medical attention, the chomped out piece of Tip's face was now looking like a large infected canker-sore. It had one half of his face swollen and red, with dried blotches of blood and puss sprinkled down his cheek.

Infuriated by his facial disfigurement, Tip spun around and flung the gin bottle into the wall across the room.

"Fucking bitch!" He roared, as the gin bottled crashed and shattered — then fell to the floor in pieces.

"I swear on everything I love!" He pulled the pistol from his waistband and aimed it at his reflection in the dresser's mirror. "I'm gonna get your old ass fo' this. I'm gonna fucking get you!" He growled, then stepped closer to the dresser and snatched up the small bottle that he kept his ecstasies in. He pried off the cap. Then turned the bottle to his head and dumped all six pills into his mouth.

As he chomped on the pills, he hurled the empty bottle across the room, and then went back to pacing. But when he was hit by a sudden thought, he stopped and then he snatched up his T-shirt from off of the bed. "You know what, fuck it. That prosecutor bitch is gonna be the one to pay fo' this shit," he snarled, as he charged towards the door.

$$\$$

After a very busy Tuesday afternoon that had her stuck at her desk for hours; Amelia finally got up, and gathered the papers that she had laid out on the desk in front of her. Once she had them all in a neat stack, she slid them back inside of the folder; and then put the folder back inside of her desk drawer.

It was now time for her to go. It was only after six, but chances are she and Kyla were the only ones still at work. After looking around inside of her office, just to make sure that everything was in order; Amelia pulled on her jacket, and left it unbuttoned. She grabbed her briefcase and cell phone from off of her desk. Then afterwards, she took another look around inside of the office, before she headed out.

As she was closing the office door behind her, she looked over at Kyla, who was at her desk reading a Black Enterprise magazine. "You ready to go?" She asked her.

"Ready and waiting," Kyla replied, as if she was bored.

Usually, Kyla would've been gone. But because her Honda Accord got stolen, just over a week ago, Amelia offered her rides to and from work.

They rode the elevator together, yapping about Bill Ferentz's visit and how pissed off he was when he left out. They got off inside of the lobby and said goodbye to the two security guards at the front desk. Then they continued on out through the door, with their conversation.

The evening was darker than usual when they stepped outside, and there was a slight chill in the light blowing breeze. The street lights were all on and shining brightly. And the surrounding area of the office building was well illuminated.

Amelia looked around inside of the almost empty parking lot, and then over across the street at the Payless shoes store and the busy Japanese restaurant.

"I feel like going out," she said. "I feel like going somewhere relaxing, where I can sit down and have something tasty to eat."

"So call Rick and let him take you out," Kyla teased jokingly.

Amelia sucked her teeth. "Oh please," she uttered in a feisty tone. "I'm so through with his sorry ass."

Kyla chuckled and then she pushed her dark hair off of her face. "So what about the guy you've been telling me about?"

"Who . . . Travis?"

"Mm-mmm. I bet that he'd take you."

"He would," Amelia said, as they walked down the steps at the front of the building; then towards the middle of the parking lot, where Amelia's truck was parked right next to a dark tinted Range Rover.

"As a matter of fact," Amelia continued, "He called earlier wanting to take me out."

"And you told him no, didn't you?"

Amelia wrinkled her nose in a very cute way. "I actually told him that I'd think about it," she said, looking at Kyla. "But now, I wish that I'd of told him yes."

"So call him," Kyla urged, all wide-eyed. "I bet that he'd be here in minutes."

"I'm not gonna call him," Amelia giggled, as she searched around inside of her bag for her keys. "I don't want him to know how much I really like him. And I'm definitely not trying to look desperate. If he really wanted to take me out, then he'll call back," she said, as she found her keys, raised her head — and then stopped dead in her tracks when she saw him.

He stepped down from the Range Rover, with his cell phone at his ear and a somber look on his face. He had a blue baseball cap pulled down over his eyes. And he was dressed casually, in dark blue jeans and a black Sean John blazer over his T-shirt.

Ice ended the conversation over his phone and set his eyes on Amelia. "What's up?" He asked in a calm tone.

She looked him over and her breathing spiked. For some mind boggling reason, she was very happy and excited to see him. She was doing a good job of masking her happy and excited feeling, but the scent of his cologne and his dapper attire had her wanting to get near him.

She took a nervous look around inside of the parking lot, just to make sure that they weren't being watched by inquisitive eyes. "Hi, Travis . . . Why do I have this feeling that you were sitting here waiting for me?"

"That's because I was," he admitted, with a tiny smirk. "I told you that I was coming to take you out."

"And I told you that I'd think about it."

"So you didn't? I gave you more than enough time to," he said, looking over at Kyla. He waved at her, before going back to Amelia. "Come on, I'm taking you out to eat."

Amelia cocked her head and then she cracked a smug grin. "You said that, as if I don't have a choice."

"You don't."

"Is that so?" She shot back.

"It definitely is," he said, in a smooth firm tone. He glanced at her truck. "You wanna ride with me, or should I ride with you?"

Amelia propped a hand on her hip and then she sized him up. She actually liked his confident aggression. It gave her a feel of extreme femininity, along with a pulsing need to be impelled.

Amelia had always been the aggressor, the dominant one, in whatever she did. But something about Ice had her feeling very acquiescent and submissive.

After a moment of silence between them, she decided to go against what she was feeling and walk away. "Tonight is not a good night for me, Trav', I've got to go home and get some sleep, because I've got a lot of work to do tomorrow. Plus, I've got to drop Kyla home."

He politely grabbed her arm and then he took her keys. "You'll be home in time for your beauty sleep," he told her. "And as for your home-girl, I'll get my cousin to drop her home... Yow, Yogi!" He turned his head and shouted at the Range Rover.

"Are you serious?" Amelia asked, while trying to disguise the bashful smile on her face. "Kyla's not going to let a total stranger drop her home."

Ice looked at Kyla. "Do you mind?" He asked her.

Kyla smiled and shrugged.

"Kyla!" Amelia laughed out loud.

Kyla's smile extended, as she replied, "You did say that you wanted to go out to eat."

Amelia scrunched up her face at her assistant and then rolled her eyes. "I'll get you back fo' that," she cackled.

Kyla smirked.

Amelia turned to Ice. "Trav', I really can't go out with you tonight," she said, trying to be firm.

He ignored her and looked over at Yogi, who had stepped down from the Range Rover with his usual toothy smile. "Yow cuz', I want you to drop home-girl home fo' me." "I can do that," Yogi replied, nodding. He turned to Kyla. "You ready to bounce?" He asked her.

Kyla gave Amelia a smiling wave, and then she started towards the Range Rover.

"Kyla! Where are you going?" Amelia shouted, while laughing.

"I'll see you in the morning," Kyla chortled, as Yogi helped her up inside of the Range Rover.

Amelia pulled her arm free of Ice's hold and tried her best to play serious. She folded her arms and watched as the Range Rover sped off. "I'm not going anywhere with you Trav'," she pouted. "So you'd better call your cousin to come back and get you."

He ignored her and opened the passenger door of the Lexus. "You getting in? Or should I lift you and put you inside?"

Brows furrowed, she licked her lips and gave him a deep penetrating stare. "You're gonna have to lift me, 'cause I'm—Hey!" She laughed out loud, when he scooped her up into his muscular arms—then with almost no effort at all, he got her seated inside of the Lexus.

CH-14

Close to an hour after turning out of the parking lot at the State Attorney's office, Ice pulled Amelia's RX350 in front of KAREEM'S and double parked. He sat for a minute and watched the small crowd outside, wondering if Shanequa or any of his cohorts were outside, or either inside of the club. He wasn't prepared for the drama that they would bring, if they saw him with Amelia. And because he found himself liking her so much, putting her in harm's way was something that he just didn't want to do.

After his visual sweep of the area outside, Ice turned to Amelia and then asked her, "Are you ready to go inside?"

Amelia kept her eyes on two thugs, who were walking by with blunts between their lips and hard looks on their faces. "Travis, I'm not really feeling this place," she said, after a light sigh. She then went back to looking around inside of the small and crammed parking lot, at all the attributes of the hood.

Ice looked at the two thugs and then sucked his teeth. "When you're with me you'll never be treated like the average chick. So don't let niggahs with their faces bent up, scare you."

"I'm not scared, but I'm definitely not trying to put myself into any hostile situations. I already told you what I'm going through and who I'm going through it with."

"Are you trying to say that I'm not man enough to protect you?"

"I didn't say that, but this is not my kind of place."

"Why? Is it because it's in the hood?"

"Stop putting words in my mouth."

"So, what are you saying?"

She turned her head to look him in the face, but had to look away. What she felt for him was so overwhelming it had her squirming in her seat. "Let's just forget everything and go inside," she finally decided and then reached for her bag.

They entered into KAREEEM'S and Amelia was blown away by the setting. Inside was nothing close to what she had just left on the outside. It was nothing like what she expected. Instead of loud expletive rap music and clouds of smoke reeking from joints, KAREEM'S was a smoke free pub, with ear friendly soul music floating around in the air.

There were small high tables and stools, black sofas with end tables against the walls, and six pool tables that all seemed occupied. The place wasn't crowded, but the vibe was extremely friendly and very appeasing.

"Do you know how to shoot pool?" Ice asked, as he stood and scanned the small crowd.

"No. I've never played before," Amelia answered.

"I'll give you a few pointers, later on," he replied, as he took her hand and pulled her along.

They got up to the bar and were immediately approached by one of the two bartenders.

"Hi Ice," the light-skinned, model-looking bartender was smiling pleasantly. "What can I get you?"

Ice hooked elbows with Amelia and pulled her close, clearly sending the bartender a message. "Where's Kareem?" He asked.

Now with a forced smile, the bartender turned her head and looked in through the open door behind her. "He's around back," she replied glumly.

"Could you go get him fo' me?"

"Sure," the bartender said, as she turned away, burning with jealousy.

Amelia watched her, as she walked away. "So, was that one of your many exes'?" She asked Ice, with a teasing grin.

"What makes you think that she is?"

Amelia pulled her arm away from his. "I'm a smart girl, Trav'. I do know jealousy, when I see it."

"So, is there a problem?"

She scrunched up her nose. "No. Not that I can think of," she replied, while shaking her head. "We may be here together, but it's not like we're together."

"As of yet," Ice chuckled, up under his breath.

"Ice, what's good playa?" A course voice echoed, inside the bar.

Ice turned and saw Kareem stepping towards him. "What's up, fam', what's the deal?" He asked, as they exchanged daps.

"Shit," Kareem smiled and nodded.

Kareem, the owner of the club, was Ice's good friend. He was short and muscular with a massive chest and arms that were ripping apart his shirt sleeves.

"What's going on upstairs?" Ice asked him.

"Not much," Kareem replied, smiling easily. "Ain't nobody up there that you're familiar with."

"*That's what I was hoping,*" Ice thought.

Kareem affixed his eyes on Amelia. "Goodnight, Beautiful. Now what can I do for you, to make your night here memorable?"

Amelia blushed. "Trav' told me that you guys make the best burgers and fries."

"He ain't lying," Kareem giggled proudly. "And just for you, I'm gonna go around back and make you one of our specials. I guarantee that you'll be back asking fo' more."

Amelia smiled. "Thank you."

"Ice, what can I get fo' you?"

Ice took Amelia's hand. "I'll have what she's having, and send up a bottle of Dom P."

"Done," Kareem smiled and then he turned away.

"Let's go upstairs," Ice looked at Amelia and suggested.

"What's upstairs?" She asked.

"You'll see."

Ice led Amelia across the room and towards a yellow metal staircase. Even though she was still in her work clothes and wasn't dressed for clubbing, she was still drawing the attention of almost every guy inside of the pub.

She walked by Ice's side with elegance. And the smile on her face seemed to be getting wider, as the seconds ticked by. She actually felt good being by Ice's side. It wasn't the drab, methodical feel that she usually got when she was hanging out with Rick. It was a pleasant, care-free feeling that had her feeling notable, accepted, and well protected. She did take notice of all the other females who were staring at Ice, as they climbed the staircase. But she didn't feel threatened in any way. The way that Ice was cuddled up on her, was enough to let her know that she was his one and only interest.

When they got to the top of the stairs, Amelia had to stop and admire the room. The area that was known as the Zen room was elegant and plush. It was levels above what she had just left downstairs.

The room wasn't large enough for a crowd. However, the cushiony leather seats and exotic coffee tables were still top tier. The walls were painted royal blue, and on each side hung a 42" plasma TV that was on but muted. There were two expensive looking pool tables across from each other. Only one was being used at the time, by the two other couples that were inside of the room.

"So this is where you usually bring all of your little hoochies, when you're trying to coerce them into bed?" Amelia asked, as Ice helped her down onto the leather sofa.

"This is my first time ever coming here with a female. But I've left here with females before."

"That makes me feel so special," Amelia crossed her legs and giggled loudly.

"You should," Ice replied with a smirk. "Because I really think that you are."

$$$$$$$$$$$$$$$$$$$$$$

Tip sat inside of his Lincoln Navigator, sipping on a bottle of Hennessy and smoking a blunt as he waited. He looked across the street at Amelia's townhouse.

"Yeah bitch, I've got something fo' yo' sexy-looking ass," he smiled and said devilishly, as he groped himself.

He was decked out in full black; black jeans, a black hoodie, and a black skull cap pulled down over his head. He was bobbing to Tupac's song, *Hail Mary*, which was playing inside of the SUV. But he stopped and sat up, when he saw a pair of headlights cruising up the street towards him.

After awhile, the headlights passed by and Tip saw that they belonged to a Jeep Cherokee and not Amelia's Lexus RX350. He slumped back down inside of his seat and then he went back to waiting, not knowing that he was being watched by the old woman, who was standing at her bedroom window — inside of the house across the street from Amelia's.

"I'm telling you Todd, there's somebody sitting inside of that truck," the old woman said, as she turned away from the window.

Her husband, a slender old man with a bald head shifted in the bed and said, "So what if somebody's in it? There's no law against you sitting in your own truck."

The old woman sucked her teeth, as she picked up the cordless phone from off of the nightstand. "As members of the neighborhood watch committee, it's our duty to keep our eyes on strangers and strange vehicles."

The old man rolled over onto his stomach, "Well, you can stay up and keep watch if you want to. I'm going to sleep."

"Well I'm not leaving this window, until I see what that person inside that truck is up to. 'Cause if I see them doing anything wrong or suspicious, I'm calling the police."

"Leave peoples' business alone, Victoria. Whatever is going on across the street has nothing to do with you."

The old woman sucked her teeth. "Go to sleep, Todd, 'cause I'm not leaving this window until I know for sure what's going on with whosoever's in that truck."

$$$$$$$$$$$$$$$$$$$$$$$$

Amelia tossed her napkin onto the empty plate, while chewing on the last of her burger.

"That's the best burger that I've ever had," she admitted, with a satisfied smirk. "I'd actually drive back over here, just for their burgers."

Ice reached over and picked up his champagne glass from off of the table. "You don't have to make the drive," he said. "Just call me and say that you need it and you'll get it."

Amelia turned on the sofa and gave him a pleased look. "You sure do talk a good one, Travis. If I didn't know any better, I'd think that you're trying to make me your woman."

"Believe me, that's my only intent," Ice muttered quietly.

It was almost nine thirty and Ice and Amelia were the only ones left inside of the Zen room. Marvin Gaye's, *Let's get it on*, was playing quietly through the mounted speakers. And the TVs were now off and the lights dimmed.

After removing her jacket, Amelia toed off her Prada pumps, crossed her legs at the ankles and then stretched out on the sofa. "I actually like it here," she admitted. "It's nothing like what I thought it would've been, when we pulled up outside."

"You thought that it would be crowded and chaotic, huh?"

"Hmm-mmm. I actually did."

"It gets like that at times, but it's mostly on the weekends. But there's never any fights or out of control altercations. Kareem puts a lot into keeping things under control." Ice took a sip from his glass. "Do you feel like playing a game of pool?" He asked.

Something flickered in Amelia's eyes, when she turned to face him. "I told you, I don't know how to play," she smiled.

He got up, took her hand and then he pulled her up next to him. "Come on, I'll show you how."

Laughing, she let him drag her over to the pool table. "What will I get, if I beat you?" She asked jokingly, watching him as he pulled down two cues from the cue rack.

He turned and offered her a cue. "You can't beat me," he said, with his eyes fixed on her mouth. He chalked up his cue and then he looked at the racked up balls on the table. "I'll make the break and go first, so that you can see what to do."

She poked him playfully in his side with her cue. "What will I get, if I beat you?" She asked again.

Ice, who was now bent over the table, turned his head and looked up at her. "Beat me and I'll go out and get you whatever you want," he promised with a confident smirk. Then with a hard steady shove of the cue, he hit the cue ball and sent it crashing into the racked up balls with a loud, heavy "Clack!"

Amelia took a seat on one of the nearby stools and watched, as the balls scattered across the table. Three low numbered balls fell into various pockets, but Ice went with the high numbered balls.

"Only because you don't know how to play," he smirked at Amelia, with his eyes fixed on the balls on the table.

Amelia, with her legs crossed sexily, shook her shoulders and chirped, "Don't get too cocky. I may've never played before, but I'm a very fast learner."

He waved her off, then leaned across the table and went on to sinking balls.

Four games and close to an hour later, Amelia was down four games to none; but she was still enjoying herself, so it didn't matter.

"You missed! You missed!" She leaped off of her stool and screamed, after Ice had finally missed a game winning shot on the eight ball.

She was laughing hysterically, because she knew with the eight ball left about an inch away from the right corner pocket, it was almost impossible for her not to make the game winning shot. She grabbed her cue from up against the wall, and then she stepped over to the pool table.
She bumped him playfully with her hip, "Get out of the way, loser," she teased.
He looked at her adoringly and cracked a smile, as she leaned across the table and took aim. She was clearly anxious, once again having difficulty gripping the cue. Ice stood and watched her. The way that she was bent over the table had him heaving and swelling.
"Goddamn," he muttered silently, as he gazed at her shapely ass and the way that she was posed provocatively.
Reaching the point where he could no longer control the urge to touch her, he stepped to her and draped his body over hers — then held her hand around the cue, while letting her feel his erection up against her firm ass.
"Trav', what are you doing?" She laughed and tried to shake him away.
"Your grip around the stick is too firm. You need to relax a bit," he instructed, without budging.
"I don't need your help. I can do this."
He brought his lips close to her ear. "Just relax and breathe," he coached, while ignoring her protests. "Keep your eyes on the spot and on the eight ball that you're trying to hit."
She tried, but it was almost impossible for her to focus on anything, other than Ice's rock solid manhood pressing against her ass.
"Concentrate," he whispered, after feeling how tense she had gotten.
It was going on three months, since Amelia had sex. So with Ice plastering his erection against her ass as he was, she just couldn't stop herself from getting horny and wet.

In a desperate attempt to ease the tormenting pulsing between her legs, Amelia set her focus; took aim, then struck the cue ball with the cue. The cue ball slammed into the eight ball with a loud "clack!" Then it stood still, as the eight ball slammed into the pocket.

"I won!" Amelia leaped and screamed. "I won! I won!" She spun around and hugged him. "I told you—"

He cut her off by pressing his lips tightly against hers. She tried to pull away, but he held her close, gripping her ass and pulling her firmly against his rigid erection. He could feel her hesitancy, but it lasted only a moment before she had her arms going around his neck and her tongue going inside of his mouth.

They kissed hard and passionately, sucking on each other's mouth as if they were both aching to be kissed. She let out a quiet moan when he started to suck on her tongue. But when he cupped one of her breasts, she shuddered and held him tight.

With a quick fluid move, he spun her around and forced her up against the wall. Then he pressed his body into hers, as they ravaged each other's mouth.

"Take this off," she gasped against his lips, as she yanked off his blazer. She then flung it down on the floor and went back to kissing him hungrily.

Their hips rocked in unison, as he pressed her into the wall— sucking on her swollen lips, while feeling on her soft velvety legs.

He finally got a hand underneath her skirt. Then within seconds, he had it bunched up around her waist with a hand in between her legs, forcing them apart just to get to her wet center.

She gasped and cringed when he cupped her throbbing mound. But when he rubbed the silky material of her thong against her pulsing clit, she arched her back and shuddered with need — need that brought her back down to earth and made her realize where she was and what she was doing. With a sudden shove, she pushed him away. "Trav' stop. Please," she uttered, with an abrupt hand at her chest and the other at her forehead. She was breathing heavily, and gasping as if she had just ended a two hundred meter sprint.
"You okay?" He asked her.
Amelia looked into his face and then she shook her head. "I'm fine," she answered, clearly shaken. "But we can't do this. Not here. Not now."
"I'm sorry."
She turned away and walked over to the sofa, to gather her things. "Please don't apologize," she said. "I was willingly kissing you."
"But I forced myself on you."
"No you didn't," she replied, as she pulled her bag straps onto her shoulder. "All that you did was gave me something that I wanted."
"So, you're not pissed off?"
"No, I'm not," she said, as she started out of the Zen room.

CH-15

It was almost midnight when Amelia pulled into her driveway and stepped down from her truck. The smile on her face was all the evidence that one would need to know that she had had a wonderful time with Ice.

She was feeling a bit woozy because of the three glasses of champagne that she drank, and her body was still tingling all over because of the way that Ice had kissed her. She could still smell the scent of his cologne, which was still oozing from her blouse. And the image of them kissing passionately was still affixed in her mind.

She was in no way prepared for what she was now feeling for him. What she had felt when they kissed, was like nothing that she had ever felt before. He gave her what she wanted, but he did it with force and aggression. And it was as if he still had his hands all over her, because the pulsing between her legs just would not go away. Neither would the image of his handsome face, which was constantly floating around inside of her head.

Amelia felt as if she was on cloud nine, when she entered into her apartment. Her time with Ice had turned out to be so much more than she had ever expected. Being with him was totally different from being with Rick. However, she still found him to be just as attentive and intelligent.

After dropping her bag, jacket, and keys on top of the lamp stand by the door, Amelia walked into her bedroom and turned the lights on. She removed her earrings and tied her hair into a ponytail, before taking her clothes off. Then after picking out a set of underwear from her dresser drawer, she sashayed into the bathroom, to take a quick shower before going to bed.

$$\$\$\$\$\$\$\$\$\$\$\$\$\$\$\$\$\$\$\$$$

"Todd. Todd. Wake up!"

"Victoria, leave me alone," the old man groaned and rolled over in bed.

"But he's sneaking into her house," the old woman blubbered quietly. She was still standing at her bedroom window, but she was now looking outside through some binoculars. "That young lady who lives across the street just got home and he's breaking in on her.

"Why can't you just leave people's business alone? Look at how late it is. You need to come to bed."

Victoria turned away from the window and then she reached for the cordless phone. "I'm telling you Todd, that mothafucka who's sneaking in on that young lady is up to no good."

"What if he's her boyfriend and she invited him over?" Victoria narrowed her eyes on her husband of sixty four years. "I know a booty call when I see it," she said, as she punched 911 into the phone. "And that shit across the street, ain't no damn booty call."

The old man sat up and then he reached for his glasses and slid them on. "What are you doing?" He asked, as he climbed out of bed.

"Are you blind?" Victoria replied, as she hurried back to the window. "I'm calling the damn police."

$$\$\$\$\$\$\$\$\$\$\$\$\$\$\$\$\$\$\$\$$$

Amelia walked out of her bathroom with a towel blotting her ponytail and a robe wrapped around her body. She had an ear to ear smile plastered across her face and glittering happiness in her eyes.

"What a night," she thought, as she tossed the towel on the bench by the foot of the bed. She then walked over to the dresser, but just as she was reaching for the bottle of Palmer's cocoa butter lotion, she heard a quiet 'click'.

She froze and then cocked her head and listened. The room suddenly sounded quieter than usual, and the air felt surprisingly dense. Another indistinct 'click' sent her pulse into a frenzied gallop. Then just as she was about to turn her head to narrow in on the source, he charged out of the closet and grabbed her from behind.

"Hel—"

He clamped a hand over her mouth, before she could get the word out. "What's up beautiful? How you been?" He snarled disgustedly in her ear.

Panic-stricken, Amelia swung an elbow in his gut. He grunted and his grip loosened a bit, but it was the second elbow that caused him to let go and double over in pain. Amelia didn't hesitate; she dashed for the door, trying to make her escape. But Tip was on her. He tackled her from behind, tripping her and sending her crashing face first to the floor.

"Somebody help me!" Amelia screamed, kicking wildly and flailing her arms in a desperate attempt to keep Tip away. But he grabbed onto her and held her firm. He wrapped both of his arms around her waist and then he pulled her up from off of the floor. "Scream again and I'll fucking kill you," he threatened, as he flung her onto the bed.

She went against his threat and screamed, "HELP!"

He backhanded her hard across the face. "I said shut the fuck up," he snarled, and then he slapped her again.

But Amelia was determined to get away, so she leaped off the bed and attacked him. She got him good with an open palm slap in the face. But it was not enough to slow him down. He grabbed the front of her robe and he ripped it open. She slapped him again. This time he smiled, before he punched her in the face. Then as she fell back onto the bed, he pulled out his 9mm pistol and then he aimed it at her head. "Stay down bitch," he warned furiously.

Amelia flinched, but she didn't get up. She stayed lying down on the bed with her eyes fixed on the gun in his hand.

He made a step towards her. "Act stupid and I'll fucking kill you. You hear me?"

"Yes. Ye-yes, I hear you," she whimpered and then nodded. "Please don't shoot me," she begged.

"You don't wanna get shot in the face?"

She shook her head frantically.

"Then take your clothes off."

She gazed at him, wide-eyed.

"I said to take off your fucking clothes!!" He barked and then stepped towards her.

In another desperate attempt to get away, Amelia scrambled off the bed and ran to the door. Only she didn't make it. Tip punched her in the back, right between her shoulder blades and sent her crashing into the dresser.

"I told you not to fuck with me!"He growled, as he grabbed a handful of her hair and pulled her up from off the floor. He bent her over at the waist and pressed the side of her face down on the dresser. "I'm not here to kill you," he said, wedging his knee in between her legs to widen her stance. "All I'm here to do is fuck."

Amelia grimaced when he started to grind his erection against her ass. She could also feel him fumbling with his zipper. But because of the gun in his hand he was having a hard time getting it down.

"Don't do this, please. I beg you," she cried, then swung a desperate elbow that connected solidly with his jaw.

He let go of her and then staggered a bit. But when she got up and tried to run away, he ran after her and struck her on the shoulder with the butt of his gun. She cried out and grabbed at her shoulder, as she crumpled to the floor in pain.

"Fucking bitch! You're just like your fucking mother," Tip seethed, as he grabbed a handful of her hair and then dragged her over to the bed.

"Pl-ee-aa-se," Amelia cried, as the surging pain from her skull trickled down throughout her body, on down to her toes. "All of this shit wouldn't be happening to you, if you had let Blood outta jail."

"Please. I'll drop the charge against hi—"

Tip jammed the muzzle of the .9mm into her jaw. "Look at me!" He growled in her face, giving her a lung-full of his stale, alcohol laced breath. "You see this shit on my face?" He pointed. "Your mother did this to me. I didn't get a chance to fuck her. But there's no way that I'm gonna let you get away."

"Ple-ease," Amelia cried weakly. "I'll drop your friend's charge."

"Shut the fuck up!" Tip barked at her. "I don't wanna hear shit about Blood and his charge. What I want is for you to take off your fucking clothes."

She grimaced and then nodded.

He let go of her hair and shoved her down on the bed. "Take off your robe," he ordered wickedly.

Sitting up on the bed, Amelia slowly started to pull off her robe. "Please, don't do this," she cried, with blood trickling from the gash across her forehead. "I've got money. I'll give you whatever amount that you want."

"I don't want your fucking money," Tip said, while unbuckling his pants. He jabbed the gun at her. "Take off everything."

Fear rippled throughout Amelia's body, when he pulled his rock hard dick out of his pants. "Please don't do—"

"What the fuck I just said?!" He barked and shuffled over to her. He grabbed her by the throat and pressed the muzzle of the gun into her forehead. "Try to stop me and you'll die," he said, as he forced himself between her legs.

The grip he had on her throat had Amelia gasping for air. She held onto his wrist, but she just didn't have the strength to pull his hand away.

"Don't fucking try to stop me," Tip warned, as he watched Amelia's eyes roll over inside her head. Because both of his hands were occupied, he couldn't get to help himself inside of her, so he leaned forward and pressed his mouth against hers. Still suffocating, Amelia felt as if she was going to throw up when she felt his tongue inside of her mouth. His rock hard erection was pressed firmly against her mound. And he was grunting and gyrating like a sex starved maniac. She knew that she didn't have the strength to stop him. Knew if she kept resisting, he would probably choke her to death. So instead of fighting against him, like her dignity was telling her to; she widened her legs, and then wrapped her arms around his neck and kissed him.

Tip got completely addled by Amelia's sudden willingness to give in. He tried to pull his mouth away from hers, but she held him down and kept on kissing him. She even started to gyrate against his erection, forcing her front against him as she dug her fingers into his shoulder blades.

Driven by compulsion and thinking that Amelia was now trying to willingly give herself to him, Tip let go of her throat and cupped one of her breasts.

She moaned and slid a hand down his back. She then forced it in between their bodies and took hold of his hard, throbbing cock. He growled when she stroked him. Then without even realizing, he let go of the gun and went in search of her pleasure spot.

"Put it in," he begged, as he fumbled, trying to get his hands between her legs.

Amelia opened her eyes and saw that he had his closed.

"Come for me," she forced herself to say, as she cupped and fondled his sac.

"Put it—FFFUUUCCK!" Tip suddenly screamed, at the top of his lungs.

His eyes flew open and got painfully wide. And his fists were tightly clenched, as he strained and trembled.

Amelia squeezed on his testicles with every bit of strength that she could conjure. She wrung, crushed and pulled, as if she was trying to rip his nuts from in between his legs.

She had him writhing in agonizing pain, and shuddering as if he was unbearably cold. When she finally let go, he toppled over and hit the floor. He was crying out in pain, with his hands clutched between his legs.

Amelia leaped off the bed and darted towards the door, running out of the room in just her panties and bra.

"Bi-itch . . . I'm gonna ki-ill you," Tip cried faintly, as he held onto the bed and then pulled himself up from off the floor. He reached for his gun. Then with a hand still cupped between his legs, he stumbled across the room and out through the door.

"Bitch! I'm gonna fucking kill you!" He roared angrily, as he looked around inside of the living room. The front door was wide open, so he barged outside — then jerked to a complete stop, when he was greeted by a sudden burst of blinding floodlights.

"Freeze! Police!" An army of police officers screamed out in unison.

They had the front of the house blocked off with guns pointed, and the streets were lined with police cars and SUVs.

Tip stood frozen, gasping as if he couldn't breathe freely. His entire body was shaking. And his eyes were wide and wild, as he searched the crowd for Amelia, who had already been placed in the back of a police cruiser and driven away to safety.

"Drop the gun!"

With tears in his eyes, Tip lowered his head and then he gazed at his feet.

"Drop the gun and get down on the ground!"

Tears started to fall from Tip's eyes. His heart was thumping relentlessly and his stomach was sour and tight.

"This is your last warning! Drop the fucking gun!"

"I can't do prison," Tip cried quietly to himself. Then with a sudden move that every single one of the police officers were anticipating, he raised the gun—but didn't get a shot off. They all opened fire at him, riddling his body with bullets that knocked him back inside of the house, killing him instantly.

CH-16

"I'm okay," Amelia told the female paramedic, who was tending to the cut across her forehead.
"You're gonna have to get it stitched up."
"I'll go to the hospital later on," Amelia said, hopping down from the gurney; then hurrying over to meet her mother and Danielle, who were walking out of her house with suitcases filled with her clothes and toiletries.
 There was a buzzing crowd of police officers and news reporters in the street, in front of the house. The house was already taped off, and a crew of crime scene investigators was inside doing what they do.
There was a channel 7 news helicopter flying around. Occasionally it would aim its light down on Tip's body, which was still on the ground in the doorway, but covered with a white sheet.
"Did you find my cell phone?" Amelia asked, just as soon as she got up to her mother.
"It's in my pocket."
 "We've got everything that you asked us to get," Danielle chipped in.
Amelia pushed a lock of hair up over her head, and then she wiped her hands on her sweatpants. "Let's get outta here," she said. "I don't wanna be around all of this."
They started towards Danielle's Honda Accord.

"Are the police through with their questioning?" Miranda asked.

Amelia shook her head. "I gave them my phone number and your address. I told them that I'll be staying at your house, so they're free to come and question me some other time."

"I hope they have the decency to wait a couple days," Danielle muttered.

Amelia looked over at her, but stopped and turned when she saw the Barolo red Benz pulling up next to a parked police cruiser. She huffed out an angry breath. Then without uttering a word, she stormed across the street.

As soon as Rick stepped out of the Benz she exploded, "What the fuck are you doing here?" She screamed at him. "I don't want you here!" She went at him with flailing arms. "You piece-of-shit! Get away from my house!"

Rick grabbed her wrists. "I just wanted to find out if you're okay."

"Why!" She yelled in his face. "You don't care about me. If it was up to you, I'd probably be dead by now."

Rick looked around nervously at the small crowd, which had suddenly gathered around them. "Do you even know what you're saying?" He held her firm and blurted. "All that I've been doing is trying to help you."

"Well I don't need your help, so get away from my house!"

"Amelia—"

"Get your fucking hands off of me!" She snapped and then yanked her arms away. She turned to a police officer, who was standing close by. "I don't want him here."

"Mam, we can't stop him from being here," the police explained. "He's in the street. Not on your property."

Amelia shot the police officer a nasty stare, before turning to Rick. "Stay away from me, you hear me?" She pointed in his face. "It would be best if I never lay eyes on you ever again."

"Amelia, I had nothing to do with what happened here tonight."

"I don't care. I just don't wanna see you again."
She turned and started away, with her mother and Danielle
trailing behind her.
"Amelia."
"Don't call my fucking name," she snapped, without even
looking back at him. She marched over to Danielle's car and
yanked the door open. "Only if he knew how much I've
grown to hate him. I can't stand his ass!" She sneered, as she
ducked down inside of the car and slammed the door shut.

$$$$$$$$$$$$$$$$$$$$$$$$$
Ice was awakened by Bob Marley's, *One love*, which was
playing on his cell phone. He rolled over in bed and looked at
the digital clock on the nightstand. It was saying 3:37am;
much too early in the morning for someone to be blowing up
his phone.
He tried to ignore Bob Marley's chanting by putting a pillow
over his head, but to his disappointment, the pillow didn't
help. After about twenty seconds, he reached for the cell
phone and answered sleepily, "Yeah . . . . Who dis?"
"Did you see it?" Yogi came on and asked.
"Niggah do you know what time it is?" Ice replied, rolling
onto his back.
"It's after three," Yogi said impatiently.
"So why the fuck are you calling me so early?"
"Because, I know you never watch the news. Turn on your
TV."
"Why?"
"Niggah, just turn on the damn TV."
Ice dry-washed his face. "This shit bettah be good," he
mumbled, as he searched around inside the sheets for the
remote. When he found it, he aimed it across the room at the
62", wall mounted plasma TV. "What am I looking for?" He
asked, as the TV came to life.
"Go to the channel 7 news."

Ice punched a button on the remote. Then he watched as the TV switched from a music video on BET, into a full bodied close-up of a beautiful Hispanic looking anchorwoman. She had a microphone up close to her lips, explaining what had happened at the house located behind her.

"Why am I watching this?" Ice asked.

"Just watch and listen, brah."

Ice watched and listened for a while, and then he sat up when a picture of Amelia appeared in the top right corner of the TV screen. He quickly raised the remote and then he raised the volume.

"—Miss Clarke did suffer minor injuries," the anchorwoman was saying. "But she appears to be okay. However, her attacker has been confirmed dead." A blurred driver's license photo of Tip appeared full-screen on the TV. "He was the *recipient* of multiple gunshots after making a daring attempt to have a shoot out with the police. We were told that his main intention was to rape the prosecutor. And to what we're being told by the police, he's one of the four men who tried to rape the prosecutor's mother..."

Ice slammed the remote down onto the bed and then he ripped away the sheets. "Fuck!" He barked angrily, as he flung his legs over the side of the bed. "I should've known that his fuck-ass would've tried that shit."

"Brah, you straight?" Yogi asked.

Ice got up and he started to pace. "I'm good, cuz. I'm just a bit ticked off, because I should've followed her home and I didn't."

"And what would you have done? Would you have faced off with Tip, only to risk Amelia finding out the truth?"

"What truth?" Ice stopped and asked. "The truth is that I'm in love with her. I've loved her ever since I laid eyes on her. And after being around her tonight, I found myself loving her even more."

"Well, you loving her ain't gonna change shit. And Tip getting killed ain't gonna stop Blood from trying to get outta jail."
"I know," Ice said, looking up at the TV. After a while, he sighed heavily and then he looked away. "Hey cuz, let me hit you back," he said, as he walked to the bathroom.
"What you plan to do?"
Ice stopped and gazed at the bathroom door. He didn't know what to say, so he said nothing. He just hung up.

$$\$$

Rick walked out of the liquor store and then he started over to his car. He was on his way home, but he had stopped to grab a bottle of Grey Goose and a pack of cigarettes. He was by no means a vowed smoker or drinker. But with things around him going as crazy as they were, smoking and drinking seemed like a very good idea to him.
The parking lot in front of the liquor store was practically empty. But there was a club across the street that seemed to be in full swing. As Rick approached his car, he uncapped the bottle of Grey Goose. But just as he was about to raise it to his head to take a swig, a black Escalade raced across the parking lot and screeched to a stop at his feet.
The passenger's side window rolled down. Batch, with a blunt between his lips, poked his head out. "Get in. Let's go for a ride," he ordered.
Rick looked at the corrupted cop with a penetrating stare. "It's three thirty in the morning, man. I'm going home. I've got to get some sleep."
"Like I give a fuck," Batch retorted, as he pulled away on the blunt. He blew a cloud of smoke in Rick's face. "Let's go, yow. Blood goes to court later on today, so I wanna straighten out a few things with you, just to make sure that we're all on the same page."
"Well whatever you've got to straighten out, is gonna have to wait. I'm taking my ass home."

Batch pulled a Glock from somewhere inside of the Escalade and then he aimed it at Rick's head. "Get in the fucking truck," he snarled, hot and impatient. "I'm not asking you if you wanna get in. I'm telling you to get the fuck inside."

$$\$$

Even after a steaming hot shower, Amelia could still feel Tip's hands all over her. She could even still smell his musky scent, seeping from her pores. She had brushed her teeth five times, and used every bit of a full bottle of Listerine, in order to rid her mouth of his lingering aftertaste. Then afterwards, she spent close to thirty minutes, firmly massaging her body with creams and lotion.

After a warm cup of herbal tea, she finally headed off to bed in her mother's guest bedroom. However, she was unable to sleep. She tossed, turned, curled and stretched, still unable to rid her mind of all that had taken place since Blood got arrested.

At one point, she was dozing off. But that was until a sudden clatter from the wooden blinds at the window, jarred her awake.

Agitated because she couldn't fall asleep, Amelia climbed out of bed and then she headed for the kitchen to fix herself another cup of herbal tea. Tea always helped her to sleep. But as she was slowly making her way across the dark living room, the quiet sniffles of someone crying caused her to stop and turn the lights on.

"Danielle?" She uttered surprisingly, when she saw Danielle curled up on the sofa with her hands over her face. She started over to her. "I didn't know that you were still here. And why are you crying?"

Danielle sat up and wiped her face on her t-shirt. But as soon as she did, she started to tear up again.

"Did I wake you?" She asked, still sobbing lightly.

"I wasn't sleeping." Amelia took a seat beside her on the sofa. "Why are you crying?" She asked again.

Danielle looked at Amelia and then she burst into sobs. "I can't tell you," she cried.

Amelia draped an arm around her. "Why can't you? I thought that we were best friends."

Danielle's sobbing got even heavier and then her shoulders started bobbing. "I'm sorry. I'm so-so sorry," she cried.

"Sorry fo' what?"

Danielle looked Amelia in the face, and then she dropped her face into her hands and continued to sob.

"What are you sorry for?" Amelia pressed.

"F-f-for what I did."

"What did you do, Danielle? Please tell me," Amelia asked, choking up.

"I can't."

"Why not?" Amelia asked, a bit loudly. She got up and sucked in a lung-full of air. "How can I help you, if I don't know what you did?"

Danielle raised her tear-stained face and then she looked at Amelia. She waited a long time before saying, "I didn't know that things would get this bad. He lied and told me that nobody would get hurt. But now look at all that's happening. I'm even scared to go home."

"What are you talking about?"

Danielle wiped her face with her t-shirt. "He gave me twenty thousand dollars to get you to drop Blood's charge. I didn't know that it was such a big deal, until I saw how determined that you were to send Blood to prison."

"*Good God Danielle, not you too,*" Amelia thought, while shaking her head. "Who gave you the money?" She asked, after a moment.

Danielle dropped her head. "I don't know his name," she cried. "All I know is that he's a police officer, with a scar below his left eye."

"Detective Batchelor," Amelia muttered quietly. She huffed out a breath and then she pinched the bridge of her nose. "Was he the one who gave you that black eye that you had, a few days ago?"

Danielle nodded. "I tried to give him his money back, but he wouldn't take it. And because you won't drop the charge against Blood, he has threatened to kill me."

Amelia sighed and then she turned away. "Goddamn, Danielle! You should've known better than to get yourself involved in all of this shit."

"I'm sorry."

Amelia started to pace. "Is there anybody around me who isn't working fo' Mike Simms?" She looked down at the floor and asked, "How much power and influence can this one man have?" She stopped her pacing and then she looked steadily at Danielle. "I'm sorry Danielle. We're good friends and all, but I can't let Mike Simms go. He's a murderer and he deserves to be behind bars."

"But I don't want you to let him go," Danielle got up and replied. "Not after all that he has had his people to do."

Amelia pushed her hair off of her face, and then she walked over to Danielle. "I really wish that you had told me this earlier. But I'm glad that you told me now."

"I'm sorry, 'Melia, I let greed get the better of me. I'm so sorry."

"Don't worry 'bout it. We all make mistakes," Amelia told her best friend, as they embraced.

CH-17

At exactly nine a.m., Amelia strode into the courthouse, in a vivacious manner. She was looking radiant in her curve-hugging skirt suit, three inch high stilettos, and her customary Chanel framed specs.

The look on her face was severe. Other than a few scratches and the band aid across her forehead, she didn't have the semblance of a person who had just been aggressively assaulted, less than twenty four hours ago.

Amelia kept her eyes straight ahead, as she strutted down the tiled hallway of the courthouse. She was trying not to be distracted by the small crowd, which was bustling throughout the hallway.

"Amelia!" Someone shouted at her from about thirty yards away. She knew who it was. Therefore she kept on walking, not wanting to talk to him.

"Amelia, please."

Agitated, Amelia stopped. She turned and then gasped when she saw him limping towards her. His left arm was in a sling, and he had a pair of large sunglasses over his eyes. However, the black and blue swellings were still visible and so was the large bruise across his left jaw. His lips were puffed up and busted. There was also a palm-sized band-aid at the right side of his face, and a smaller one on his forehead, just below his hairline.

"What the fuck happened to you?" She asked, removing her glasses.

"Can we talk?" He ignored her question.

She looked at him scornfully and then she shook her head.

"There's nothing for us to talk about, Rick. You've chosen your path and I'm staying on mine."

"Amelia, please."

"Rick no. I'm through listening to you."

"What I have to say will only take a minute, I swear."

"You swearing don't mean shit to me anymore. You're a liar. I don't believe anything that you say and I don't trust you."

"Do you hate me that much, that you can't even give me one minute of your time?"

"You had a lifetime of it, yet you threw it away!"

"I made a mistake. Don't we all make mistakes?"

"That's what you call it, a mistake? Was it a mistake when your friends tried to rape me and my mother?"

A few people walking by were now starting to stare. Feeling a bit embarrassed, Rick grabbed Amelia's arm and then he dragged her towards the bathroom.

As soon as they entered through the door, Amelia ripped her arm away. "What the fuck's wrong with you, Rick? I don't wanna talk to you."

"Would you rather to see me dead? They're threatening to kill me, Amelia."

She propped a hand on her hip. "So, what did you expect? When you lay up with dogs you catch fleas, so deal with it."

"So you don't even care?"

"No. I don't give a fuck. And I definitely don't care about you," Amelia protested with much attitude. She shoved her head forward and then rebelled, "Why should I care? When all that you care about is stacking your bank account with drug money. Your only reason for doing what you did was greed, Rick. And what do you think is gonna happen to you, when Mr. Barrett finds out? You think that he's gonna let you keep your job? He's gonna fire you. And you need to pray to God that you don't go to jail."

"Are you saying that you're gonna tell him?"

"If that was my intention, then I would've done it a long time ago. But if you don't stay the fuck away from me, then I probably will."

"Amelia, I had nothing to do with what happened to you and your mother."

"I don't believe shit that you say. You're a liar and a money hungry bastard. I don't put shit pass you."

"You just don't know what I was going through."

"Were you homeless? Were you starving? For Christ-sakes, Rick, you were driving a brand new Lexus, right before you bought that Be—" She stopped and gazed up into his face. "Did Mike Simms buy you that Benz?"

He gazed back at her, with tears tumbling down his cheeks. "It doesn't matter if he did or not, because if he goes to prison, then I'm dead."

"Well, you should've thought about that before you started taking his money." Amelia rolled her eyes, clearly agitated. "There's no chance of me letting Mike Simms go. Not after he had my house destroyed and then had my mother beaten and almost killed. Then, if not for my neighbor, I would've probably been raped and killed last night." She sucked her teeth. "Mike Simms' ass is going to prison."

"And I'll be dead."

"Would it make you feel any better if I was killed?"

He raised his head and looked at her, but he didn't answer.

"Just as I thought," Amelia said, as she turned and then started away with her face scrunched up.

He watched her for a while. Then when his anger got the better of him he shouted, "Do you think that I'm the only one at the office working for Blood? This is bigger than what you think, Amelia. It's much bigger than you."

She stopped, turned, and then she walked back over to him. "I don't care how big it is. I have a job to do and I'm gonna do it. So if I was you, I'd gather up all of those who are involved and move outta town."

He glared at her. "Are you threatening me?" He asked, with his jaws tight.

"Call it what you will," she replied.

He stepped towards her. "When did you turn into such a bitch, Amelia? When did you get so fucking arrogant?"

She cocked her head alarmingly. "You know what?" She flicked a palm up in his face. "Stay the fuck away from me."

Amelia turned and then she started off, but he grabbed her by the arm. "Don't fuckin' walk away from me. Bitch, I'm talking to you!"

She spun and then she swung her briefcase at him.

He blocked it with his disabled arm and screamed out in pain. "You fuckin' bitch!" He yelled and then he shoved her hard. She stumbled backwards, dropping her briefcase. Then with flailing arms, she fell on her ass, banging the back of her head on the wall by the sink.

Holding onto his dislocated arm and grimacing, Rick turned and started out of the bathroom. "You can't change the fucking world, Amelia. You don't have the power to do it." Amelia sat on the floor and watched him leave. Her ass and the back of her head were aching, and it had her wanting to get up and chase after him with clenched fists.

"Fucking asshole!" She grimaced, as she got up slowly.

It took her about ten minutes to put herself back together and walk out of the bathroom. She was only a few steps away from Judge Silverman's courtroom, so she hurried over, pulled the door open and then stepped inside.

"Glad you could join us, counselor," the Judge greeted Amelia, with a miserable frown.

"Please forgive me, your honor. But I got held up outside," Amelia said, hurrying down the aisle.

As she took her seat next to Kyla at the prosecutor's table, she looked over at the defense table and caught Blood glaring at her angrily. He was chained and shackled, with the words MAXIMUM CUSTODY INMATE written across the back of his orange jumpsuit.

He had Bill Ferentz seated on his right, and three other high paid lawyers huddled together on his left.

"What took you so long?" Kyla asked, as she offered Amelia a file folder.

Amelia took it. "It's too long of a story to tell you right now," she answered.

"Miss Clarke, are we ready?" The judge asked, with his beady eyes fixed on Amelia.

"Yes your honor, I am."

"Then let's get this hearing started, so that I can get on to another," the judge said, as he took a file folder from the clerk. He read it over and called the case. Then he looked over at the defense table. "Mr. Ferentz, I assume that you've been briefed about your client's situation?"

Bill Ferentz got up and he straightened his pink silk tie. "I have your honor and I find it absurd that my client wasn't given a bond."

Amelia got up instantly. "Your client is a menace to society," she lashed out calmly. "That is why I have requested that he be held without bail."

"My client's criminal history is just as spotless as yours, Miss Clarke. That is unless you don't believe in innocent, until proven guilty."

"What do you mean by almost, Mr Ferentz? Not because he wasn't convicted of his priors, that doesn't mean that he's a saint."

"And who are you, to say that he's not?"

"I'm the one who filed the charge against him, just in case you haven't noticed."

"Don't get slick with me young lady, I'm old enough to be your father," the lawyer sneered loudly.

The judge intervened with a bang of his gavel. "You two need to cut it out," he said, pointing the gavel. "I won't tolerate such bickering inside of this courtroom... Am I understood?"

"Yes, your honor," Amelia and Ferentz muttered in unison.

The judge shoved his specs up against his face. "Miss Clarke, I see where you've filed another charge against Mr. Simms."

"Yes your honor. I—"

"Is this bitch fo' real!" Blood got up and snapped. He then started over to Amelia, but he was quickly held back by his lawyers. "Get the fuck off of me!" He barked, as he tried to break free. "This bitch is gonna keep going, until I break her fucking neck!"

"You won't be breaking anything, Mr. Simms!" The judge barked, as he banged his gavel. "I've heard about your outbursts inside of judge Horne's courtroom. But just so you know; you act like that again, and I'm gonna have you thrown out."

"We do apologize, your honor." Ferentz pleaded, as he helped to lower Blood back into his seat. "But as you have seen, my client's outburst is due to Miss Clarke's vindictiveness."

"How am I vindictive?" Amelia glared at Ferentz and asked.

Ferentz glared back at her. "We all know that this new charge is because you think that my client is responsible for all that has been happening to you. So don't act as if it's anything else." Ferentz looked up at the judge. "Your honor, I really think that Miss Clarke has been overstepping her bounds as a state prosecutor. She's got this hatred for my client, which has her abusing her power. It's as if she's got a personal vendetta against him."

The judge looked over at Amelia.

"Your honor, all that I'm doing is my job," she said, speaking softly.

"Miss Clarke, I'm quite aware of all that has been happening to you," the judge said. "But until you can prove that Mr. Simms is behind those incidents, I'm advising you to keep your personal feelings to yourself."

"I know that he's behind them," Amelia muttered. "The night that my mother was abused; he called me and told me to drop his charge. He said that if I didn't, that he would make something even worse happen."

The judge looked over at Blood. "Mr. Simms, is this true?"

"I'm in jail; I ain't got no fucking phone to call that ho."

"You're such a damn liar!" Amelia barked at Blood. She turned to Bill Ferentz. "Mr. Ferentz, didn't he tell you that we had spoken over the phone?"

"I don't know what you're talking about." Ferentz lied. He looked up at the judge. "Your honor, could we continue?" The judge pulled off his glasses. "Miss Clarke, please control your temper," he said, cleaning the lens with a napkin. "I know that you're going through a lot. However, you know the law. Without proof, you can't blame Mr. Simms for what you're going through."

Amelia dropped her head. "I understand your honor," she replied dolefully.

"Your honor, is there any way for my client to get a bond?" Ferentz asked.

"Are you serious?" Amelia blurted out, looking angrily at Ferentz.

"Just like everyone else, he's entitled to a bond," Ferentz shot back.

"Not with all that's been going on," the judge chipped in.

"Thank you, your honor," Amelia smirked.

"So my client is being singled out?" Ferentz asked loudly.

"Your client is an accused murderer." Amelia replied, just as loudly.

"He's accused, not convicted!"

"Well, all of the accusations against him are more than enough to keep him off of the streets, until a jury decides his future."

Amelia and Ferentz went on for a few more minutes, until the judge said, "Mr. Simms will be held in custody until this case is settled." He glanced over the sheet of paper inside of his hand. "Mr. Ferentz, how does your client plea to the charge of first degree murder?"

Ferentz hesitated, while glaring at Amelia. "Not guilty, your honor."

The judge turned to the clerk. Then he accepted a sheet of paper that she had received from Amelia. He read it over, and then he looked at Ferentz. "You saw this?" He asked.

"I have, and I think that it's ridiculous."

"Miss Clarke, this is a very... severe plea deal," the judge said, with his brows raised. "Life without the possibility of parole... Am I seeing right?"

"That's the state's offer, your honor. And I do think that the offer is appropriate," Amelia said confidently. She then took a deep settling breath. "The state has reviewed Mr. Simms' case, and will be pushing for the death penalty, if he is found guilty by a jury."

"Fuck you, Bitch!" Blood got up and raged. "You'll be fucking dead, before a jury can find me guilty!" He shoved Ferentz out the way. Then he started to wrestle with the other lawyers, while trying to get to Amelia.

Chairs were being tossed out of the way and the defense table was tipped over. Sheets of paper were flying around in the air, and Ferentz was on the floor holding onto Blood's leg.

"Get the fuck off me!" Blood was growling, as he fought against his lawyers.

"Order! Order! Get him outta here!" The judge barked, banging his gavel.

Security was streaming into the courtroom like ants. And Amelia and Kyla were huddled together, up against the wall across the room.

"Bitch, you'll never get me to do time!" Blood screamed, as he fought off the many hands grappling at him. "I'm bigger than prison, bitch! You hear me! I'm Blood! I'm fucking bigger than prison!"

Despite all of the chaos, the judge was still seated at his bench and banging his gavel. "Get him outta here!" He was shouting, with spittle flying from his mouth like darts.

Ferentz was amongst the group that was forcing Blood out through the door. He had blood trickling down from a gash on his forehead, and his navy blue Armani suit was soiled and ripped.

When they finally got Blood out through the door, Ferentz stopped and looked across the courtroom at Amelia. "Do you really think that I'm gonna let my client take a plea deal for a life sentence? You must be out of your mind," he snarled viciously.

Amelia sucked in a couple of deep breaths, in order to slow down her adrenaline. "You've got other options," she said to Ferentz. "However, me lowering my offer is not one of them." Ferentz didn't reply, but he did shoot Amelia a nasty glare, before storming out of the courtroom.

CH-18

Ice stepped down from the Range Rover with his cell phone at his ear and a white baseball cap pulled down over his eyes. He stood for a while and listened to Amelia's cell phone as it rang in his ear. She hadn't answered his two previous phone calls, and by the sound of her voicemail that came on for the third consecutive time, it was evident that the third wasn't gonna be answered.

"She still ain't picking up?" Yogi asked, as he walked over.

Ice hung up and stuffed the phone down inside of his pocket. He slammed the truck door closed, and then he turned to Yogi. "Who is she?" He asked complacently.

"Niggah, don't try to play me," Yogi snorted. "I've known you too long, not to know you well. So stop acting like it ain't Amelia that you've been calling. Shit, seems like you're about to go crazy worrying about her."

Ice looked over at Yogi but said nothing. He knew that he couldn't hide much from him. Decades of being close had them capable of reading each other like books. After about five seconds of silence, Ice took a deep breath then uttered, "So, shouldn't I be worried? Blood got her going through hell, brah. She doesn't deserve to be going through all this shit. I've been around her, so I know what she's about. She's not only that hard-nosed prosecutor that everyone sees her as. She's also very funny and caring." He pulled the cap down closer to his eyes. "You've seen her; you've seen how sexy and beautiful she is. The woman is straight up wife material. What man in his right mind wouldn't be worried about her, if he was in my shoes?"

"She is a stunner," Yogi agreed, nodding.

Ice sighed and then he looked at the restaurant in the distance. Frustrated, he then sucked his teeth and started across the parking lot. "Come on, yow, let's go find out what these niggahs are talking about," he said dauntlessly.

As they were walking, Yogi glanced across his shoulder at Ice. "Have they found out about Tip?" He asked.

"They should've," Ice answered, as they approached the restaurant. "It's been on the news like a dozen times, ever since it happened."

Yogi placed a hand on Ice's shoulder. "I know that Tip was your good friend and shit. But on the real, he got what his fuck-ass deserved."

Ice gave his cousin a blank look, but he didn't say a word. Instead, he huffed out a breath and then stepped inside of the restaurant.

The small Jamaican restaurant wasn't crowded. Only a handful of customers were there, chatting quietly amongst themselves. There was a Sean Paul joint playing in the background, along with the smell of fried fish floating around in the air.

Ice scanned the restaurant before making his way to the back, where he saw Rebel and Rev seated at a table. Rebel was flirting playfully with a big ass Jamaican chick, and Rev had his head down over his plate of oxtail and rice.

"What's up, fool?" Rebel greeted Ice with a smirk, when Ice got up to the table. He slapped the Jamaican chick on her ass, as she walked away. Then threw his head back and laughed, when she cut her eyes at him. "I'm so fucked up about that bitch," he said, while reaching for his Heineken. He took a sip and then he glanced up at Yogi. "What's up Yogi Bear?"

Yogi didn't answer; he just stood next to Ice, with his face stern.

"You always trying to play tough," Rebel giggled over his Heineken.

Ice took a seat at the table. "So, what's up? You said that you wanted to talk to me. Here I am. What's good?"

Rebel took another sip from his Heineken. "You heard about Tip?" He asked.

Ice nodded.

"I heard that they lit his ass up light a Christmas tree," Rebel giggled. He glanced up at Yogi, and then looked steadily at Ice. "You know that Blood went to court yesterday, right?"

"So, what happened?"

"Shit . . . the bitch is still playing hard ball. She even tried to hit him with another charge."

Ice gritted his teeth when he heard Rebel call Amelia a bitch, but he kept his cool and said, "It seems as if she has her mind made up about sending him up the road."

"The bitch is stubborn as fuck," Rebel sneered. "But we'll get her to change her mind. That's why I called you." He glanced up at Yogi, and then leaned over to Ice and lowered his voice. "Blood wants us to kidnap and kill the ho if he's not released."

Ice's heart slammed against his chest. He fell back in his seat, before glancing up at Yogi. Then he narrowed his eyes on Rebel. "You've got to be joking?" He argued. "After what happened to Tip, you niggahs still wanna go after this prosecutor?"

"You know how it is, brah. It ain't no stopping, until Blood is outta jail."

"Or we're all in there with him," Ice lashed out. "Better yet, we could all end up like Tip."

Rev raised his head from his plate and then he looked at Rebel, with his face twisted viciously. "I told you that this niggah would be on some suckah ass shit."

Ice shot Rev a hard stare. "Call it what you will, brah. I'm not trying to spend the rest of my life in prison because of you, Blood, or no other niggah."

"So what you trying to say, Ice? It sounds like you're trying to turn your back on Blood?"

Ice looked at Rebel. "I'm just looking out fo' me, brah. I ain't trying to end up like Tip," he retorted.

Rebel got serious. "After all that Blood has done fo' you?" He gritted out and stared.

"Done fo' who?" Ice fired back, with a hard stare of his own. "Niggah I ain't obligated to Blood. I was giving him upfront cash fo' mine."

Rebel pointed a finger at Ice and then he warned firmly, "Lower your voice when you talk to me, yow."

"Niggah, you've got me fucked up!" Ice snapped and got up. "Rebel, you ain't no fucking John Gotti or Al Capone. You can't order me around. Niggah, you're just living in your brother's shadow. We all know you a pussy, brah. You just a wanna-be-gangsta."

Rebel got up.

Rev got up.

Yogi stepped next to Ice.

"I ain't on that shit that you niggahs are on," Ice said, stepping away from the table. The few customers inside the restaurant were all looking on worriedly. But Ice ignored them and continued with his rant. "Whatever you niggahs wanna do to help Blood, then go ahead. But leave me the fuck out of it."

"So, you want out?"

"Niggah, I've been out," Ice shot back at Rebel. "I ain't risking my life fo' Blood. Do you think he'd risk his life fo' me? Blood ain't any different than those other niggahs, who copped to deals to stay outta prison. Everybody got a fucking breaking point. And I'm sure if Blood could, he would snitch on one of us just to keep his ass out of the joint."

"Seems as if you've forgotten who Blood really is?" Rebel said, gritting his teeth. "But if that's how you wanna play, we'll play."

Ice didn't miss Rebel's threat. He locked eyes with him and said, "I ain't got no beef with you, yow. But whatever you wanna bring, bring it." He then turned away. "As I said before, I want no part of what you niggahs are trying to do."

"Don't worry 'bout it, brah. I'll just let Blood know."

Ice stopped and turned to look at Rebel. "I don't give a fuck," he growled quietly. "You can also let him know that I said it's fucked up what he did to Bam. I ain't trying to go down with his ass fo' that shit. As a matter of fact, you can tell him that I said *fuck you*."

Rebel stepped towards Ice.

Yogi stepped in front of him. "Calm down, brah. Don't be spitting gasoline on fire."

"This ain't got nothin' to do with you, yow; so back the fuck up."

Yogi clenched his fists and then he glared at Rebel. "Be careful asshole," he threatened coldly. "Go try that tough shit with some other niggah. I'll break yo' fucking neck."

"Niggah, you ain't bullet proof."

Yogi looked over at Rev and saw him with a Beretta pressed firmly against his thigh. He started towards him.

Ice grabbed him by the arm. "Let that shit go, cuz. This ain't the time or the place."

"You better let his big, goofy-ass know," Rev scoffed.

Yogi stared angrily at Rev for a very long time, and then he surprised everyone with a coy grin. "It's all good," he said calmly. "You got the better of me today."

"And I'll have it tomorrow too," Rev scoffed.

Ice knew that if Yogi was to lose control of his temper, Rev would have to kill him to stop him from killing him. So he stepped in front of Yogi and shoved him away. "Let's go cuz. We don't need to be here, right now."

Yogi hesitated before turning away. "I'll see you fools around," he said, as he walked towards the restaurant's exit.

"Just hope that we don't see you first," Rev warned.

"You fucked up, Ice. You fucked up big time," Rebel said, while watching Ice and Yogi as they walked away.

"Pussy-ass niggahs," Rev added.

$$\$\$\$\$\$\$\$\$\$\$\$\$\$\$\$\$\$\$\$$

After work, Amelia decided to go by Danielle's house in Coral Springs to hang out for a while. As she drove, she mused over all that was going on between her and Blood. The feud between them was just as intense as how it had started, but she had no intention of backing down. She had made up her mind to do all and everything that she could to send him to prison. Yet she was trying her best not to worry about the repercussions behind it.

After seeing all that was going on because of Blood's detainment, Amelia knew better than to take his threats lightly. The truth was that she did get a bit scared at times. She had come to the realization that Blood was a powerful and cruel individual, who was capable of getting to her in more ways than one.

He had proven that he wasn't afraid of the law or the judicial system. He had also showed her that he was a fearless mortal, who lived by his own rules. But Amelia had her mind made up to do one thing. And that one thing was to prove to him that he wasn't above the law.

It was close to six o'clock when Amelia pulled up next to Danielle's Honda Accord, which was parked in front of her two bedroom townhouse. The nose tingling smell of barbeque chicken was emanating from the kitchen, and it had Amelia hurrying out of her Lexus and rushing up to the house.

The front door was unlocked, so she pushed it open and then strode through the sparsely furnished but immaculately kept living room. "Danielle!" She yelled, as she approached the kitchen. "Danielle where are you?!"

"Goddamn 'Melia, why are you shouting?" Danielle uttered, as she stepped out of her bedroom in a skimpy red thong and a wife beater.

"My bad," Amelia giggled. "I thought that you were inside of the kitchen." She dropped her bag and keys inside of the sofa and then she pulled off her jacket. "What's that smell?" She asked.

"What smell?"

"I smell barbeque chicken. Was your mom here?"

"She just left," Danielle said and then she turned away. "She cooked enough food to last me forever. So if you want, you can take some home."

"Sure will," Amelia said, as she followed Danielle into her bedroom. She walked over to the four-poster king-sized bed and took a seat. She then crossed her legs and watched Danielle, who was in front of the dresser applying make-up to her face. "Are you going out?" She asked her.

"Hmm-mmm, Dane asked me out to dinner."

"Dane?" Amelia wrinkled her nose suspiciously. "Ain't Dane that mechanic from across the street, who's been chasing after you for over a year now?"

"Yep."

Amelia started laughing. "So, you've finally decided to give him a chance?"

"Might as well," Danielle giggled. "It's time that I move on from the fast money making kind. They're all like ticking time bombs, waiting to explode."

"I'm so glad that you finally figured that out."

"It took me too damn long to figure it out," Danielle replied. She looked back at Amelia "I almost lost my best friend because of one of those ticking time bombs. So because of that, I've decided to leave them all alone and give the hard working, civil brothers a chance."

"Ain't nothing wrong with that," Amelia said, getting up. She walked over to Danielle and embraced her. "Just so you know," she whispered in her ear. "You weren't about to lose me. We're best friends fo' life."

Danielle cocked her head and then she showed off a coy grin. "I wasn't talking about you," she sassed jokingly.

Amelia pushed her away playfully. "Whatever ho . . . I'm the only friend you've got," she replied laughing.

"And the only one that I need," Danielle responded, while reaching over to kiss her best friend on the cheek.

Just then, Amelia's cell phone chirped from inside of the living room.

"I'll be right back," Amelia told Danielle, as she turned and hurried away. She quickly got her cell phone from her handbag. Then she checked the caller ID and answered with a warm smile. "Please, don't be mad at me," she cooed.

"But I've been calling you fo' the whole damn day."

"I know, but I was busy at work."

"But you could've at least called me back after work."

"I'm sorry," she apologized, as she walked back inside of the bedroom, and found Danielle, twisting her way into a pair of low-rider jeans.

"Where are you?" Ice asked.

"I'm at Danielle's house."

"I'm coming to get you. I'm taking you out to dinner."

"No, you're not," Amelia scrunched up her face and said flatly. "I told you that I'm at Danielle's house. I'm not dressed."

"Then, I'm giving you an hour."

"An hour to do what?"

"An hour to take your ass home and get dressed."

Amelia giggled. Then she took back a seat on the bed and crossed her legs. "Are you taking me back to Kareem's?"

"Is that where you wanna go?"

"I'd like to. But if you've got something else planned, then I'm cool with whatever.

"I've got another place in mind. You've got an hour."

"Trav', an hour is not enough time for me to get home and get dressed."

"How much time you need?"

"At least two hours."

"Okay then; you've got two hours. Dress nice."

"Don't I always?" Amelia giggled, right before hanging up.

CH-19

Ice took Amelia to an exclusive poetry club that entertained and catered to its guests in the most awe-inspiring way. The club was decorated beautifully with high stools and tables for two, burgundy love seats against the walls, and dining tables that were all fully occupied.

There was a small dance floor that was covered with blue imported mosaic tiles, along with a semi-circular bar, located next to the stage at the front of the room. The vibe inside of the club was pleasantly soothing, yet lively. It was close to being jam-packed. But Ice had paid a small fee to get a table inside of the V.I.P section, away from the crowd and up close to the stage.

After enjoying a tasty serving of curried lamb and white rice, Amelia got comfortable on the sofa next to Ice and took sips from her glass of apple martini. She had her shoulder pressed lightly against his chest, while listening to Brian McKnight's soothing voice.

Her legs were crossed sexily, and a foot of her black Jimmy Choo pumps was dangling in the air. She was looking radiant and sexy in her black sequined mini, which was giving Ice an eyeful of her sexily toned legs. Legs that he was hoping to get in-between, before the night ended.

After a slow sip of apple martini, Amelia placed a hand on Ice's knee and said, "I didn't know that you were into poetry."

"I'm not," he replied coolly. "I'm only here because of you."

She sat up and turned her head to look at him. "Because of me?" She blurted with a quiet giggle. "What makes you think that I'm into poetry?"

He shrugged. "I just thought that it would help to get your mind off of things, for a while."

She glanced around at the beautiful setting and the well-mannered crowd inside of the club. "I've never been to a poetry club before," she said. "But I must admit that I like it here." She surprised him with a quick, steady kiss on the lips. "Thank you. I really needed this."

"No problem," he replied, while taking a sip from his Hennessy.

Amelia got back comfortable on the sofa, by pressing her shoulder back against his chest. "So, how was your day today, Trav'? What did you do, other than blow up my phone?" She giggled.

He laughed a little. "I really didn't do much. I spent the majority of my day hanging out with my cousin… What about you?"

She held onto his thigh and then squeezed it lightly. "I had a crazy day. But let's not waste our times talking about it. I'm having too much fun, as it is."

"Whatever you say lady, you're the boss."

After about two hours of appeasing the patrons with a variety of old school R&B hits, the DJ allowed the MC to take the dimly lit stage, while introducing the first poet. The theme for the night was love. And the MC let it be known that anyone could take the stage and recite a rehearsed or a concocted poem.

For about thirty minutes, Amelia sat wrapped up inside of Ice's arms and enjoyed the performances of four poets. They were all professionals, so it didn't take them long to have the entire club in a daze. Everyone listened intently, while trying to grasp onto all that they were saying.

The fifth poet was introduced as Mama Dynamite. She was a heavy set black chick, with long flowing dreadlocks that stopped just above her ass. She was dressed in a black, green, and yellow sarong, some black gladiator sandals, and a bundle of colored bangles were bunched up around each arm. She was clearly a favorite at the club, because the entire room stood and greeted her with joyous hand-claps and loud shouts of approval. She took the stage, laughing. Then after she took the mic, she turned and jiggled her wide ass like a paid stripper.

This got the entire room to explode with laughter, and it took about two full minutes after that moment for the club to settle down. But just as the club got quiet, she started her poem.

"What di fuck is love?" She wailed comically, in her strong Jamaican accent. "I don't kno' what love is, an' I don't t'ink that I've ever felt it. Is love the cause of these pulsin' tinglin's between my legs? The same pulsin' an' tinglin's that sometimes leave I wet. Somebody ansa mi nuh!" She snapped, with a sudden thrusted fist into the air. "Tell me if it's love, why my nipples get so perky an' hard? Or if its love, why I'm always willing to hunch ova like a dawg...?"

The entire club was now in stitches. Mama Dynamite was only at the beginning of her performance, yet she had everyone laughing hysterically and grabbing at their sides. Even Amelia was laid out in Ice's lap, laughing uncontrollably. She had tears leaking from both eyes, and her beautiful face was looking bright and blissful, as she enjoyed her night.

$$$$$$$$$$$$$$$$$$$$$$$$

"I'm telling you dawg, I'm gonna put it on that niggah Ice, whenever I see him. I just feel like his fuck-ass tried us," Rebel bickered loudly. He took a pull from the blunt that he was smoking and then he blew a cloud of smoke out through the window of the speeding Porsche Cayenne. "I'll see his fuck-ass again. And when I do, I'll show him that I don't only talk gangsta; I live that shit fo' real."

Rev glanced over at Rebel, and then went back to gunning the Porsche down Atlantic Blvd. "I told you that his ass wasn't down with Blood," he sneered. "We should've dropped that fuck-niggah, a long time ago."

"Fo' real."

Rev gave Rebel a skeptic glance, before racing by a slower moving Dodge Ram truck. "So what we gonna do about this prosecutor ho. We gonna snatch her up, or what?"

"That's what Blood wants us to do, but I've got a better idea," Rebel said, gazing at the scenery outside. "Where the fuck we going?" He asked, as Rev turned off of Atlantic Blvd.

"To get something to eat . . . that blunt I smoked earlier got me hungry, like a mothafucka."

"So why didn't you just slide by the Mirage? They've got food there."

"I know. But I've been hearing mad shit about this little spot. I just thought that we'd stop and check it out," Rev said, as he turned the Porsche into the huge strip mall. He made an immediate right, then coasted towards the club-like scene at the east end of the parking lot.

"What the fuck is this, a club?" Rebel asked, as soon as they got to the front of the building, where there were a couple of tux'd out bouncers and a few lingering patrons.

Rev double-parked next to Ice's Range Rover, without even realizing it.

"It's a poetry club. They just opened it up, a few weeks ago."

"A poetry club?" Rebel challenged. "Niggah, I ain't going into that shit. Gangsters don't get into poetry."

"There's a lot of hoes in there, dawg. Just look at that bitch standing by the door." Rev pointed, at a thick, red-bone chick, whose ass was ripping apart her skimpy white skirt.

Rebel looked at the red-bone and then he sucked his teeth. "Man, I ain't even trying to get caught inside of no damn poetry club."

"So, you don't wanna go in?"

"Fuck naw. Let's go to the Mirage, where the women walk around naked."

"If that's what you wanna do," Rev said, as he slid the Porsche back into drive and pulled away from next to Ice's Range Rover.

$$$$$$$$$$$$$$$$$$$$$

After Mama Dynamite's hysterical performance, the MC announced a break that sent the DJ back to playing a slew of R&B hits. Amelia utilized the break by making a quick trip to the ladies room, to freshen up.

She had to. Because she had laughed so hard during Mama Dynamite's performance that her hair got tousled and her joyful tears left her with streaks across her face. She was clearly enjoying her night with Ice. And as expected, Ice was doing all of the right things to have her feeling special.

When she got back to their table inside of the V.I.P section, he greeted her with a third glass of apple martini.

She took it, after taking her seat. "So did you miss me?" She asked jokingly.

He flashed a smile. "More than you know," he told her, while sipping on his Hennessy and watching the crowd out on the dance floor. They were getting down to R. Kelly's, *Step in the name of love*. "Do you feel like dancing?" He asked a bit timidly.

She cocked her head and eyed him leerily. "I thought they say that thugs don't dance," she giggled.

He took her hand and then got up. "People say a lot of things," he replied, as he pulled her up from her seat. Then while keeping a hand at the small of her back, he led her out onto the dance floor. Then without missing a beat, they stepped into the Fugees' song, *Killing me softly*, which had just come on.

They danced as if they had practiced together for years, swaying their hips with slow but firm synchronization and moving in-sync to the beats that played. Ice had his hands just above the upper curve of Amelia's ass, keeping her tightly against his body as they drifted away

Then.

"Hell-fucking-naw!"

Ice cringed to the loud familiar voice that blared above the music. When he pulled away from Amelia, his blood curdled. It was obvious that she wasn't ready for him to let her go.

"Ice, this is how you do!" Shanequa snapped, as she charged over. The crowded dance floor parted for her. And even though the music was still playing, it was as if it had completely stopped.

She was dressed daringly in some barely there jeans shorts, knee high Coach boots, and a pair of huge chandelier earrings dangling from her ears.

"You can't find the time to call my fucking phone, but you are out here wilding out with this sadity bitch?"

Amelia cocked her head and then she looked at Shanequa, with her eyes narrowed. "Excuse me?" She snapped scornfully.

Shanequa flicked a palm up in Amelia's face. "I'll get with you in a minute. Wait your turn," she said snaking her head, with her eyes on Ice.

Amelia sneered at Shanequa and then she spieled, "Trav', I'm giving you two minutes to get rid of this little tramp, before I get rid of her fo' you."

Ice quickly stepped up to Shanequa. "What the fuck you doing, yo, are you out of your fucking mind?"

"What the fuck do you mean?" Shanequa asked defensively.

"What did I tell you about trying to show out, whenever you see me?"

"So, what you want me to do? How would you feel if I was up in here, grinding on some other niggah?"

"I wouldn't give a fuck!" Ice said hotly. "I told you that it's over between us, yo. What part of that don't you understand?"

A crowd had now gathered around them and it had Ice feeling a bit embarrassed but extremely pissed off.

Tears blurred Shanequa's eyes. "After all that we've been through, Ice; after all of the time that we've spent together?"

"We were together for three months, Shanequa. Stop acting like we were a married couple."

"So that is why you're here with this ho?"

"Ho!" Amelia snapped and then she started to unlatch her Jimmy Choos.

"Let's go then!" Shanequa fired back loudly, as she ripped out her earrings. "I ain't gonna let you beat me, over what's mine."

Ice shoved her away. "Get the fuck outta here!" He spieled, while holding onto Amelia.

Shanequa leaped at him, but leaped into the arms of a bouncer instead. "Let me go!" She raged. "I'm tired of this niggah treating me like a raggedy jump-off."

The crowd had gotten bigger and the music was turned off.

"Travis, I'm ready to go," Amelia said hotly. She had her nose flaring and her eyes fixed on Shanequa.

"You better go!" Shanequa yelled. "And you ain't going nowhere with my man!"

"I don't know who your man is, but it ain't me," Ice said, while draping an arm around Amelia. He kissed her on the cheek. "We don't have to leave, if you don't want to. You know that I'm about you and you alone."

"Aaaahhhhhh!" The crowd cooed.

Amelia couldn't help but to smile. She put an arm around Ice's waist and then she pulled him close. "Take me home," she said, just to taunt Shanequa. "We've had enough interruptions for one night."

Ice took Amelia's hand and then they started away.

Embarrassed, Shanequa burst into tears. "Fuck you, Ice! Fuck you!" She screamed angrily. "You may think that you're all that, but niggah you ain't!"

"That's a lie," Amelia looked back at Shanequa and said. "He's all of that to me."

"Fuck you!" Shanequa yelled.

"Same to you, baby girl," Amelia replied, smiling.

CH-20

They drove in complete silence, Ice with his hands gripped tightly onto the steering wheel of his Range Rover, and Amelia with her arms folded and her lips tight. She was furious; pissed at him for putting her through such embarrassment inside of the poetry club.

Ice sighed and then he glanced over at her. The hostile look on her face had him wanting to get into another slew of apologies. He had already apologized numerous times. But Amelia ignored him the entire time and kept her mouth shut.

The smile that she had thrown at Shanequa as she was walking out of the club had disappeared, the very moment that she stepped out through the door. It was all a facade, nothing but a show.

With his eyes fixed on the road ahead, Ice reached over and placed a hand on Amelia's knee.

She slapped his hand away. "Don't fucking touch me!" She growled at him.

"Amelia, I'm sorry."

She cut her eyes at him and then she went back to the passing scenery outside.

"Could you at least talk to me?"

"I don't wanna talk to you."

He sighed. "'Melia, I'm sorry. I know that I fucked up, but could you please forgive me?"

"Why should I? You don't deserve my forgiveness. Not when you just had your little girlfriend trying to get up in my face."

"I wouldn't have let her. And besides, you made it clear to her that I'm your man."

"That was all a show. I said what I said, because I was trying to hurt her feelings."

"Well it felt good hearing you say it."

"Well you'll probably never hear me say it, ever again." She spun in her seat, in order to face him. "You really embarrassed me, Trav'." She glared at him. "Just because of you and your little hoochie, I was in the middle of a crowd acting just like a hood-rat."

"I know that's not who you are."

"Lucky you, 'cause I don't know who you are," she said as she folded her arms and then went back to pouting. "You could've at least said something about her."

"Said what?" Ice uttered, trying to keep his voice low and even. "I stopped talking to Shanequa, before I even met you."

"Well, she's still in love with you."

"And what am I supposed to do about that?" He shot back. "I can't stop her from loving me. And I'm not gonna let her stop me from loving you."

"You don't love me, Travis. You don't know enough about me to love me." She sat up and gazed out of the window. "And where are we going? This is not the way to my mother's house."

"You said to take you home, so I'm taking you home."

Amelia's mouth fell open and her eyes got huge. "I meant my mom's house, Travis. Don't play with me."

Because he knew that Rebel and Rev were out to kidnap Amelia, Ice was determined to stay by her side. He knew that he couldn't watch over her, twenty four hours a day. But his plan was to watch over her, just as much as he could.

"I'm just doing what you told me to do," he glanced over at her and snickered.

She folded her arms and then she pouted, "Travis, please take me home. I've got to get up early in the morning and go to the gym. I also have to take my car to the carwash."

"I'll take your car to the carwash fo' you."

"I'll do it myself. Just take me home."

"No," he said flatly. "You're spending the rest of the night at my apartment."

"Are you fo' real?"

He kept his eyes straight ahead, with his lips twisted devilishly.

She sat and stared at him. She so badly wanted to flip on him — snap and tell him to leave her the fuck alone. Only she just couldn't find it in herself, to do it.

The way that he stood by her side at the club had her convinced that his liking for her was truly genuine. But she wanted more from him, just a little bit more, to fully convince her that he was in it for the long haul.

"Travis, I don't wanna go to your house," she said twisting in her seat, with a show of attitude.

"Well, it's too late now, 'cause we're already at my crib," he said with a smile, as he turned the Range Rover through the automatic gates which led up to the prestigious Alvarado Tower, a twenty four story condominium high rise, which featured elegant European interiors and offered a breathtaking view of the Atlantic.

It took Ice close to thirty minutes to get Amelia out of the Range Rover and up to his nineteenth floor, bachelor-like pad. But as soon as they stepped off the elevator, she then got back into her ranting.

"I'm never going out with you, ever again," she sassed, as they walked down the corridor. "I'm much too old to be at a club wildin' out."

"You're not old," he said, as he pushed his front door open for her to step inside.

She did.

"I'm much older than your young ass," she snipped, while looking around the foyer and checking out the polished marble floor and the abstract paintings on the walls.

Ice's apartment was very neat, unique, and equipped with all of the latest electronics and an over stocked wet bar.

"Just so you know, I'm not staying long," Amelia said, as she dropped her keys and purse down onto the nightstand by the door. "I don't even know why you brought me up here, 'cause we're not doing anything."

He ignored her, as he walked across the living room. "Would you like something to drink?" He asked.

"No," she answered dryly, while gazing at all of the framed photos on the wall.

"I've got fruit juice and your favorite, V8."

She didn't answer; she stayed checking out the photos. After about two minutes, she asked, "Who are all of these people?"

"Mostly family."

She cringed, when she heard how close he was. He had walked up on her, without making a sound. And his close presence had her covered in goose bumps. Her gut tightened with pleasure, when she felt his hand on the small of her back. And she had to wet her suddenly parched lips, in order to hide the surge of lust that was now swirling around throughout her body.

"That's my mother." Ice pointed at the largest of the framed photos.

"Sh-she's beautiful," Amelia admitted shakily, desperately trying to control her raging libido.

He stepped closer and held her arms. "I'm really sorry about what happened tonight."

She flushed. His hands on her arms sent sexual warmth throughout her body. And within a couple heartbeats, it found that spot between her legs. She knew that it was lust and desire, because a part of her was crying for him.

She wanted him all over her, in the most erotic way. But there was another part of her that was still saying no. That part was saying to be careful and wait; *you don't know enough about him.*

She turned to face him, and then she looked up into his eyes. "You should be sorry," She said after a long pause between them.

"And I really am," he whispered, and then he pulled her close.

Amelia felt her pelvis throb, when her front touched against his. The temptation to rip his clothes off was overwhelming. And her libido was begging to be appeased. But she didn't want him to see how dangerously in need she was, so she closed her eyes and then dropped her head.

He put a finger below her chin and raised her head back up. "Please don't get mad at me for doing this."

She locked eyes with him and her entire body quaked, "Doing wha—"

He cut her off by yanking her body up against his and then pressing his lips tightly against hers. Their lips locked and they started to kiss each other, as if they were starving. They sucked at each other's mouth, while moaning loudly in pleasure.

Already wet and throbbing, Amelia forced her front against his hard manhood, wanting to have him inside of her, thrusting and pounding away. She eased up on her toes when he grabbed her ass cheeks. He pierced them with his fingers, as he pulled her into him. They were going hard and fast, gyrating into each other as if they were trying to make their bodies' one.

They shuffled across the room and then they tumbled onto the sectional, Amelia with her legs wide and Ice in between them.

"Take your clothes off," she gasped against his mouth, and clawing at his t-shirt, as if she was trying to tear it away.

He yanked the t-shirt up over his head. Then he kicked off his shoes, jeans, and underpants. She was completely naked before he was. Her sequined mini was strewn onto the floor at her feet, and her panties were thrown across the room.

She fell back down onto the sectional. Her full, firm breasts were pointing at the ceiling with her nipples looking perked and hard.

He gazed at her in awe, stunned by all of the blessings that she had in between her legs. He tore his eyes away just long enough to race for a condom. Then as he covered himself, he watched her as she gazed at his hard, bent, ten inches.

"I swear; you're the most beautiful being that I've ever laid eyes on," he said, as he approached her with his dick hard, erect, and covered.

She put a foot on the sectional and then she spread her thighs. "Don't talk Trav'. Just give me what I need, before I change my mind."

His dick thrummed, when she said this. It was all that he needed to hear, for him to grab her legs and pull her to the edge of the sectional. He passed the head of his dick over her glistening slit to lubricate them both. Then he drove his entire length down inside of her core, with a slow, yet firm thrust.

She gasped and yelped, but he held her legs inside the crook of his arms and buried himself, slow and deep.

She had her teeth gritted and her eyes squeezed shut, with her hands clawing at the cushions on the sectional as if she was trying to rip them apart. It took her a while, to adjust to his size. But when she got adjusted and was taking him with less pain, she started to thrust up against him with raging force. She wrapped her legs around his waist and pulled him closer. She wanted to feel him against her swollen breasts, as he dug and plunged into her.

Ice pounded away as if he was a man possessed. He was carrying on, as if it was his very first time. Amelia was no different. She was writhing and squirming, with her eyes closed and her mouth wide open.

"Trav'," she called his name, when he buried his full length down inside of her. She tried to pull her legs free, but he wouldn't let her. "Trav' you're hurting me!" She cried out. But he ignored her cries and pleas and continued thrusting. His steady pounding was painful for her, but it had her cloaked in a cloud of unfamiliar pleasure.

Every bit of fear that she had for painful sex went away the moment that he reached down and started to kiss her. She started to accept his pounding willingly. Needing more, she held onto the back of her thighs. That way he could thrust freely down into her, as she thrust up to him.

"Fuck!" Ice groaned, as his body started to convulse.

She was thrusting up at him so fiercely, that he lost every bit of control. But he didn't want to cum before she did, so he gritted his teeth and tried his best to hold on.

"Aawwwe-shee-iit," Amelia forced out in trembling pleasure, clawing at Ice's back as she peaked. "Travis!" She screamed his name as she quaked, writhed, and squirmed in sexual bliss. She was cumming, while gasping and screaming to let the world know.

She pounded a fist into the sectional, as she erupted. She then wrapped her arms around him and pulled him down on top of her. Hugging him tightly, she kissed him fiercely. Then allowed him to pound and thrust as she shook and quaked.

Thirty minutes after her three explosive orgasms, Amelia stood inside of the huge octagonal shower with the surging warm water from the six spray heads, slapping against her body. She was thinking about Ice. She found herself missing him, even though he was only a few steps away. He seemed to be the only solution for her problems. Whenever she was around him, she tended to forget that she was a state prosecutor, who had a maniac trying to hurt her.

In spite of all the chaos that was going on around her, at the moment all she was craving for was Ice and his aggressive lovemaking. She just couldn't figure out what it was about him that had her so hooked. She just seemed to lose all control, when she was with him.

His thuggish attitude had her overwhelmed. And after having sex with him, she wasn't sure if she could step away from him for good. In an attempt to clear her head of Ice and her need for him, Amelia gazed up into the cascading water. She was grateful for its powerful surge and skin tingling warmth, the feeling of soothing pleasures slapping against her blemish less skin.

After a couple minutes of allowing the warm water to soothe her, Amelia picked up the bar of soap that was inside of the console on the wall, then went on to rubbing it all over her breasts, her stomach, her ass, and in between her legs. She was lathering her inner thighs, when the glass doors slid open. A welcoming smile broke out across her face when she saw him, gazing at her lustfully, with a straining erection.

"I couldn't wait any longer," he said, as he stepped inside of the shower and closed the door.

She glanced down at his manhood and she felt her body quake. "I was on my way out," she replied, with a perceptive shrug.

"Let's stay a bit longer," he told her, as he took the bar of soap and went straight for her breasts.

She closed her eyes and allowed him to have his way. She was aching to have him for a second time, so she dared not complain. She moaned, as he brought the soap down to her taut stomach, rubbing it over her pelvis, before going between her legs and then over her pleasure spot.

He started to kiss her as he lathered her mound, caressing her soft frilled folds and teasing her nub. She pressed against him, as sexual purrs left her throat. But when she reached for his manhood, he forced her around so that her back was against his chest.

"Oh Trav', what are you doing to me?" She whimpered, as she eased her ass out to him, aching to have him penetrate her core and douse her flames.

He granted her wish by forcing her against the tiles. He then nudged her legs apart with his right knee, and then he slowly entered her tight, warm wetness.

 She cringed and groaned, when she felt him. But she wanted him. So she pressed her palms up against the tiles and gave him what he wanted.

CH-21

When Amelia pulled inside of the carwash early Saturday morning, the taxi that she had called to pick her up was already there. It was parked at the Southside of the parking lot, right next to a payphone. The driver was leaning against it, with a newspaper up-close to his face.

Amelia waved happily at him, as she pulled up to the attendant behind the check-in podium. The smile on her face was as bright as the early morning sun. Her sex-filled night had left her pleased and satisfied, beaming as if she had just won the lottery.

Her many trips to the gym hadn't prepared her for Ice's never ending need. He was like the energizer bunny, with an energy pack on his back. She could still clearly remember how he had put it on her, inside of the bathroom. He had ignored her cries and pleas, and ravaged her from behind with slow aggression. Her most memorable moment was when he had her up against the wall — with her legs wrapped tightly around his waist, and his entire length up inside of her. Having sex with Ice was like everything that she had imagined it to be. It was tense, it was fulfilling, and it was satisfying.

It was only 9:23 in the morning, yet the carwash was crammed with cars, motorcycles, and SUVs. The smell of grease, wax, and cleaning chemicals were strong in the air, and every single employee was busy at work. The majority of those who brought their cars to be washed were inside of the lounge area, chilling in the A/C. But there were a few who opted to stay outside in the heat.

Amelia stepped down from the Lexus, dressed in a pair of black low-rise jeans and a yellow snug fitted t-shirt with a sketch of Bob Marley on the front. She retrieved her black Chanel handbag from the passenger's seat. Then she took a quick look around inside of the SUV, before turning to the attendant. "What's up Sam? Good morning," she greeted him pleasantly.

"What's up beautiful?" The pot-belly attendant smiled. "Getting the usual?" He asked.

"Yep, and if you can get Roger to change the oil and rotate the tires, I'd really appreciate it."

"For you beautiful, I'll do anything," he flirted, as he logged her in on the register. He ripped out the page that he had written on and handed it to her. "Give it about two hours," he told her.

"I'll be back to pick it up at about twelve," she replied, as she took the sheet of paper. She looked it over and then she smiled at the attendant and turned away. "Bye Sam. I'll leave something with Simone fo' you."

"I appreciate it," The attendant responded, with his eyes all over Amelia's voluptuous ass.

Amelia pushed open the glass door of the lounge area, and then she stepped inside. The room was a bit more crowded than usual, but everyone seemed to be occupied with a magazine, or locked in on the music video that was showing on the TV.

Amelia ignored her few admirers, as she strode up to the pay counter. "What's up Simone?" She greeted the cashier. "Busy morning, huh?"

"Too busy fo' my liking," Simone replied, with her nose scrunched up.

Amelia slid the sheet of paper that she had gotten from Sam, over to her.

"I bet Roger ain't complaining."

"Hah. If his boney ass could, he would have us all working eight days a week."

Amelia chuckled, as she pulled her wallet from her bag. She popped it open and then she pulled out her bank card. "The man is just trying to secure a future for you both, so you'd better stop complaining. There ain't much better out there than Rog', believe me."

Simone took the bank card. "You already know that I love his boney ass," she said, as she worked the cash register. "But I'm gonna stay complaining, until he puts a ring on it."

"I'll relay the message," Amelia laughed.

"Please do," Simone chuckled, as she gave Amelia back her bank card, along with a receipt.

Amelia took them and slid them both inside of her wallet. She then pulled out a ten dollar bill and placed it on the counter. "This is for Sam," she said, with a warm smile.

Simone rolled her eyes. "You need to stop spoiling his old, retarded ass."

"I can't help it," Amelia chortled, as she turned away. "Bye gurl. See you later."

"Later," Simone waved.

Smiling broadly, Amelia strutted across the room and out through the door. She pulled her bag straps up over her shoulder, as she stepped down the three levels of steps. But just as she was about to hurry over to where the taxi was waiting, someone grabbed onto her arm.

Startled, she yelped and then she spun around. "Can I help you?" She asked, as she looked up into the face of her accoster.

"Didn't mean to startle you, but ain't you that prosecutor who's trying to send my dawg, Blood, to prison?"

Amelia felt her stomach move, as she cocked her head and looked him over. He was about six-two, slender and jet black with a mouthful of gold; and tall reddish-brown dreads, dangling above his shoulders. His baggy jeans were barely up over his ass. And you could see the imprint of his gun at his waist, through his wife beater.

She shot him a black look. "Could you let go of my arm, please."

His grip got tighter. "I asked you a question, yo. I wanna know if you're that prosecutor who's trying to put Blood away, 'cause you do look like her."

Amelia tried to pull her arm away, but he held on firmly. "What's your problem?" She asked steadily.

He smiled a cocksure grin before looking over at his two friends, who had suddenly appeared by his side. "The bitch fine, ain't she?" He asked them.

The shorter of the two nodded, with a perverted smirk.

"This is the last time that I'm gonna ask you to let go of my arm," Amelia said firmly.

"Damn dawg, seems like she's catching an attitude," the other friend jeered.

Amelia looked over at him and cut her eyes.

They all giggled loudly, as if they found it amusing.

"So what's up, yo, you ain't gonna answer my question? If you don't, then I ain't gonna let you go."

Amelia shook a lock of hair from in front of her face and narrowed her eyes. "I don't have to answer anything that you ask me. Who the hell do you think you are?"

He yanked her towards him. "I'm Blaze, bitch. So you'd better check your fucking tone," he snarled, with his face twisted.

Amelia frowned irritably. *"Is this really happening?"* She wondered, as she looked around at the close by faces around her, some of which seemed to be masked with fear. She suddenly got the feeling that no one was going to do or say anything to help her, so she decided to calm down and try a different way out.

After taking a deep breath, she forced a smile at Blaze and said in a calm, low tone. "Hey listen, I'm not trying to be a bitch or anything, but I've got a taxi cab waiting on—"

"I don't give a fuck!" Blaze snarled arrogantly. "I asked you if you're the prosecutor bitch, who's trying to send Blood to prison."

That's when Amelia lost it. A burst of anger shot through her body and she ripped her arms out of his grip. "Get your fucking hands off of me!" She barked and then she backed up several steps. She then propped a hand on her hip and poked her head forward. "Yes, I'm the prosecutor who's trying to send your dawg to prison. And if you know what's good for you, you'd better leave me the fuck alone."

He stepped after her, with murder in his blood red eyes. "Bitch, you got shit mothafuckin' twisted—"

"Just chill out man! Just chill the fuck out!"

Blaze stopped and turned his head. Then he glared at the cab driver, who was hurrying over to Amelia's aid. "Who the fuck is you? Her knight in fucking armor?" He gritted out fiercely.

The cab driver stepped in front of Amelia. "Listen man, I'm not trying to get into it with you—"

"You already did, fool."

"Yeah fool. You already did," Blaze's taller friend chipped in.

The cab driver looked over the faces of the three thugs. "Well I apologize," he said humbly. "But I can't just stand by and let you guys harass this young lady."

Blaze reached underneath his wife beater and pulled out a Glock 40 pistol, which caused a loud gasp in the crowd.

"I swear on everything that I love," he threatened. "If this Haitian mothafucka don't trot his ass back to Haiti where he came from, I'ma show him what being gangsta is all about."

"I won't let you harm her," the cab driver stated firmly, but clearly in fear.

"Jean just go back to the car," Amelia shoved him.

Jean stood his ground. "I'm not leaving you here, Miss Clarke," he said, while staring at Blaze.

There was a fearful buzz in the gathered crowd. A few onlookers were standing behind cars and walls, trying to stay clear, just in case gunfire ensued. Blaze was known throughout Ft. Lauderdale to have a short temper and two idiotic friends who did whatever he asked. So the majority of those at the carwash knew that he wouldn't be hesitant, to show out in front of a crowd.

"So what you gon' do, pussy? You wanna get your fucking brains blown out because of this ho?"

"I-m not le-leaving her."

There was a loud 'clack!' then a gasp in the crowd when Blaze selected a round in the chamber of the Glock. The crowd quickly started to disperse, and a deathly feeling started to swirl around in the air.

Blaze who was showing signs of rage, aimed the gun at Jean's head. "Didn't I tell your bitch-ass to bounce?"

Jean shuddered, but he held his ground. He wasn't known to be a violent person, but he had his mind set on protecting Amelia.

"Fuck this niggah!" Blaze snapped and then stepped at Jean.

"Goddamn Blaze! What the fuck are you trying to do, shut my shit down?"

Blaze stopped and looked over at Roger, the owner of the carwash. He was hurrying over with a greasy towel dangling from the back pocket of his greasy cover-all. His girlfriend, Simone, was by his side, looking pissed.

"How you gonna violate my business place like this, brah?" Roger questioned, as he got up to Blaze.

Blaze, with the gun at his side, scowled at Roger before turning to Jean. "I've got to give it to this fool, yow. He seen me hollering at this bitch and he's trying to sho' out."

"I ain't nobody's bitch!" Amelia snapped.

"You are, what the fuck I say that you are," Blaze spat and then stepped towards her.

Roger grabbed onto him. "Leave that shit alone, man. Amelia's one of my best customers. So you can't chase her off like this."

"Fuck that ho! She's the one holding Blood in jail," Blaze announced.

"I'm not the one holding him," Amelia uttered. "The law is."

"Fuck the law!" Blaze growled.

"Fuck Blood! I hope they fry his ass!" Someone shouted from the crowd.

"His ass is getting what he deserves!" Someone else shouted.

Blaze looked around at the crowd. "Fuck all of y'all!" He spat fiercely, when he couldn't pin point the two who had voiced their hatred for Blood. "We make our own laws in the hood. And when niggahs violate they get taken care of." He looked steadily at Amelia. "You're violating, bitch. You need to let the boss go or else."

"Or else what?" Amelia asked, a bit timidly.

Blaze pointed a finger in her face. "You'll see," he threatened.

"You're always on some shit, Blaze." Simone propped a hand on her hip and chipped in loudly. "That is why I hate when your ass is here. You're always causing shit. One of these days, you're gonna fuck with the wrong person."

"Ain't nobody out here to punch me in my shit, Simone. So fuck you."

"I've got Roger to do that," Simone fired back at him. "Your black ass will never get the chance."

Blaze glared at her, and then pointed a finger in her face. "You should be glad that I'm cool with Roger."

"And if you wasn't—"

"Simone!" Roger snapped, wanting to put a stop to the commotion at his business place. He looked over at Amelia. "Amelia, I'm really sorry about this. I promise that this shit won't ever happen again."

"It's all cool Rog'," Amelia said, picking up her bag that had fallen from her hand. "I don't blame you for any of this. It's all arrogance."

"Arrogance and ignorance," Simone uttered, as she cut her eyes at Blaze. She took Amelia's arm and started off. "Come on gurl; let me follow you to your ride."

"You can't protect her, Simone," Blaze said, as he slid the Glock back into his waistband. "Now I know who she is, so you can't protect her. I'll see her again."

Neither of the two women answered. They kept their heads straight, as they walked away.

The moment that Amelia was seated in the back of the taxi, Jean asked, "Do you want me to call the police?"

Amelia sighed and looked at him. "Please don't. Roger and Simone are good friends of mine. Having the police running up into their carwash would make it bad for them and their business."

"Are you sure?"

"Hmm-mmm," Amelia nodded, as she reached over the driver's seat and hugged Jean from behind. "Thank you so much for stepping up and defending me the way that you did."

Jean smiled. "No sweat at all," he said proudly. "That's what real men do. We protect our women."

$$$$$$$$$$$$$$$$$$$$$$$

Inside the small visiting room was dead quiet, with the air heavy and tense. There was a can of soda in the middle of the small metal table, and a pack of cigarettes next to the filthy ashtray.

Batch sat across from Blood, with his arms folded and his eyes fixed on nothing. He didn't want to look at the irate drug dealer. He knew if he did, that he would only be adding fuel to the already blazing situation.

Blood was glaring angrily. The look on his face was that of a man who was about to explode. He had a lit cigarette between the fingers of his right hand, and every so often he would take a hard pull and let the smoke filter out through his nostrils.

"So, what you want me to do?" Batch asked, with his eyes bouncing everywhere except for on Blood. "You know that it's whatever you say."

Tight faced, Blood got up and then he started to pace. "What I want is to get the fuck outta here. I'm tired of eating fucking bologna and cheese."

"I told you to let Jackson bring you in, whatever food you want."

Blood turned and slapped the soda can off of the table. "Fuck the food!" He barked. "You think that I enjoy sleeping inside of a fucking cell?"

"I know you don't."

"So, why the fuck am I still here?"

Batch dropped his head and then he exhaled. "We're all trying to get you out," he muttered bleakly. "But Miss Clarke is proving to be a lot more stubborn than we all had anticipated."

"So kill the bitch!" Blood barked.

Batch dry washed his face. He wanted no part of killing Amelia, but he wasn't about to say it. He knew that her death would only make the situation even worse. Because then the Feds would get involved and Blood and all those affiliated to him, would all be suspects — including himself.

Blood went back to pacing. He took a hard drag from the cigarette and then he blew the smoke up at the ceiling. "So what about that niggah, Rick? Ain't he the one fucking the ho?"

"They're not together anymore."

Blood stopped and turned to face the corrupted cop. He stared at him, from across the room. Then after about ten quiet seconds he exploded, "One of you mothafuckas better do something to get me the fuck outta this shit! I don't care who's got to die or who's got to get paid, but somebody had better do something and do something fast. With all of the money that I was giving you fuckers, I should've been outta here a long time ago."

"I'm almost sure that you'll be outta here by next week."

"What the fuck you mean by almost?" Blood scowled. "He flicked the lit cigarette at Batch and then he stormed over to him. "Listen here, you mothafucka," he snarled in his face. "I was giving you thousands of dollars to keep me outta shit like this."

"Rick is the one who fucked up," Batch said, with a dismayed look on his face. "He's the one who lost track of your case file."

Blood leaned closer to Batch. "I don't give a fuck about all that," he said, through clenched teeth. "You're the one who said that he was reliable. You're the one who said that he could be trusted. So if I go down, then I'm taking your greedy cock-sucking ass with me. You hear me?!"

Batch swallowed the lump inside of his throat and nodded.

Blood turned away and then he started out of the room. "And you can tell the others, I said it," he said, before stepping out through the door. "Ain't nobody getting spared, if I've got to go to prison! If I've got to do time, then all of y'all mothafuckas gone do time with me!"

CH-22

The salon was buzzing, like it was a holiday weekend. All of the hairstylists were busy at work and the three barbers had their hands full. There was a small crowd lounging around inside of the waiting area, and there were a few waiting customers hanging out outside.

The chattering inside of the salon was loud, but this was how all of the workers liked it. To them, a noisy salon was a busy salon.

"So, what are you gonna do?" Danielle asked. She was seated at the manicure station, putting the finishing touches on Amelia's airbrush design.

"I'll just call another cab," Amelia answered. She already had her hair washed, blow dried, and wrapped. Her pedicure was done to perfection, and Danielle was spending more time than necessary on her fingers. "I'm just not gonna take the risk of having Jean confront that idiot, for a second time."

They were talking about Blaze and what had happened at the carwash. Amelia was still a bit bothered by the ordeal. But she was determined not to let it get her down. She had spent the last two hours giving Danielle a rundown of what had happened. And now they both were trying to figure out how to go back and get her truck, without confronting Blaze.

Even though Jean had dropped her off and told her to call him whenever she got done, she decided that she wouldn't call him. She just didn't want him facing off with Blaze and his two idiotic friends, for a second time.

"You want me to give you a ride?" Danielle asked, as she examined her artwork on Amelia's fingernails.

Amelia took a look around inside of the bustling salon. "I can't have you to leave the salon now," she demurred. "Just look at how busy it is."

"And it will be just as busy, when I get back."

"That wouldn't be fair to the customers that you've got waiting. I'll just catch a cab."

"You sure?"

Amelia nodded. Then just as she reached for her cell phone to call a taxi, it began to vibrate and ring. Thinking that it was Jean calling to find out if she was ready to go, she hesitated. But when she saw Ice's number on the screen, a smile broke out across her face.

"Hello," she answered, after accepting the call.

A few seconds ticked by before Ice came on and asked, "Yo, whassup?"

His husky voice caused Amelia's smile to stretch wider. "I'm at Danielle's, getting my nails done. What's going on?"

"Are you into basketball?"

"Somewhat. Why?"

"I was gonna get us a couple of tickets to go to the Heat Knicks game tonight. That's if you wanna go."

Amelia's stomach churned with excitement. She had never been to a professional basketball game, but it was something that she had always wanted to do. More than anything, she wanted to scream, "*Yes, I wanna go!*" But instead, she took a deep breath to compose herself, and then she said, "Can I think about it and let you know later on?"

"I've got to know now, so that I can go get us the tickets."

She hesitated and sighed, as if she was a bit annoyed. "Okay then. I'll go," she droned, but the toothy smile on her face was showing how happy she was.

Danielle squeezed Amelia's hand, to get her attention. "Is that Travis?" She mouthed, when Amelia looked at her.

"Yes," Amelia mouthed back at her.

"Tell him to come and get you," Danielle whispered, wide-eyed.

Amelia shook her head.

Danielle slapped her on the hand, in a playful way. "Bitch, tell the man to come and pick you up!" She said loudly.

Amelia threw her head back and laughed.

"Who are you talking to?" Ice asked her.

"Danielle," Amelia answered, giggling. She raised her hand and then she examined her nails that were finally finished. "Trav', where are you?" She asked timidly.

"Close by... Why?"

"Can you come and get me? I need a ride to go and pick up my truck at the carwash."

There was a brief delay, before Ice asked, "What are you wearing?"

Taken aback, Amelia's smile disappeared. "Wh-what?" She asked tentatively.

"Take a chill pill, yow. A niggah ain't on no freaky-ass phone sex shit. I just wanna know if you're wearing a dress or not."

"I've got jeans on... Why?"

"Don't worry about it."

Amelia smiled and then she waved at three younger females. They were saying goodbye to everyone, as they left the salon with fresh, off the chain hairdos. "So are you coming to get me?" She chirped into the phone.

"I'll be there in a few."

Before she could respond, he hung up. She rolled her eyes happily. "He's on his way," she said to Danielle, who was slouched back in her seat with a mischievous grin on her face.

"I just bet he is," Danielle teased. "So where are you two going later on?"

Amelia shot her friend a playful scowl. "Were you listening to everything that we were saying?"

Danielle smiled and shrugged.

Amelia did the same. "He wants to take me out to a basketball game."

"The Knicks heat game?"

"Hmm-mmm, that's what he said."

Danielle sighed loud and heavily. "I'm so fucking jealous of you right now," she pouted.

Amelia looked at her and chortled, "There's no reason for you to be jealous. I'm sure if you had asked Dane to take you out to the game, then he would've found a way. What's up with you and Dane anyway?" She asked, as she examined her fingernails for a second time.

Danielle tilted her head slightly. "We a'ight, so we ain't gonna waste our time talking about me and Dane. I wanna talk about you and Ice."

"There's nothing to talk about."

"Liar," Danielle poked her head forward and said. "It's all over your face, 'Melia, so stop lying."

"What's all over my face?"

"That after-good-sex glow."

Amelia laughed. "Your eyes are deceiving you, gurl. You need to get them checked out."

"Yeah right," Danielle drawled, with her lips twisted crookedly. "I know you, 'Melia. I can always tell when you get some."

"Keep telling yourself that," Amelia giggled.

"So, you didn't get some last night?" Danielle pressed. "And don't lie."

"Get what?"

Danielle inched her head forward and then she widened her eyes.

Amelia did the same.

"Come on 'Melia, stop playing."

Amelia rolled her eyes. "Is it that obvious?" She asked with a toothy smile.

"Sure is," Danielle cooed. "Gurl, you were glowing like a bulb, when you were talking to Ice just now."

"Was I?"

Danielle nodded.

Amelia fell back in her seat. "I just don't know what it is about him. But whenever I'm around him, I'm so damn happy."

"So you two had sex last night?"

Amelia looked Danielle dead in the eyes. She smiled and then nodded. "I can't even tell you how good it was. I'm still tingling all over."

"The tingle that you are feeling is love," Danielle said, reaching for her can of Red bull. She took a sip. "It's been a while since I've seen you this happy. So Ice has got to be doing a couple of things right."

"He is," Amelia admitted, with a content smile stretched across her face.

Danielle got up, and then she turned the can of Red bull to her head. When she lowered it she then asked, "Did you tell him about what's going on between you and Blood?"

"He knows. We've spoken about it a few times," Amelia said, as the thunderous roars of speeding motorcycles caught her attention.

Within seconds, the roaring motorcycles jerked to a stop right in front of the salon. There were two of them. Each one gleaming beautifully with each rider decked out in colors to match his ride.

The entire salon stopped to watch the riders, who were both wearing helmets. No one knew who they were. That was until Ice pulled off his green and black helmet and hopped off of his green and black Kawasaki Ninja 650.

"Gurl, your ride is here," Danielle turned to Amelia and sang.
"My ride!" Amelia uttered, with a hand at her pounding chest.
"I don't know where he's going with that thing, 'cause I'm not getting on it."

Just then, Ice pushed the salon's door open and he stepped inside. He looked around, before popping the latches on his gloves. Then he slowly walked over to where Amelia was standing, right next to Danielle. "What's up, you ready to bounce?" He greeted Danielle with a light squeeze on her shoulder, as he addressed Amelia.

"Trav', I'm not getting on that bike."

He looked outside at the Kawasaki, before cracking a sinister grin. "What. You don't trust me?" He asked.

"Of course, I trust you. I just don't trust that," she pointed at the bike.

He took her hand. "If you fall, I fall. And believe me, I'm not gonna fall."

She stood her ground. "Trav', I've never been on a motorcycle before."

"Then, you don't know what you're missing."

She leaned to the right, to look at the bikes outside. "I'm scared," she muttered.

"Scared of what? If you're not scared to drive, then you shouldn't be scared to ride. Car crashes are much more prevalent than motorcycle accidents."

She laughed a bit, as he started to drag her to the door.
"Danielle, I'll call you," she giggled, just before stepping outside. The closer that she got to the motorcycles, the faster her heart pounded. She had never in her life ridden on a motorcycle. So the thought of her now getting on one, had her scared stiff.

"Put this on," Ice offered her his helmet, when they got up-close to the bikes.

"Trav' I—"

"Amelia, just put on the damn helmet," he demanded, as he flung his leg over the Kawasaki, then pulled some green and black goggles, down over his head and eyes. He took her bag and placed it on the gas tank, directly in front of him. "Get on," he told her, as he fired up the bike.

Amelia took a deep breath, before she hesitantly climbed up behind him.

"Hold on!" He shouted above the loud and powerful engines of the two motorcycles.

Amelia quickly wrapped her arms around his waist and plastered her body up against his back. Then the motorcycles, one after the other, thundered out of the parking lot, then roared away down Oakland Park Blvd.

Less than ten minutes later, Amelia's knees buckled and she fell into Ice's arms, when she climbed down from off of the back of the Kawasaki. Her adrenaline was still surging powerfully, and her heart was thumping much too heavily for her to take control of her breathing.

She was smiling though. Beaming like a little girl, who had just stepped off of her favorite ride at the amusement park. Being on the back of the Kawasaki, as it sped up to the speed of 130 mph, had been quite an experience for her. It was wild, it was frightening, and it was intense . . . . But she loved it. Loved it so much; she just couldn't wait to do it again.

"Give it a minute," Ice told her. He was still seated on the Kawasaki, with his goggles up on his forehead and a hand around Amelia's waist.

She leaned into him, unable to move because of her wobbly legs.

"You've got to ride with us more often," Yogi grinned. He was standing next to his red and white Ducati, with his red and white helmet in his hand. "After your first couple of rides, that feeling usually goes away."

Amelia laughed. "I think that I'd better stay away from you two and these motorcycles," she said. "Because I'm here already craving to go again."

"So let's go," Ice suggested with a smirk.

She eased away from him. "Let's ride to the game later," she proposed, as she reached for her handbag. She then eased forward and whispered in his ear, "I'll even wear something *really-really* sexy."

Ice felt his dick twitch. Just the thought of seeing her in a pair of skimpy short shorts, was enough to have his gut twisting with pleasure. His eyes lingered on her mouth. "I'll be at your steps at eight," he said

"And I'll be ready and waiting," she smiled, as she turned away. "Bye Yogi," she chirped. She then hurried towards Sam, who was watching her from the check-in podium.

Ice sat on his motorcycle and watched her, as she walked away. He just couldn't pull his eyes away from her and her provocative ass. He had grown to enjoy watching her. Just looking at her had him fantasizing about them in the most erotic way. He wanted her badly, wanted to make love to her again and again, until she begged him to stop.

After Amelia stepped through the door of the lounge area, Ice took a deep breath to clear his head. He then took a quick look around the busy carwash. Things were in full swing, and music was thumping from a parked Denali. There were a few females standing around, but the men outnumbered them, by at least two to one.

"You ready to go?" Yogi asked.

Ice adjusted his goggles. He wasn't quite ready to leave. Something was pulling at his gut, telling him to chill out for a while; sit back for a minute and watch Amelia drive out. He had no idea what was the cause for the adverse feeling in his gut. But with Rebel and Rev out there wanting to kidnap Amelia, he wasn't about to ignore what he was feeling. Therefore he pulled off his goggles and dismounted from the bike.

"Let's head inside," he said. "Let's go and grab something to drink, before we ride out."

" —I held him tight, the entire time," Amelia was telling Simone, about the ride to the carwash.

"Gurl, I don't know how you do it," Simone responded, with excitement in her eyes. "I don't think that I could ever get on a motorcycle. It's just too scary."

"It's scary, but I love it," Amelia beamed. "I just can't wait fo' tonight."

"So, you guys are riding to the game?"

"Hmm- mmm," Amelia nodded.

"I do hope that you enjoy yourself," Simone said. "I'm no fan of basketball. But I'd love to attend one of the games, just for the experience. Roger promised—"

Simone stopped, when she saw them, walking towards her with mischievous grins on their faces, as if they were heading for trouble.

Amelia noticed the sudden change in Simone's facial expression, and she turned her head. Her heart flipped over inside of her chest, when she saw them. And a sour feeling started to develop inside of her stomach. She wanted to turn and run out through the door. But that thought quickly dissipated, when Blaze got up on her and placed a hand on her ass.

Amelia slapped his hand away and then she spun in his face. "What's your fucking problem?!" She screamed at him. "Why can't you just leave me the fuck alone?"

"You know what time it is," Blaze snarled, with two fingers pointed down in Amelia's face. "Didn't I tell you that I'd catch up with your ass?"

"I'm not trying to go through this again," Amelia said, and then she tried to walk away.

He stepped in front of her.

"Goddamn, Blaze!" Simone charged, from behind the counter. "Are you fucking deaf? Didn't you hear the girl say to leave her the fuck alone?"

Blaze snapped his head around, to face Simone. "Be careful bitch. Roger ain't here to save your ass."

"Bitch?" Simone erupted, with her head cocked. "Niggah, the ho that pissed you out is the bitch."

This caused rage to hit Blaze like a sledgehammer. He charged at Simone, but didn't get to her. That's because a solid right fist from Ice, connected with his temple and sent him crashing into the counter.

A bit stunned, Blaze spun around, and then he reached for his gun. Only he got a large fist in the mouth from Yogi for trying—then another in the gut that knocked the wind out of him. This caused him to double over, in gut-wrenching pain. But his pain intensified when Yogi snatched up the gun from off the floor, and then used it to slap him across the face.

At that very same moment, Blaze's friend charged at Ice. He got him good, with a fist to the jaw. But that one blow was all he got off, because Ice spun around and punched him square in the face and broke his nose.

He grabbed at his face, but that didn't stop Ice from pulling his Beretta M9 from underneath his biker jacket, and then used it to smack him across the head. He grunted and groaned. Then as his eyes rolled to the back of his head, he crumpled down to the floor like a wet towel.

REPERCUSSIONS by SHAWN STARR

By now, the majority of those who were lounging around were out through the doors. A few of Roger's workers had charged in to see what was going on. Only when they saw Yogi with a gun in his hand standing over Blaze, they fell back and kept their mouths shut.

Nursing his aching jaw, Ice kicked Blaze's close to unconscious friend, dead in the gut. "Niggah, you punched me in my shit!" He snarled furiously, and then he kicked him again.

After walking up and seeing what was going on, Blaze's other friend charged into the room like a mad man — but he slid to a stop and flung his hands up in the air, when Yogi turned and aimed the gun to his head.

"Please don't shoot me, man. I ain't got nothing to do with this," he begged.

"You better not," Yogi warned him.

Still nursing his aching jaw, Ice walked over to where Amelia and Simone were standing. "You straight?" He asked Amelia. A bit shaken, she nodded.

He looked over at a smiling Simone and got a confirming nod, before going back to Amelia. "What's up with you and dude?" He asked.

Amelia waited, trembling slightly, as she tried to regain her composure. She looked over at Blaze. He was glaring at her bitterly, as he struggled to get up from off of the floor. "He's been messing with me, ever since I got here this morning," she said.

"So, you don't know him?"

Amelia shook her head.

"He's a damn low-life, who's trying to be recognized," Simone quipped noisily. "His ugly ass deserves exactly what he got."

"He sure does," an old woman voiced, from the gathered crowd at the door.

211

Ice turned to Blaze. He then narrowed his eyes on him, thinking that he had seen him before. "You got beef wit' my girl, yo?" he asked firmly.

Blaze didn't answer him. He just glared at Ice with hatred. He started to get up, but when Yogi steadied the gun at his head, he went back down.

Ice walked over to him and said to his face, "Let me explain something to you, playa. I don't know who the fuck you think you are—"

"I'm Blaze, niggah. And I'm connected to Blood. So you had better back the fuck up."

Ice looked over at Yogi and got an "I don't know this fool" shrug, so he brought his attention back to Blaze. "I don't care if you're connected to the damn Pope," he said bitterly. "Don't you ever make the mistake of even looking at my girl again!"

Blaze's gaze remained fixed on Ice's face. He narrowed his eyes a bit, and then he tilted his head slightly when recognition hit. "Niggah, I know you," he said, as his eyes widened. "You be hanging with Rebel and Rev." He wiped his bloody mouth with the back of his hand, and then he gave Ice a cold once over. "If you down with Rebel, then how the fuck are you hanging with that ho?"

"That who?" Ice asked, with his head angled and a disturbed look on his face.

"That ho, niggah. I called the bitch a ho. She's the one who's got Blood loc—"

"Clack!" Echoed loudly across the room, when Ice cracked Blaze in the jaw with the butt of the Beretta, and stopped him short of what he was saying.

"Don't you ever..." Ice raged, as he grabbed a handful of Blaze's dreads and slapped him again. "Call her a ho or a bitch!" Another slap caused blood, saliva, and a couple teeth to fly from Blaze's mouth.

"Beat his ass!" Was yelled from the crowd

"Call her a ho again!" Ice threatened furiously, and then raised the Beretta to slap Blaze a third time.

But before he could, Yogi grabbed onto his arm and pulled him away. "Ease up, cuz. You're about to kill that fool," Yogi implored apprehensively.

Just then, Roger barged in.

"What the fuck is going on, man?!" He yelled.

Ice with the Beretta still in his hand and his face masked with rage, looked over at Roger.

Roger looked back at him; looked at Yogi, then took a step back when recognition hit. He looked at Blaze, and then at Simone and Amelia. "What happened?" He asked, running a hand down over his face.

Simone stepped to him. "Blaze tried to hit me, just because I told him to leave Amelia alone."

Roger took a deep breath and then he turned to Yogi. "Yogi what's going on?" He asked respectfully.

Hushed mumblings started in the crowd.

Blaze's eyes got wide, when the name Yogi connected with his brain. He gazed at Yogi steadily, and then he looked over at Ice before dropping his head. He was worried. He didn't know Yogi. But just like everyone else across Broward County, he knew of him and his deadly past.

Yogi glanced down at Blaze, as he stepped towards Roger. "What's up fam', this your spot?"

"Yeah man, what happened?"

"Fool violated," Ice lashed out, as he slid the Beretta back underneath his biker jacket. He stepped next to Yogi. "Sorry about your spot. But we had to put that fool in check."

Blaze turned up his bloody face and looked at Roger.

Roger looked back at him and shook his head pitifully. "You see what you get for playing stubborn. I told you to leave Amelia alone."

"I didn't even touch her, "Blaze muttered weakly.

"That's because you got punched in yo' shit, before you could," Simone exclaimed, with an arm draped around Amelia. "I told your big black ass, that one of these days you'd fuck with the wrong person. Now look at your bitch-ass, down on the floor, crying like a ho."

Blaze didn't say a word. He was too embarrassed.

Ice stepped towards Roger. "You know that fool?" he asked him.

Roger nodded and then said, "Unfortunately."

"Well, try to talk some sense into him," Ice warned, as he stepped away. "Cause it could get worse, the next time around."

"He knows." Roger replied, looking at Blaze pitifully.

Ice walked over to Amelia. "You ready to get away from all of this shit?"

She nodded.

He wrapped an arm around her. "Come on, let's go and get your truck," he said, wiping away perspiration from her forehead.

CH-23

Amelia was laid out on the back of the Kawasaki, with her arms wrapped tightly around Ice's mid-section. She had her upper-body pressed tautly against his back, her ass scooted out, and her ponytail out in a straight line at the back of her head.

This time, she had the goggles on. But she could barely make out anything, because of how fast they were going. The last time she checked, they were speeding at about 165 mph, with everything flashing by them in an unrecognizable blur. The I-95 was just about empty, at two o'clock in the morning. Therefore Ice had the bike roaring like a stolen fighter jet—flying by whatever vehicle popped up in his path.

Amelia felt as if she was flying. Her adrenaline was at a relentless surge, and her heart was pounding out of control. She was scared shitless, yet she still felt excited and alive. It was as if her life had sprung into an outer-worldly peak. Her and Ice had only moments ago left South Beach, after watching the basket ball game. They had a great time together. And Ice saw a side to Amelia that had him loving her even more. He felt good having her by his side and seeing her so happy. And as he raced towards his condo in Ft. Lauderdale, the only thing on his mind was another long session of unbridled sex.

When the Kawasaki jerked to a stop at the main entrance of Ice's apartment building, Amelia could still feel her adrenaline surging, and the blood in her ear pounding as she declined from her high. She waited a while, before pulling her arms from around him. Then she waited a while longer, before stepping down from the bike.

She stumbled, as her legs gave way. But Ice was off the bike, just in time to grab hold of her and pull her close to his body. She made a childish giggle, as she wrapped her arms around him.

"I don't think that I'll ever get used to this," she said.

"You will. Just give it time," Ice replied, staring at her beautiful face and thinking how badly he wanted to kiss her. Realizing just how dangerously close that their lips were, Amelia tried to pull away but failed.

"Give it another minute or so," Ice told her, as he held her against his chest. "It usually takes a while to get your blood fully circulating."

"I bet it does," she said, getting comfortable inside of his arms. She placed her head against his shoulder. "Trav', we really need to talk about what happened at the car wash today."

"Do we have to, especially right now?"

She sighed, against his chest. "Why do I get the feeling that you're hiding something from me? I just feel like there's more to you, than you're saying."

"There is more to everyone than what they say, Amelia. It's not only me."

"I know that," she raised her head and said. "But what I don't know is who you really are. I do know that you care for me. But if we're going to be together; then you have to trust me enough, to tell me everything about yourself."

"That could take a very long time," he said, palming her ass and pulling her up against his oncoming erection.

She felt it and giggled. "Is that your gun?" She asked, with her brows raised.

"No. But it's just as lethal," he smirked.

She threw her head back and laughed. "If that's the case, then I need to get away from you," she chortled and then forced her way out of his arms.

He pulled her back against his chest, then waited a few seconds before asking, "Are you ready to go upstairs?"

She glanced back at his apartment building. "Are you sure that you want me upstairs? You know there's no telling what I'll do to you and that." She then glanced down at the bulge in the front of his pants and giggled.

"I think that I can handle whatever you throw at me."

"You sure?"

He snickered.

She cracked a grin and then she stared at him adoringly, before turning and hurrying away.

He quickly eased away from the bike and followed after her — his eyes locked-in on her shapely ass. She was looking sexy as hell, in her panty-fitted jean shorts and Miami Heat jersey with the knot at the back. She chose a pair of red and white Nike shox, over her customary high heels. But the style gave her such an innocent look, that it had Ice craving her even more.

They took the elevator up to Ice's apartment and strode straight into the bedroom. Then as if they were burning with desire, they latched onto each other and kissed—hard and passionately.

Ice backed Amelia up against the wall, without breaking the onslaught on her mouth. He pulled her hands up above her head and held them there—feeling on her breasts and not wanting to stop. She was gasping and panting; squirming, as if she was on fire. She pulled a hand away from his and then she turned the lights off.

He switched them back on. "You're too beautiful, to be kept in the dark," he whispered against her lips.

She shuddered with pleasure when he said this — then she grabbed the back of his head and slammed his mouth against hers. Soaking wet, she gyrated against his erection, begging for something to douse the sexual flames inside of her.

She wrapped her arms around his neck when he grabbed onto her ass, lifting her up from off of the floor and taking her over to the bed. He laid her down and then climbed on top of her, while settling himself between her legs without separating their lips.

He continued to kiss her just like a man possessed. He kissed her even harder when she wrapped her legs around his waist. Amelia was now completely wrapped up in ecstasy. Her body was throbbing so hard, she felt as if she was about to explode. Ice moved from her mouth, down to her neck. Then he went back up to her mouth again, when she let out a quiet carnal, "Mmmm . . . ."

He had her soaring through a haze of sexual bliss, surging to that outer-worldly peak that she had found on the motorcycle. She was so hot between the legs, that she grabbed him by his ass and pulled him further into her; and then she moaned, "Oh God!" when his rock solid shaft rubbed against her mound. She forced her pelvis firmly against his front. Then when he started to gyrate against her, she let out a loud, "Oh Shit!"

Things between them got wild and fast. And neither of them knew when it was that one of her breasts got pulled from underneath her jersey, and found its place inside of his mouth. She shuddered with pleasure, as he sucked on her nipple. Then she arched her back, when he groped and freed her other breast.

The heat inside of her was still rising. She was thrusting out her front, in a wild and animalistic way. She was aching to feel his bare shaft, up against her bare flesh; get it to ease the tormenting pulsation inside of her.

She grabbed a handful of his braids and pulled him away from her breast. "Kiss me," she begged, and then immediately got what she asked for.

He went back to kissing her hungrily. Every single nerve in his body was begging for release. He didn't know how much longer that he could go on, without exploding. So he snaked a hand down inside of her shorts and cupped her opening. Lights exploded behind her eyes, when she felt his hand against her bare flesh. The pleasure that she felt was so outer-worldly, that it had her shuddering. She eased her ass up off of the bed, when she felt him tugging at her shorts. He then quickly got them off, and then tossed them across the room.

"Good God," He gasped quietly, when he saw her flesh, spilling out through the sides of the crotch of her thong.

More than anything, he wanted to attack her. Make love to her as if he would never get another chance. But he knew for sure that it wasn't his last time. So he stepped to her and gently cupped a hand over the fist size lump between her legs.

She shuddered. Then spread her legs wider when he teased her perked clit with his thumb. She started gasping and writhing in bliss; while thrusting her front against his hand, as he drove her to insanity.

"Don't tease me Trav'," she begged, and then she grabbed him by the front of his shirt.

He went down on her, kissing her across her stomach; around her navel, and then down to the waistline of her thong.

"Don't stop, please," she whimpered, with a hand at the top of his head, urging him to go lower.

As his lips got closer to hers, he pulled the crotch of her thong, over to the side, and then he slid a finger inside of her vast wetness.

"Oh God! Trav'! Why are you doing this to me?"

"Isn't this what you wanted?" He asked, from down between her legs.

"Yes!" She answered shakily.

He inserted a second finger into her wetness.

She cringed as he stroked her. But when he pulled out his fingers and inserted his tongue, she grabbed his head, arched her back, and then started shuddering uncontrollably.

$$\$$$

Rick sat on the back seat of the Escalade, nursing his broken rib. He had gotten another beat down from Batch and his partner. But this time, he had been tied to a chair and blindfolded. The beatings had left him with several broken bones and lacerations. His face was now an unrecognizable mess. And he was also having difficulties breathing through his broken nose.

"Yo, it's time baby," Detective Morris said, as he stopped the Escalade in front of Amelia's apartment. Morris, Batch's partner, was a high-yellow, over weight rookie cop with a bald head. Chewing rapidly on his spearmint gum, he turned to Batch. "If this shit don't work, then nothing will."

"It better work," Batch replied. "I'm getting tired of beating up on this asshole."

The two detectives looked back at Rick and busted out laughing. But Rick wasn't amused; he just sat there staring at Amelia's Lexus truck; and wondering how he had gotten himself in so much shit, and what he could do to get himself out of it.

Snickering grossly, Batch turned in his seat to face Rick. "You ready to go?" He asked him.

Rick wiped away a streak of tear, from his right cheek and sobbed. "You know that she could go to jail for this, right?"

"Who gives a fuck?" Batch snickered and snatched up the manila envelope, which was on the dashboard. He then pulled it open and looked inside, before tossing it over to Rick. "Go do what you're supposed to do and we'll take care of the rest."

"What if somebody sees me and then call the police?" Rick asked glumly.

Batch grabbed Rick by the front of his bloody t-shirt. Then he yanked him between the two front seats. "Do you want us to go over this again?" He asked, with his face twisted.

Grimacing, Rick shook his head.

"Good," Batch hissed, and then he shoved him against the back seat. "Now get the fuck outta here," he spat.

Crying, Rick picked up the envelope from off the floor, and then he popped the back door open. He took a brief look around outside, then stepped down from the Escalade and then limped up the driveway towards the Lexus.

SSSSSSSSSSSSSSSSSSSSS

Kyla stepped out of Peppers night club and shuddered, when a light gush of cool breeze swept across her bare skin. She hugged herself and then she rubbed her upper arms, mad at herself for leaving her jacket inside of the car.

As she started across the parking lot, she looked up at the starless sky. It was almost five o'clock in the morning, but there was no sign of daylight anywhere.

She had a tremendous time inside of the club. However the glass of cosmopolitan that she had drank, left her feeling a bit woozy. Kyla knew that she wasn't good at holding her liquor. One glass was enough to have her acting a fool. But the guy that offered her the drink, just wouldn't take no for an answer. He kept pressing and pressing, until she eventually gave in and took it.

Trying to stay upright in her Christian Louboutins; Kyla made her way towards her brand new Honda Civic, which was parked only a few yards away. She was searching around inside of her clutch purse for her keys, when the silver Infiniti Q45 pulled up next to her.

"Well hello there, beautiful. Can I give you a ride somewhere?"

Kyla looked over at Rebel and smiled politely. "No thank you," she told him. "I've got a car."

"Is it that Honda Civic over there, with the flat tire?"

Kyla turned her head to check out the wheels on her car. But before she could get a good look, the back door of the Q45 flew open and Rev jumped out. He clamped a hand over her mouth, grabbed her around the waist, and then quickly dragged her into the back of the Infiniti, without anyone seeing.

CH-24

Early Sunday morning, Amelia was awakened by Jaheim's, *Put that woman first*. It was playing quietly on the stereo, inside of Ice's bedroom. She cracked her eyes open and looked out through the window. The sky was cloudless, and the freshness from across the Atlantic was blowing into the room. Sighing pleasingly, Amelia pulled the sheets up over her bare shoulders and then she rolled over in bed. Ice wasn't there next to her, so she immediately felt disappointed. She wanted him to be there; wanted to roll on top of him and wrap her naked body around his.

"Trav'," she called out to him, but he didn't answer. She listened for running water inside of the bathroom, but she heard nothing. "Travis!" She called out to him again.

"I'll be there in a minute! Just stay in bed," he finally answered, from somewhere inside of the apartment.

Amelia smiled, when she heard his voice. And just like whenever he was around her, her body shuddered with need. *"What's happening to me?"* She wondered, then giggled childishly, as she snaked a hand down in between her legs and cupped her twitching mound.

Ice had her deeper in love than she had ever been and she knew it. She just couldn't get over his thuggish charm, along with his aggressive lovemaking.

She knew that there was more to him than he was saying; Knew that they had a lot to talk about. And because she was now starting to consider him as her man, she was now aching to find out every bit about him.

"Breakfast fit for a queen," Ice announced, as he entered the room with a large, silver breakfast tray.

Amelia sat straight up in bed, and then she cupped both of her hands over her mouth. "Trav', what did you do?" She asked, overwhelmed with surprise.

"I made you breakfast," he replied, as he placed the tray on the bed next to her. "I ain't no chef," he admitted. "But I do know my way around the kitchen."

"I can tell," she said, while uncovering a dish of scrambled eggs. She looked at him lovingly. "So does this mean that I never have to cook?"

"No. it means that I'll be cooking for you, at times," he said, as he moved in for a kiss.

She snapped her head away and then she clamped a hand over her mouth. "Don't do that," she protested. "I haven't brushed my teeth, as of yet."

"So what?" He tried to pull her hand away. "My love for you is unconditional."

"Yeah, right... you say that now; but you'll be saying something different, when I gain a couple of pounds and add a few wrinkles."

"Won't make a difference; I'll love you even more," Ice said, and then he pressed his mouth against hers.

He kissed her as if nothing mattered. But when he pulled the sheets down from over her breasts, she scooted away and hopped down from the bed, naked.

"Can I please brush my teeth first?" She chortled, as she turned away and ran towards the bathroom.

Twenty minutes later, they were cuddled together in bed and nibbling on what was left from their breakfast. "What's on your mind?" Ice asked, after watching Amelia gaze at a slice of toast for about two full minutes.

She looked at him and cracked a tiny grin. "Just thinking, that's all."

"Thinking about what?"

She bit into the toast. "You and if you love me, as you say you do."

He gave her a strange look. "Where did that come from?" He asked.

She reached for her glass of orange juice and took a sip, before saying, "I just feel like there's so much more to you, that I don't know. But yet here I am in your bed, trying to convince myself that you love me."

He jammed his fork into a sausage. "So because you don't know everything about me, you don't think that I love you?"

"I know that you've got a lot of feelings for me. But I also feel that if you really love me, then you shouldn't be afraid to tell me just about anything."

"Who says that I'm afraid?"

She locked eyes with him. "You don't tell me anything, Trav'. The little that I do know about you, is the little bit that I've figured out for myself," she said in a low, yet even tone. "I'm not stupid, you know. I know that you're into selling drugs."

"I *was* into selling drugs."

She hesitated. "So what, you stopped?"

"Yes, I stopped," he said, stuffing a forkful of eggs into his mouth. "And I have no intention of starting again. That is the main reason why I'm trying to get this car dealership, up and running."

She dropped her head and then sighed loudly. "You don't even talk to me about this car dealership. It's like I'm not a part of your life. At times, I just feel like it's all about the sex."

"If that's what your feeling, then your feeling is wrong. I really do love you."

"So why are you afraid to open up to me?" She raised her head and then gazed at him. "Trav', I'd be lying if I was to say that I don't love you. I've fallen for you so hard and quickly, I'm still puzzled by it. But I need to know more about you. Not just the little that I can see."

He stared at her long and hard. Then when she cocked her head and stared back he asked, "So what do you wanna know?"

She allowed a few seconds to tick by, before she pursed her lips and looked away. "You probably won't tell me the truth," she mumbled.

"Do you really think that I'd lie to you?"

She looked at him. "I don't know, Trav'. Would you lie to me?"

"No, I wouldn't," he replied strongly.

She stared at him through slits. She waited and waited, for several moments. Then she asked, "Why do you have to walk around with a gun? If you gave up selling drugs as you say that you have, then why can't you give up walking around with a gun?"

He bit into his lips before saying, "It's just a bad habit, a very bad one. But if it will make you feel any better, then I'll drop it."

She looked at him adoringly. "You don't have to drop it, if you don't want to," she said, putting a hand on his arm. "But it would make me feel a whole lot better, if you don't keep it around me."

He reached over and then he kissed her on the cheek. "You won't have to tell me twice," he said with a grin. He then picked up a slice of pine from off of the tray. "So what else would you like to know?"

She studied him for several beats, and then she scrunched up her nose and asked, "Who is Rebel?"

Ice almost choked on the pine. He quickly swallowed what he had inside of his mouth, and then he eyed her curiously. "Who told you about Rebel?"

"Nobody," she shrugged nonchalantly. "I heard his name from the idiot that you had the fight with yesterday. I heard him say that you be hanging with Rebel. So I thought that Rebel was one of your good friends."

"We ain't friends," Ice said, with his voice laced in hatred. "We were business associates and nothing else."

"It sounds as if you don't like the guy."

"I don't, and I'd really rather not talk about him," Ice said, as he flung his legs over the side of the bed. He got up and then he offered a hand to Amelia. "Come on, let's go and take a shower; I wanna take you somewhere."

She took his hand. "Where are we going?" She asked, while crawling across the bed.

"You'll see when we get there."

"Why can't you just tell me now?"

"Because . . . if I do, then you won't be surprised when we get there."

$$\$$

Rev turned his Yukon Denali inside of the small strip mall, and pulled up in front of the liquor store. He slid a pair of dark Versace sunglasses over his blood red eyes, then stepped down from the sparkling black SUV, with a lit joint dangling at the corner of his mouth

"Hey Rev!" She called out to him, just as soon as he started towards the liquor store.

He stopped and turned his eyes on her.

"Haven't seen you in a while," Shanequa smiled, as she pranced up to him.

Rev gave her a skeptical look over, before pulling the joint from his mouth. "That's because I haven't been clubbing, like I used to," he informed her. "You know how it is with Blood in jail . . . So what's up with you, what you doing out here?"

Shanequa looked back at her girlfriend, who was about ten yards away. "I'm out here with my gurl, Nicole. She's trying to go to the beach, but I wanna go home."

"So what, you need a ride?"

She nodded, and then said, "I would've called Ice, but we haven't been like that lately."

Rev took a pull from the joint and then he blew a cloud of smoke up above his head. "You two are always going through some shit," he muttered. "You must really love him, to be hanging on like this?"
Shanequa rolled her eyes. "It ain't got nothing to do with love," she replied, with a bit of attitude. "I just don't like being alone."
Rev pulled off his sunglasses and then he stared longingly at her bulging cleavage. "I don't see how a girl like you could ever be alone," he emphasized. "There's got to be at least a thousand niggahs out there, waiting for a chance to get with you."
"I wish I knew them," Shanequa flirted. She propped both hands on her backside and then she tilted her head to the side. "So what's up, Rev, you gonna gimme a ride home?"
"Sure," he said, with a treacherous smile etched across his face. "Just gimme a minute; Let me grab something from inside the liquor store."

$$$$$$$$$$$$$$$$$$$$$$$$

"So, where are we goin'?" Amelia asked, from the passenger seat of the Range Rover. She had one legged pulled up underneath her, a hand at the back of Ice's neck, and her eyes fixed on the passing scenery outside.
"Just sit back and relax," Ice told her. "We're almost there."
She started to massage the back of his neck. "My mom asked about you earlier this morning," she said calmly.
Ice took his eyes off the road and gave her a worried look. "Your mother asked about me?" He asked leerily.
She squeezed the back of his neck lightly. "Stop being so paranoid," she giggled lightly. "My mom is the sweetest person in the world. I can't wait for you to meet her."

Ice took a deep settling breath before setting his eyes back on the road ahead. *"I've already met her,"* he thought sadly, as memories of the night that Miranda almost got raped and killed by Tip, floated around inside of his head.

Ten minutes later, Ice turned off of Pembroke Road and drove through a pair of wide open wrought iron gates.

"Here we are," he announced, parking the Range Rover right next to a blue Toyota Tundra.

Amelia sat up in her seat. She looked out at the recently paved car lot, over to her right; then over at the smaller one to her left. She then looked up at the two-story office building in front of her. "Is this place yours?" She asked.

"As of last week, yes," Ice answered, with a proud smirk. He popped his door open. "Come on, let's go check it out," he said, as he stepped down from the Range, and then hurried around to the other side. He pulled the passenger door open. "I've got people painting and upgrading a few things, so be careful," he warned, as he took her hand and helped her down.

"I really wasn't expecting this," Amelia said, as they started towards the office building. "This place is not only big, it's beautiful."

"But it's still not where I want it to be," Ice informed her.

As soon as they stepped through the double glass doors, a fat white man wearing a yellow construction helmet hurried up to them.

"Travis, I wasn't expecting you until tomorrow," he beamed, with a hand outstretched.

Ice took his hand and shook it. "What's up Pat? How's everything going?"

"Good man, good," Pat replied, elated. He looked over at two of his employees, who were walking by with buckets of paint and rollers. "Hey Chris, make sure that you catch that little spot inside of the bathroom upstairs."

"I already did."

Pat flashed his employee a thumbs up, before turning back to Ice. "As you can see, we're way ahead of schedule," he said. "We're just about through with the tiling and the painting."

"I see that," Ice said, while looking around. He then draped an arm around Amelia and pulled her close. "Hey Pat, I'd like for you to meet my girlfriend, Amelia."

"Nice to meet you," the overweight white man said, as he took Amelia's hand and shook it. He then looked her dead in the eyes and said, "I've been around a lot of beautiful women in my lifetime. Please believe me when I say, that you top them all."

Amelia actually blushed.

"Thanks for the compliment," she replied, then snuggled up to Ice, with her lips curled gracefully.

Pat turned his attention to Ice, while rubbing his palms together. "So what's up boss? You guys wanna check out what we've done so far?"

"That's why we're here," Ice replied.

Pat clapped his hands together. "Then come on, let me show you around" he said, as he turned away.

With an arm still wrapped around Amelia, Ice followed behind the contractor. He waited until they were a few steps away from the showroom, before he put his lips close to Amelia's ear and asked, "Do you feel like you're a part of my life now?"

She paused, and then she leaned into him and said, "Not completely, but I do feel like I'm getting there."

CH-25

Monday had never looked better for Amelia. It seemed as if the sun was shining extra bright; the birds were chirping extra loud, and the air was a perfect seventy eight degrees. Even the radio host on 99 Jamz seemed to be in a good mood. Ever since Amelia turned on the radio inside of her truck, he had been cracking jokes about the high jobless rate and the diving economy.

After her wonderful weekend with Ice, Amelia was back at work with a bundle of energy and a wide toothy smile plastered across her face. She parked the Lexus at her usual parking spot; and then hopped out looking radiant in a beige pantsuit and black peep-toe pumps. She strutted across the parking lot, like a model parading a runway. Her hair was tied back into a neat and tight ponytail, and her make-up was sparing, but well applied.

The bustling of her co-workers and affiliates greeted her, just as soon as she stepped inside the state attorney's office.

"Good morning— Good morning— Good morning," she chirped happily, strutting towards Selena Estefan and three other prosecutors, who were huddled together at the front desk.

They all turned their heads to look at her. "Good morning," they all replied dryly.

Still smiling, Amelia stopped and shot them a questioning look. "Damn. Y'all sound as if y'all ain't happy to be at work," she challenged lightly.

Selena raised an eyebrow. "I think that you're the one who sounds a bit too happy, to be at work," she said

"I am happy to be here," Amelia responded delightfully. "It's a beautiful day, and I had a wonderful weekend." She turned and then swished off. "Wish I could tell you guys about it, but I can't... See y'all later," she chortled and waved, as she sashayed across the lobby.

She was about to get on the elevator, when frank Hibbert ran up to her and told her that their boss would like to see her inside of his office ASAP. She told Frank Hibbert, "thank you," then she hopped onto elevator and rode it to the sixth floor.

When she got to her boss' office, the door was opened, so she knocked, stepped inside, and then chirped, "Good morning Mr. Barrett, you called for me?"

Albert Barrett leaned all the way back inside of his seat and looked steadily at Amelia. He then sighed heavily before saying, "Please close the door behind you and have a seat." The tone of his voice took away Amelia's smile. She had no idea of what it was that he wanted to talk to her about. But she just knew that it had something to do with the high-yellow, bald-headed guy that was sitting at his desk; along with the two uniformed cops, who were standing by the wall across the room.

Once the door was closed, Albert Barrett introduced the bald guy as detective Carl Morris. Amelia shook his hand, as she took the seat next to him. Sensing a bit of tension inside of the room, she looked at her boss and asked, "What is this about?" The overweight state attorney sighed, as he removed his wire rimmed glasses. "Detective Morris, you wanna tell her what's going on?"

Morris nodded and then he turned in his seat, to face Amelia. "Miss Clarke," he started out. "I'm here because the police department got an anonymous phone call this morning."

"And?"

"The call was about you accepting bribes."

"That is absurd," Amelia cocked her head and said. "Why would I do such a thing?"

"You tell me," Morris said. "We don't wanna make a stink about this, without solid proof. But the caller did say that he paid you a hundred thousand dollars to let Mike Simms go."

"What caller? What hundred thousand dollars?" Amelia scrunched up her nose and spieled. "I've never made an illegal dollar in my entire life. So whoever made that phone call is lying."

"So you don't know anything about the hundred thousand dollars, which he said that he paid you to let Mike Simms go?"

"Hell no!" Amelia blurted and she shook her head in disgust. "Is this a damn joke?" She narrowed her eyes and asked.

Morris shook his head. "I wouldn't dare play around with you and your career, like this. This phone call was actually made. The caller said that he gave you the money last night and that you promised that Mike Simms would be released on his next court date, which I just found out, is tomorrow."

"All that you've said just now, sounds so ridiculous," Amelia snapped. She then turned to her boss. "Mr. Barrett, do you really believe all of this nonsense?"

Barrett shook his head. "I don't, but it is a very bad accusation."

Amelia whipped her head around to face Morris. "Is this some kind of a set-up?" She asked, with her eyes narrowed on him. "Is this another one of Mike Simms' ploys to get outta jail?"

"I don't know Mike Simms," Morris lied. "And just so you know, I'm on your side with this. But please, try to understand that I have a job to do."

"And I would like to get to mine," Amelia said, getting up. "I refuse to waste my time talking about this."

"So you're saying that you don't know anything about what the caller said?"

Amelia shot Morris a black look. "I'm saying it's the stupidest thing that I've ever heard. My job is to send criminals to prison, detective. And if you check my record, then you'll see that I'm very good at it. Plus, I'm quite satisfied with what I'm being paid by the state. Therefore, I have no reason to accept bribes."

"I would really like to believe that what you're saying is all true. But until this whole mess is cleared up, I really have to keep on with my job."

"Then don't let me stop you," Amelia said hotly. "My life is an open book, feel free to read."

"So then, you don't mind if we search your office and your car?"

She tossed her keys at Morris. "Feel free, I have nothing to hide."

"Amelia, calm down," Barrett said, while leaning across his desk. "The detective will get to the bottom of this, so there's no reason for you to get all riled up."

"Mr. Barrett, I know that Mike Simms is behind this."

"You're probably right, but the detective does have a job to do. So let him go ahead and do it."

"I'm not stopping him," Amelia exclaimed.

Morris tossed Amelia's keys to one of the uniformed officers. He then turned to Amelia and asked, "Would you like to watch, while they do the search?"

"I don't need to, because I'm sure that they won't find anything."

"As you wish," Morris said, while signaling the two uniforms to go ahead and do the search. When the two officers stepped out and closed the door behind them, Morris turned to Amelia and said, "We'll get to the bottom of this. If this is all bullshit as you say, then there's no need for you to worry."

"Believe me, I'm not worried one bit," Amelia said and then she started away.

"Amelia," Barrett stopped her. "Don't leave. I want you to be here when the officers return."

Amelia walked back over to the desk and took back the seat next to Morris. "I just feel like this is a big waste of my time," she said, crossing her legs.

"I feel the same way," Barrett said.

Morris pulled a pack of spearmint gum from his pocket. He made offers to Amelia and Barrett. They both declined. "So who is this Mike Simms guy?" He asked, while tossing a gum into his mouth.

$$$$$$$$$$$$$$$$$$$$$$$$

Not even close to being satisfied, Shanequa lay naked on the bed and watched as Rev sucked on a cigarette. His naked body was glistening with sweat, and he still had on the condom that he had used on her.

The smirk on his face was that of a champion lover, who had just brought his woman to multiple orgasms. But let Shanequa tell it, and she would tell it totally different. To her, Rev was slight and boring in bed. He hadn't brought her to the orgasm, which he bragged that he could deliver. And having sex with him was too brief for her to enjoy. But it was her way of getting even with Ice, so she felt as if the disappointment was worth it.

"Are we gonna go again?" Shanequa asked with a hand massaging her breasts, and the other between her legs.

Rev turned away from the window to look at her. "Maybe some other time," he said uncaringly. "I've got somewhere to go and I can't be late."

"But I haven't cum yet."

"I'm sure that you can do that without me."

She cut her eyes at him, and then she sucked her teeth disgustedly as she reached for the TV's remote. She switched the TV on. Then she started to dig around under the sheets for her panties. After about a minute or so, she found them and then she slipped them on. But as she was reaching for her bra, an article on the front page of the newspaper on the nightstand caught her eyes.

Curious, she reached for the week-old newspaper and she read the headline. She then went on to staring resentfully at the picture of Amelia, which was midway through the column.

"The fucking bitch is a prosecutor," she muttered to herself, as she read through the bold, capped section below Amelia's picture.

Rev heard her turned around. When he saw what she was looking at, he stepped towards the bed. "That's the bitch that's got my dawg in jail."

Shanequa looked up at him. Looked at Amelia's picture; and then looked up at him again. "She's the prosecutor that's holding Blood in jail?" She asked, pointing at Amelia's picture.

Rev nodded.

Shanequa flung her legs over the side of the bed, and then she shoved the newspaper up in Rev's face. "This is the same bitch that Ice is fucking!" She disclosed loudly.

Rev looked at Amelia's picture for a thoughtful moment, and then he took a pull from his cigarette. "It couldn't be," he said, as he shook his head slowly. "That bitch is a prosecutor."

"I see that she's a damn prosecutor," Shanequa pressed. "But I'm telling you; she's the one that Ice is with now. I saw them together at that poetry club on University drive. We even got into a fight."

Rev looked steadily at Shanequa, before turning away. "You probably saw him with some other ho, that looks just like her," he said, while picking up his pants and boxers.

"You think that I'm dumb?" Shanequa snapped, with her head snaking. "This is the same bitch that I saw Ice with."

"And I'm telling you that's not her," Rev said, while stepping into his pants.

Shanequa sucked her teeth and then she started to gather up her belongings. "You can believe whatever you want," she lashed out loudly. "I know who I saw, and this is the same bitch that I saw Ice with."

$$$$$$$$$$$$$$$$$$$$$$$$

About twenty minutes after leaving Albert Barrett's office, one of the uniformed cops returned with a brown manila envelope in his hand. Amelia got up from her seat, and watched him as he walked over to detective Morris, who was leaning against a file cabinet across the room. He whispered something in Morris' ear, and then he gave him the envelope. As if she could sense that something was wrong, Amelia's spine stiffened and her mouth got dusty dry. Her heart did a little flip, when Morris opened up the envelope and peeked inside. But when he started over to her, her breathing got heavy and labored.

"Miss Clarke," the detective started to say, before he even got up to Amelia. "Have you ever seen this envelope before?" Amelia exchanged glances with her boss, before saying, "No. I doubt it."

"Are you sure?"

"Of course I'm sure. I'm not dumb," Amelia fired back, in a feisty manner.

"Well, it was found underneath the passenger seat of your car," Morris sneered. "And guess what's inside?"

"How the fuck am I supposed to know?" Amelia growled anxiously. "I just told you that I've never seen the damn envelope before."

"Well, have you ever seen this?" Morris asked, as he dumped all that was inside of the envelope onto Barrett's desk.

Amelia gasped and stiffened in shock, when she saw the banded stacks of fifty and one hundred dollar bills. She glared at detective Morris with her body engulfed in heat. "Is this a fucking joke?" She snapped.

"You tell me," Morris responded. "To my estimation, I'd say that there is about a hundred thousand dollars, right here. Now my question to you is . . ." He looked straight at Amelia. "Is this the one hundred thousand dollars that the anonymous caller said that he gave to you?"

"Amelia what's going on?" Barrett got up and asked.

Amelia looked over at her boss. "Mr. Barrett, you know me well enough to know that I'd never do such a thing. This has got to be a set up. It has to be Mike Simms."

Morris stepped over and held onto Amelia's arm. "In spite of all that you're saying, I'm still gonna have to place you under arrest."

She ripped her arm away. "You can't arrest me! I didn't do anything!"

"Please, don't make this hard fo' me, Miss Clarke. I can cuff you and drag you out, if you want me to."

"Are you serious?!"

"Amelia, wait," Barrett said, walking over. He turned to Morris. "Detective, I do know that you've got a job to do. But please try to understand that this could very well be a set up."

"If it is, then we'll get to the bottom of it. But until we do, Miss Clarke has to be placed under arrest."

"I didn't do anything!" Amelia cried.

"For your sake, I hope you didn't," Morris said, as he reached inside of his shirt pocket. He pulled out a plastic card, and then he went on to read Amelia her rights.

"This can't be happening," Amelia muttered quietly. She was a wink away from tears, but she was trying her best not to cry.

Barrett charged over to his desk and snatched up the telephone receiver. "Hold up," he said to Morris. "Let me call captain Martinez. I'm sure that we can work this out without her being arrested."

"Go ahead and do what you have to do, Mr. Barrett. I'm doing what I'm supposed to do," Morris said, as he raised the card and went back to reading Amelia her rights.

Amelia was now in tears. She couldn't stop herself from crying. She knew the law well enough to know that resisting and protesting would do her no good. So she dropped her head and tried to tune out the nightmare that was going on around her.

The uniformed cop, who had walked up behind her, tugged her arms around to her back. She grimaced when she felt the cold metal going around her wrists. She knew this whole situation was Blood's doing. Only what good would it do to say it, when Morris and his colleagues weren't trying to believe her.

"Take her down to the car," Morris told the uniformed cop, when he saw that Amelia was fully cuffed.

Amelia looked up at him. "Please don't do this to me," she cried. "I'm telling you, it's a set-up." She turned to her boss for help, but he was talking animatedly on the phone.

"Take her down to the car," Morris repeated.

"Mr. Barrett," Amelia cried out for help, as she was being tugged towards the door.

"Hey wait!" Barrett raised a quick hand and said. He offered the phone to Morris. "Captain Martinez wants to talk to you."

Morris sucked his teeth quietly, as he walked over and took the phone.

Barrett walked over to Amelia. "It's gonna be okay," he assured her.

Amelia dropped her head shamefully. "I didn't do it," she cried.

"I know you didn't," Barrett held her arm and said.

Morris' conversation over the phone was brief. When he cradled the receiver, he said to the uniformed cop, "Take off the cuffs."

Amelia breathed a heavy sigh of relief. She then raised her teary eyes to detective Morris, "Thank you," she whimpered.

"Don't thank me, just yet," Morris said, as he put the money back inside of the envelope. "The captain didn't say to drop the charge. He just said to let you go and to continue on with the investigation."

"We don't have a problem with that," Barrett said.

"You shouldn't," Morris snickered. He then turned to Amelia. She was out of the cuffs and rubbing her wrists. "The captain also said that you'll be placed on leave until—"

"What!" Amelia blurted suddenly. She snapped her head around to face her boss. "Mr. Barrett, what is he saying?"

Barrett sighed, "I had to agree to put you on leave, until the issue is settled."

"But I have to be at court in the morning. Tomorrow is Mike Simms' hearing."

"I didn't have a choice." Barrett pinched the bridge of his nose and said. "It was either leave, or jail."

"But what about Mike Simms' hearing?"

"I'll get someone to cover for you."

"You can't do that." Amelia hurried over to her boss and she grabbed his arm. "You know what's going on. You know that if I step away from that case, that Mike Simms will walk free."

"Is there a problem with what the captain suggested?" Morris interjected. He looked steadily at Barrett. "If there's a problem, then I could always call him back."

"No need to do that," Barrett said. "As of right now, Miss Clarke is on leave, until I say that she's not."

"Mr. Barrett."

"Go home, Amelia," Barrett looked at Amelia and said. His expression was flat and unreadable. "I'll call you back to work, once all of this is cleared up."

"Mr. Barrett, I can't—"

"Miss Clarke!" Barrett snapped firmly. "I just gave you an order. Are you refusing?"

Amelia was flushed with anger. She wiped her teary eyes, and then shot her boss a fiery stare. "This is bullshit!" She spat, and then she turned and stormed out of the office.

"You'll thank me later!" Barrett shouted at her.

Amelia didn't answer. She charged towards the elevator, with her teeth gritted and her lips quivering. Her heart was pounding just like a drum inside of her chest. She felt as if Blood was finally getting what he wanted. And even though the feeling was painful; at the moment there was nothing that she could do about it.

As she approached the elevator, she shook her head in disgust. She was about to press on the down button by the elevator door, when her cell phone suddenly rang. After pulling it from her jacket pocket, she brought it up to her ear and answered, "What?"

"Damn. Now is that any way to answer your phone?"

Not recognizing the rough male voice, Amelia pulled the phone away from her ear and looked at the screen. The number was restricted.

"Who is this?" She asked.

"Amelia, he-he-help."

Amelia cringed and shuddered, when she heard Kyla's whimpering voice. Kyla sounded as if she was in pain. She sounded as if she was writhing and sobbing uncontrollably.

"Kyla?" Amelia's voice came out soft and caring.

"Kyla is a bit tied up, right now."

"Who is this? What do you want?" Amelia asked, as worry lines raced across her forehead.

"You already know what I want, bitch. Let Blood go. If you don't, then you'll be getting pieces of your assistant through the mail. And don't even think about calling the fucking police…"

CH-26

"I raced over, just as soon as I got the call," Bill Ferentz said, as he stepped inside of the visiting room and saw Blood sitting behind the small metal table.

Blood, in his now customary orange jumpsuit, took a pull from his cigarette and then blew a cloud of smoke up at the ceiling. "So, what's gonna happen now?" He asked.

"We appear in court tomorrow," Ferentz said, as he took the seat across from Blood. He placed his briefcase on the table and then he loosened his tie. "The hearing is set for nine o'clock. Let's try to get there early, so that you can be out of this place by noon."

"That's what's up," Blood grinned.

Ferentz shifted around in his seat before saying, "I'm gonna need you to be on your best behavior tomorrow. You know that Judge Silverman's got it out for you. So let's not give him any reason to throw us out of his courtroom, or reschedule the hearing."

"Fuck that cracker."

Ferentz looked at Blood warily. "We can't afford a postponement, Mr. Simms. That could keep you here for another month or so."

Blood shot Ferentz a hard stare. "You don't have to tell me shit, mothafucka. I know what to do, so stop talking to me like I'm fucking stupid."

Ferentz fell back in his seat, with an inane look on his face. He sighed heavily and then he waited awhile before saying, "I spoke to Frank Hibbert, on my way over here."

"Who the fuck is Frank Hibbert?"

"He's the prosecutor who took over for Miss Clarke."

"So what happened to Montgomery?"

"I didn't ask, but if you're worried about Hibbert, then don't." Ferentz leaned forward, with a devilish grin etched across his face. "He told me that he has worked with you before. He said that he's willing to squash everything, if he's paid right."

"What's right?" Blood asked.

The lawyer let his eyes wonder for a while, before saying, "He's asking for two hundred thousand dollars in cash."

A quiet grunt left Blood's throat.

"I could talk to him and get him to go lower," Ferentz said quickly.

Blood closed his eyes and sucked on his cigarette. He stayed with his eyes closed for a while, musing over his freedom and how badly he wanted it.

After about a full minute of saying nothing, he opened his eyes and looked steadily at Ferentz. "Give him what he asked for," he said calmly. "But let him know that if I'm not out here by midday tomorrow, I will have someone kill his ass."

Ferentz swallowed the lump in his throat. "As you say," he said, with a forced smile. He checked the time on his wrist before asking. "So how did you do it?"

"Do what?" Blood asked, with his eyes hard and narrowed.

"How did you get Miss Clarke off the case?"

Blood leaned across the table and got up in the lawyer's face. "Do me a favor, cracker," he sneered aggressively. "Stay out of shit that doesn't concern you."

$$$$$$$$$$$$$$$$$$$$$$$

Amelia was sitting on the front steps of her house, when Ice's Range Rover pulled up behind her Lexus. Before he was even fully out of the vehicle, she was hurrying over to meet him.

"Oh Trav'," she cried, as she clung to him. "They've got Kyla. They kidnapped Kyla."

Not understanding what she had said, Ice held her at arm's-length and asked, "What?"

Amelia's eyes were bloodshot red and her face was matted with tears. Sobbing, she said, "Kyla's been kidnapped."

"Fuck," Ice cursed quietly, as anger eased through his veins. He knew for certain that it was Rebel and Rev who had kidnapped Kyla. He also knew that they would never let her go, unless Blood was released from jail. Wanting to comfort Amelia, he pulled her close and hugged her. "Did you call the police?" He asked.

"No. They said that they'd kill her, if I do." Amelia wiped away a snaking tear. "They want me to let Mike Simms go. They want me to drop the charge against him and I can't."

After a thoughtful moment, Ice pulled away from her and said, "Amelia you have to." He knew that Rev would surely kill Kyla, if Blood wasn't released. And even though he didn't want Blood to get away with what he had done to Bam, he just didn't feel as if keeping him in jail was worth Kyla's life. "Amelia, listen to me," he said, while holding her by her shoulders and looking her dead in the face. "You're gonna have to let Blood go."

Tears started to race down Amelia's cheeks. "I can't let him go," She cried.

"Why?" Ice shook her.

Amelia dropped her head. "Because . . . I'm no longer the prosecutor handling his case; I was laid off from work today." Ice's face crinkled with confusion. "What are you saying?" He asked.

Amelia looked at him, and then she leaned back against the Range Rover, looking pitiful. She inhaled deeply as she wiped her eyes. "Someone lied on me, Trav'. Someone set me up. They put a hundred thousand dollars inside of my truck. Then they told the police that I was taking bribes."

"Bribes? Bribes fo' what?"

"They say that the money was payment to let Mike Simms go," she mumbled, while shaking her head. "If it wasn't for my boss, then I would've been arrested and taken to jail. He had to make a deal with the police, to lay me off until the investigation is over." Amelia closed her eyes and she winced, as if she was in excruciating pain. "I know that it was Mike Simms who set me up. I know that he's the one who had someone put that money inside of my truck, and then made the call to the police."

"That's gonna be very hard to prove," Ice replied.

"I know," she dropped her head and said tearfully. She then bit into her quivering lip and looked up at Ice. "I don't care about being laid off. I just wanna save Kyla."

"We will," Ice assured her. He then placed a caring hand against her cheek and used his thumb to wipe away her tears. "After we find Kyla, we'll try to find out who broke into your truck—"

"I saw who did it."

Amelia and Ice turned their heads and they saw Miss Victoria—the old lady from across the street, walking towards them.

"I stood at my window and I watched the whole thing," the old lady said with a little grin, as she stepped closer. "I wasn't spying on your house or anything. But when I saw that truck turn inside of your driveway, I just knew that something was up."

"What kind of truck?" Ice asked.

"I don't know the name, but it was one of those big expensive trucks that drug dealers love to drive."

"What color was it?"

"It was black. And as soon as it pulled up, I went and got my new digital camera."

Amelia's eyes got wide. "You've got pictures?"

Miss Victoria nodded. "I thought the mothafucka was trying to steal your car," she said. "But he only went inside and spent a few seconds before getting back out."

"Where are the pictures?" Ice asked.

Miss Victoria patted the pocket of her housecoat. "I would've told you about it," she said, while looking at Amelia. "But I haven't seen you since the police killed that guy inside of your house."

"I've been staying with my mom," Amelia said, with her eyes on the old woman's housecoat pocket. "May I see the pictures?" She asked anxiously.

"Sure," Miss Victoria smiled, as she pulled a small digital camera from her pocket and then she offered it to Amelia. "They're a bit dark. But your eyes are better than mine, so you should be able to make out the little buggah's face."

Amelia took the camera, turned it on, and then went to the photos that were saved on it. The first one that came up was very dark, but she was still able to make out the black Escalade that was parked in her driveway.

"I don't know whose truck this is," she muttered, looking thoughtfully—and then she quickly narrowed her eyes in on the photo that followed. She pulled the camera up to her face and gasped when recognition hit. "Oh my God!" She blurted, with her eyes wide. "Trav', this is Rick."

$$\$$$

"I'm coming!" Danielle shouted, as she ran out of her bathroom, giggling like a love-struck little girl.

The look on her face was blissful and her eyes were teary, because of how hard she had been laughing.

When she got up to the front door, she wiped her hands on her skimpy cotton shorts. Then without even checking to see who it was that had knocked, she unlocked the door and pulled it open. She immediately tried to close it shut, when she saw Batch in the doorway.

"Don't do that," Batch smirked as he stuck a foot in the doorway, to stop the door from closing in his face. He shoved it open and then he stepped inside. "It seems as if you're not happy to see me."

The blissful look that was on Danielle's face, only moments ago, was now replaced with one of pure dread. Her eyes were now big and filled with fear, and her lips were quivering around her gaped mouth.

"Did I pop up at a bad time?" Batch asked playfully, as he closed the door behind him.

"What are you doing here?" Danielle asked fearfully, as she backed away. "I told you that I'm through trying to help you."

"And I told you that you're never through, until I say so."

Worry lines raced across Danielle's forehead. "I told Amelia about you," she said, after swallowing the lump that had developed in her throat. "She knows about you and all that you're doing."

"Your friend is the last person that I'm worried about. Believe me; she's got her hands full right now." Batch gave Danielle a lustful once over, and then he walked over to the living room couch. "So what's going on?" He smirked, as he took a seat and crossed his legs. "Why are you still hiding from me?"

Danielle shot him a black look. "Please leave." She pointed towards the door. "If you don't, then I'm gonna call the police."

Batch sucked his teeth. "Yeah, whatever," he snorted and then he patted the couch next to him. "Come here. Come sit next to me."

Danielle shook her head. "I want you to leave," she said firmly.

Batch grinned, a devilishly cocky grin. "Stop playing around, yow. You know why I'm here."

Danielle clenched her fists and glared at him. "I'm giving you ten seconds to leave my house," she demanded.

Impatience pulled Batch's brows together. "Bitch, I said to come the fuck here!" He snapped, while pounding a fist into the couch.

"No!" Danielle shot back. "I said for you to get outta my house, now!"

Batch got up, but as he started towards Danielle, a six-six, two hundred and forty pound, Dwayne 'The Rock' Johnson look-a-like, stepped out of the bathroom with a towel in his hand and no shirt on.

"What's going on?" He asked looking steadily at Batch, as he wiped his hands inside of the towel.

Batch tossed a dirty look over at the much younger man, who seemed to be about twice his size. "Who the fuck are you?" He asked rudely.

"He's my man," Danielle announced, as she hurried over to Dane and clung onto him. She placed a hand against his chest and looked up in his face. "Baby, this is Batch. He's the one that I've been telling you about."

Dane wrapped an arm around Danielle and then he locked eyes with Batch. "So you're the dirty ass cop that I've been hearing about," he spat venomously. "Look here, pop, if you know what's best fo' you, then you'd stop sniffing around my woman. She may be scared to report your ass, but I'm not."

Batch stood across from Dane and stared at him with unmoving eyes. "Don't bite off more than you can chew, young cat. What's going on between me and Danielle has nothing to do with you."

"It has everything to do with me," Dane fired back, shooting Batch a cold stare. "Danielle is my woman, so she's my responsibility. And I'm not gonna keep telling you to stay the fuck away from her."

"Sounds as if you're threatening me?"

"That's exactly what I'm doing," Dane said, shoving Danielle aside.

Batch matched Dane's fiery stare. "Ain't this some shit?" He said with a little grin. "I came here to take care of my business and looked what I stumbled into."

"What business do you have to take care of?" Danielle barked. "I told you to leave me the fuck alone!"

"So it's like that?" Batch scowled at Danielle.

"That's exactly how it is," Dane interjected. "As a matter of fact," he stepped towards Batch. "Get the fuck outta here, before I have to throw you out and then call the police to come pick you up."

Batch gave Dane a menacing once over. He knew that he was no match for Dane in a physical fight. However with the Glock on his hip, he knew that he could take him down without breaking a sweat.

"You really don't know what you're stirring, huh?" He said, looking Dane dead in the eyes and suppressing the urge to pull his Glock. "I'm gonna leave. But just remember that this shit ain't over."

"I'm cool with that," Dane replied, as he pulled Danielle into the safety of his arms.

Batch sucked his teeth and then he turned away. "I'll see you around," he said, as he headed for the door. "You too Danielle, I'll be keeping an eye out fo' your ass."

CH-27

Consciousness returned with a throbbing headache for Kyla. The blow that she had received to the head from Rev had knocked her out instantly. She winced and grimaced, then slowly opened her eyes. Her mouth was as dry as she had ever felt it, and her tongue felt as heavy as lead.

As the fog cleared from her brain and her eyes adjusted to the bright lights inside of the room, she tried to move her arms but she couldn't. It was the same with her legs – they too were tied to the bed that she was laid eagle across.

"It's about time that you woke your little sexy ass up."

Kyla moved her eyes around in the direction of the voice. She heaved and shuddered, when she saw Rebel and Rev, standing across the room, staring down at her.

"Well, hello there," Rebel smirked devilishly. He stepped across the room and then he took a seat on the bed next to Kyla, who was staring up at him through fear-filled eyes. "There's no need for you to be looking so scared, yo. We're not gonna hurt you," he said.

"Hmmm -mmm," Kyla tried to talk, but could not. The duct tape across her mouth was stopping her.

Rebel placed a hand on her leg and then he slowly inched his way up underneath her dress. "You'll be outta here, in a few hours. We're waiting on your boss lady." He smiled, as he went inside of her panties.

"Mmmm-mmm," Kyla whined as she jerked and twisted, while whipping her body in an attempt to get Rebel's hand from inside of her panties.

"Ain't you a feisty little thing," he said, as he pulled his hand away. He then gripped her cheeks and screwed up his face viciously. "Your boss lady has less than twenty four hours, to let Blood outta jail," he rasped. "If she doesn't; then only God knows what we're gonna do to you."

"Mmmm-mmm!"

"What? I can't hear you." His grip on her cheeks intensified, as he brought his ear down to her face.

"Mmmmmmm!"

"You want me to take the tape off?"

"Mmmmm!" Kyla nodded vigorously.

Rebel glanced over at Rev, before looking into Kyla's fear-filled eyes. "I'm gonna take the tape off," he told her. "But if you scream, then I swear to God that I'll have Rev punch you in the face again."

Fear pulled Kyla's brows together.

Rebel ripped the tape away, and then smirked when she winced in pain.

She looked up into his face, with her eyes pleading. "Please," she whimpered quietly as tears tumbled down her cheeks. "Please, let me go. I promise that I'll get Amelia to let your friend go."

"We can't do that beautiful. We need you."

"Please."

Rebel got up from off the bed. "We're gonna let you go," he smirked. "But it will be after Blood gets released from jail."

"Let who go? The bitch saw my face, so I'm not gonna let her leave here alive," Rev thought, as he walked across the room. He looked out through the window. "I wonder what's taking that mothafucka G-man so long," he muttered quietly.

"G-man?" Rebel turned his head and asked. "You got G-man coming over here?"

Rev turned away from the window. "I told him to swing through with an ounce. I need something to smoke."

"Niggah, you trippin'!" Rebel blurted, as he walked up to Rev. "We can't let G-man see her." He pointed at Kyla. "That mothafucka don't know how to keep his fucking mouth shut."

"I feel you on that," Rev replied dryly. "But I'm feening for some weed, brah."

"Then go out and get it yourself. We can't have G-man running up in this shit, like what we're doing is legal."

"G-man ain't gonna say shit to nobody."

"We don't know that," Rebel frowned. He walked over to the window and then he looked outside. "Call that niggah and tell him to meet me at Kareem's in twenty minutes. I'll get the weed from him and then I'll pick up something to eat, on my way back."

"If that's what you wanna do," Rev said, as he pulled his cell phone from his pocket.\

Rebel walked over to the bed and then he looked down at Kyla. "You want me to get you something to eat?"

Kyla shook her head. "Will you just let me go, please," she cried. "I won't tell anybody about this. I promise. I swear to God I won't."

"You can swear all the fuck you want, bitch. We ain't letting you go, until Blood is outta jail," Rev snorted from across the room.

Kyla turned her eyes on him. "Please," she begged.

Rev sucked his teeth. "You're just wasting your fuckin' breath," he snarled. "If Blood ain't outta jail after his court hearing tomorrow, then your boss lady will be getting bits and pieces of you in the mail."

$$$$$$$$$$$$$$$$$$$$$

"Who dat?" Yogi yelled, as he got up from the couch in front of the TV.

"Who do you think brah? Open the door.

Yogi pulled the door open and gave Ice a skeptical look. "How the fuck did you get here so fast? I thought that you said you were with Amelia, over in Pembroke Pines."

"I was," Ice answered, as he stepped inside of the living room.

Yogi watched him through slits, as he walked across the room and then started to pace. "What's up with you, brah? You straight?"

"I need your help, man," Ice said, still pacing. "Rebel and Rev kidnapped Amelia's assistant, and now they're threatening to kill her if Blood ain't released from jail."

"Who they kidnap, Kyla?"

Ice nodded.

"Shit," Yogi cursed quietly. He closed the door and then he started over to Ice. "You think they're serious, about killing her?"

"I know Rebel ain't got it in him. But knowing that niggah Rev, I'm almost certain that he'll kill her, if Blood ain't released."

"So why doesn't Amelia just let Blood go? Kyla's life ain't worth keeping him in jail."

"Her boss took her off the case," Ice replied, as he took a seat on the couch. "Her ex set her up to get arrested, because he wanted to get her off of the case."

"Her ex?"

Ice nodded. "The niggah's also a prosecutor, but he's one of those working fo' Blood."

"This whole shit is crazy as fuck," Yogi exclaimed. He ran a hand down over his face. Then he picked up the TV's remote from off of the couch and turned the TV off. "So if Amelia's off the case, there's no guarantee that Blood is going to prison?"

"He probably won't. But right about now, Amelia's more worried about Kyla."

"So, where's Amelia at now?"

"She's on her way to see her boss, to tell him about Kyla and her ex." Ice dropped his head and then he dry washed his face. "But I've got to do something to help Kyla, brah. I know that niggah Rev. He'll kill Kyla whether Blood gets outta jail or not."

"So what you wanna do?" Yogi looked at Ice and asked. "You know me, brah. I'm down fo' whatever."

"Ice rose from the couch and then he went back to pacing. "I don't know where they've got her," He said. "Rebel may be dumb, but he ain't that dumb to have her at his apartment." "But they've got to have her somewhere," Yogi uttered quickly. "You and I both know that Rebel and Rev ain't the type to stay cooped up indoors fo' too long. Let's hit the streets and find these niggahs. I guarantee; if we find any one of them, then we'll find Kyla."

$$$$$$$$$$$$$$$$$$$$$$$

When Amelia pulled up in front of Rick's house, her boss was already there. He was leaning up against his Lincoln Navigator, with his cell phone pressed tightly against his ear. It was close to six o'clock and the sun was on its way down. Yet there still was a searing heat, traveling along with the light blowing evening breeze.

Still dressed in her beige pantsuit and black peep-toe pumps, Amelia stepped down from her truck and then she walked up to her boss. "How long have you been here?" She asked him. "Just got here," he answered. He then pulled his cell phone down from his ear. "I spoke to detective Morris. He didn't sound pleased, but he's on his way."

"So you're gonna wait for him to get here?"

"Hell no," Barrett said, shoving the cell phone down into his pocket. "I wanna talk to that bastard, before I have his ass arrested."

"So let's go," Amelia said, as she ran up to Rick's front door and rang the bell.

After about a minute, Rick appeared looking battered, depressed, and haggard. "Amelia," he said, completely surprised. He then looked over at his boss and saw the resentful look on his face. He swallowed hard. "Mr. Barrett? What are you doing here?"

Amelia shoved him out of the way and stepped inside the house. "You son-of-a-bitch!" She exploded loudly. "How could you? How could you do this to me?!"

"Amelia wait," Mr. Barrett said, as he stepped inside and closed the door behind him. "Let's hear what he has to say, before the police get here."

"The po-police?" Rick stuttered, very nervously.

"Yes Rick, the police," Barrett said. He loosened his tie before saying, "Rick, we know that you're the one who put that envelope with the money inside of Amelia's truck."

"Wh-what envelope?"

"You know what envelope, you bastard!" Amelia raged, as she leaped at him. "I've got pictures of you—"

"Amelia!" Barrett shouted and grabbed her around the waist. He pulled her across the room, away from Rick. "If you can't control your temper, then we're gonna have to wait until the police get here. You hear me?!"

"But—"

"You hear me?" Barrett cut her off loudly.

Breathing heavily, Amelia shoved her hair from in front of her face. "I'm okay. I'm okay," she gasped, while looking angrily at Rick, who had his head down.

Barrett turned his eyes on Rick. "You wanna tell us what's going on?" He asked, holding onto Amelia's arm.

Rick raised his head.

"There's no need to lie about anything," Barrett said. "We already know that you're working for Mike Simms. And we know that you're the one who set up Amelia, by putting that money inside of her truck."

Rick shook his head, as tears tumbled from his eyes. "I'm sorry," he muttered quietly. "I didn't want to do it. But if I didn't, then they would've killed me."

"I almost went to jail!" Amelia screamed.

"I'm sorry," Rick said, wiping his face. He took a deep breath. "Can we talk about this inside of my office?"

"Are you gonna tell us the truth about everything?" Barrett asked.

Rick nodded and then he turned away. He started across the living room, leading Amelia and Barrett through the arched doorway by the wet bar. They walked down a small corridor and stopped at a small arched oak door. Rick took a deep breath before he pushed the door open, and then stepped aside, so that Amelia and Barrett could walk in.

The room was small, but neatly kept. There was a small desk with a computer shoved up against the wall, and a filing cabinet to its right. There was also a small gray sofa, a 19" plasma which was mounted onto the wall, and a bookshelf, with about three dozen hard cover books.

"You guys can have a seat," Rick said, as he slowly lowered himself down into the swivel chair behind his desk.

"I don't wanna sit," Amelia said hotly.

Barrett held onto her arm, to calm her down. "What's going on with you, Rick?" He looked at Rick and asked. "What impelled you to go out and work for Mike Simms? And didn't you know that setting up Amelia, the way you did, would've sent her to jail?"

Rick looked at Barrett through teary eyes. "I wasn't trying to send her to jail. All I wanted was for her to let Mike Simms go."

"How long have you been working for him?" Barrett asked.

"For about a year," Rick said, and then he broke out into loud sobs. "I tried to stop, but they wouldn't let me!" He cried.

"Who wouldn't let you?"

Rick shook his head. "I can't tell you. If I do, then they'll kill my parents."

"We can't help you, if you don't tell us everything, Rick. You're a prosecutor. You know how the process works."

"I don't need your help," Rick cried.

Amelia stepped forward, with her face bent in disgust. "Who were the guys who broke into my house, Rick? What are their names?" She asked, thinking that whosoever it was that broke into her and her mother's house, were the same ones that had Kyla.

"I don't know," Rick dropped his head on top of his desk and sobbed.

"You're a fucking liar!"

"I swear. If I knew, then I would tell you."

"Stop fuckin' lying!" Amelia yelled furiously.

Barrett held her back. "Tell us who else at the office is working for Mike Simms," he queried.

"I don't know," Rick answered sheepishly.

"What the fuck do you know?!" Amelia screamed at him. Her voice was spiked with rage.

"Tell us something, Rick," Barrett pressed persistently. "Tell us something to help you out, before the police get here."

"I don't need your help. You can't protect me. You can't help me."

"So you'd rather to go to prison?"

"I'm not going to prison," Rick muffled out, as he raised his head with the nozzle of a chrome 10mm pistol, stuffed inside of his mouth.

"Rick, what are you doing?!" Amelia screamed, as a single shot rang out—and a bullet from the chrome handgun tore its way through Rick's brain—then exited through the back of his head, along with blood, bits of skull and brain tissue.

Rick fell back from the chair and hit the floor hard. He twitched a couple of times. Then after a sudden heave, the gun fell from his hand and he went completely still and lifeless; with his eyes wide open and blood oozing from his mouth.

CH-28

As Yogi steered the Range Rover north on 441, Ice sat in the passenger seat with his cell phone at his ear. He had a pensive look on his face, and had a 9mm rested across his lap, while his eyes were fixed steadily on the road ahead.

They were cruising the streets, looking for Rebel or Rev. So far; they hadn't seen or heard anything on either of them, and impatience had Ice just about ready to drop the search and go home.

"Still nothing?" Yogi asked, after seeing Ice pull the phone away from his ear.

Ice shook his head. "It's like they're hiding. Ain't nobody seen either of them."

"You tried the Mirage?"

"They ain't there," Ice answered, getting more and more frustrated. "That's the first place that I called."

Yogi glanced over at his cousin. "Don't lose patience, brah. If we search long enough, we'll find them," he said, as he pulled up next to a yellow Porsche Carrera, which was sitting at the red light on Commercial Blvd. "We have to find them and find Kyla," he continued quietly. "Because shit could get real crazy, if that niggah Blood gets outta jail. You know that, right?"

"I know, but I ain't worried about it," Ice said, while leaning back in his seat. "I'd rather to see Kyla alive and Blood outta jail, than to have her dead and him doing a bid."

"That's real," Yogi muttered.

Ice sighed heavily, as he raised his cell phone to call Amelia. Then as he was scrolling through his contacts, he was interrupted by the loud honking of the Porsche's horn.

"Yo. Yow Ice! Wha'sup, main man?" The driver of the Porsche yelled.

Ice turned his attention to the Porsche. That's when he saw G-man sitting behind the steering wheel, while smiling up at him. "What's up, G? What's good?" He asked, as he looked out through the passenger side window of the Range.

"I can't call it," G-man replied, with a toothy smile. "It seems like you've been laying low? I haven't seen you in a minute."

"I've been kicking back," Ice replied. "Ain't shit going on in the streets."

"You right about that. But you know me, I stay on the grind."

"Somebody has to."

G-man looked up at the stoplight and saw that it had changed from red to green.

"Anyway main man," he said looking back over at Ice. "I'll hook up with you, some other time. Got that fool Rebel waiting for me at Kareem's. Rev needed something good to smoke and you know I'm the man who's got it," he chuckled.

As the Porsche sped off, Ice looked over at Yogi and smiled.

"I heard him," Yogi smiled back, and then gunned the Range Rover, straight through the green light.

$$\$$

"What the fuck happened here?" Batch asked, as he and Morris barged inside of Rick's office, after pulling up outside and hearing the single gunshot.

With teary eyes, Amelia turned to face him. "He shot himself in the head," she whimpered.

"He's gone," Morris looked up at Batch and said. He had two fingers pressed against Rick's neck. "You want me to call it in?" He asked.

"Yeah, get on it," Batch replied, as he shoved Amelia out of the way and stormed across the room. When he got a close look at Rick, he huffed out a breath. Rick was still laid out on the floor, behind his desk with his eyes wide open.

The gun was on the floor next to him, and his head was in a pool of blood that was still spreading.

"Will somebody tell me what the fuck happened?!" Batch snapped.

"The idiot swallowed his gun," Barrett informed him.

Batch turned and looked at him, and then he looked over at Amelia. "For some strange reason I don't believe that," he quipped, with his nose flaring and his chest heaving. He then reached out and grabbed Amelia by the arm. "You're going to jail, Miss Thang. I know that you're the one who did this." Barrett grabbed Batch by the front of his shirt. "Get your fucking hands off of her. I was here when the idiot shot himself. Amelia didn't touch him."

"How do I know that you're not lying, just to protect her?" Amelia ripped her arm away from Batch's hold. "As much as I hated Rick, I never wanted him dead!" She shouted. "He chose to put a gun in his damn mouth. I had nothing to do with that."

Batch glared at her angrily. "Don't you think for one minute, that I'm gonna let this rest," he flared up. "I'm gonna get to the bottom of this, young lady. And if I find out that you have anything to do with it, your ass is going to jail."

"Just like how you'll be going to jail, for working for Mike Simms!" Amelia fired up in his face. "Danielle told me everything, detective Batchelor. I know about you and all that you've been doing."

"I don't give a damn, about what you know. You think your little whore for a friend is enough to send me to prison?"

"You'll see!" Amelia yelled.

Barrett grabbed onto her arm and then he pulled her away. "Calm down Amelia," he told her. "There's too much going on right now, for you two to be going at each other like this."

"He's one of the reasons why Rick killed himself!"

"Rick killed himself because of you!" Batch snapped and pointed. "He was trying to fucking help you!"

"Detective, that's not true," Barrett said, holding onto Batch's arm.

Batch yanked his arm away. "Get off me!" He shouted, unable to calm down. "If she had let Blood go, then Rick would still be alive."

Amelia glared at Batch furiously. She was about to get in his face, but Morris walked into the room and announced, "There's an ambulance outside, and a few of ours just pulled up."

Barrett stepped over to Morris. "Detective, may I have a word with you?"

Morris looked at Batch, and then back at Barrett. "If it's related to that," he pointed at Rick's corpse. "You can say it in front of my partner. I've already told him about what happened this morning."

Just then, six uniformed cops barged into the room and got things louder than what it was. One of the cops, after seeing Rick, immediately clamped a hand over his mouth and ran off in search of a bathroom.

"What the fuck happened? Did he shoot himself in the head?" Another cop asked, while the others looked on with their eyes and mouth wide.

Barrett ignored them and turned back to Morris. "Just for the record, Amelia has nothing to do with what happened here," he said. "As I told you over the phone, we found out that Rick was the one who put that envelope inside of Amelia's truck, and we were talking to him when—"

"What are you getting at, Mr. Barrett?"

Barrett glared angrily at Morris, for cutting him off. "I'm putting Amelia back on Mike Simms' case," he announced seriously.

"You can't do that!" Batch blurted.

"I already did, Detective," Barrett said, glaring at Batch. "I don't know how many prosecutors and police officers that Mike Simms has working for him; but on everything that I love, I'm gonna find out." Barrett turned to Amelia. "Come on, let's get outta here. We've got a few indictments to put together," he said and then he started off.

REPERCUSSIONS by SHAWN STARR

Batch ran after him and grabbed him by the arm. "You can't leave!" He raged. "This is a crime scene, and you just witnessed the crime."

Barrett looked Batch dead in the eyes. "Get your hands off of me," he said fiercely.

Batch hesitated.

Barrett's lips got tight, as he glared at him.

Morris walked up behind Batch and put a hand on his shoulder. "Let him go, partna," he said calmly. "He's the State Attorney, so you already know what will happen if you press too hard."

Batch huffed out a loud breath, before letting go.

Barrett grabbed Amelia by the arm and they both charged out of the office. As soon as they stepped outside, Barrett pulled out his car keys and said, "I want Mike Simms convicted, you hear me? I want him in prison for all of this. And I want you to get the name of every single state worker, who worked for him."

Amelia stopped and then she stepped out the way of two police officers, who were making their way into the house. "How am I gonna do that?" She asked bleakly.

Barrett looked at her steadily. "If anyone can find out all that's going on, it's you Amelia. You're the best at the office. So get this mothafucka, Mike Simms, convicted and find out what's going on."

Amelia dropped her head and then she wiped her teary eyes. "I was thinking to let him go," she whimpered sadly.

"What?" Barrett asked, looking confused.

Amelia covered her face with her hands. "They've got Kyla," she began to sob. "They kidnapped Kyla and now they're threatening to kill her, if I don't let him go."

"Holy shit," Barrett cursed quietly.

$$$$$$$$$$$$$$$$$$$$$

Ice and Yogi sat in the parked Range Rover, at the south east corner of Kareem's parking lot; about fifty yards away from the entrance of the club. They hadn't seen Rebel since they pulled up, ten minutes ago. However, his blue Aston Martin Volante was parked next to G-man's Porsche, so they sat and waited patiently, with their eyes fixed on the exit of the club.

"There he is," Yogi nudged Ice in the side and pointed at Rebel. He had finally walked out of Kareem's, with a toothy smile on his face and a bag filled with food in his hand.

"I see him." Ice replied, sitting up in his seat. "Let's follow him and see where he leads us," he suggested.

Yogi waited until Rebel was inside of the Aston Martin, and on his way out of the parking lot, before he turned his lights on and drove off.

It was minutes after 7pm, and the shadows of a bleak night had already taken over the county. But Kareem's parking lot and the surrounding streets were well lit, so Yogi didn't have a problem following the Aston Martin from a safe distance.

After about fifteen minutes of driving, the Aston Martin turned off of Atlantic Blvd and onto Coral Ridge drive. It made the immediate left through the open gates of a small apartment complex. Then it cruised towards the back, where there was a large play ground. The complex was dark and graveyard quiet, but there were lights in the windows of most of the apartments.

"Damn," Ice muttered, when the Aston Martin cruised to a stop and parked. "The mothafuckas got Kyla inside of Tip's apartment. How the fuck, I didn't think of that?"

"Doesn't matter now, 'cause we found out," Yogi said, pulling the Range into a parking spot, between an Escalade and a Benz truck. He kept his eyes on Rebel, who was now out of the Aston Martin and making his way across the parking lot towards Tip's apartment building. "He's on his way inside," Yogi informed Ice.

Ice took a deep settling breath, and then he gripped the handle of his 9mm pistol. "Let's do this," he said, as he unlocked the passenger door.

They both slid out of the Range Rover. Then they moved quietly and quickly across the parking lot, just like assassins. They waited until Rebel stepped inside of the building's lobby, to move in after him.

"What's up fool?" Ice called out to Rebel, from a few steps away.

Rebel spun around, looking startled.

"Don't even think about running," Yogi gritted out, with his Glock raised and aimed. He quickly covered the short distance between him and Rebel. "Why you looking so surprised?" He asked.

Rebel's face creased viciously. "Mothafu—"

He almost bit off a piece of his tongue, when Yogi struck him across the face with the butt of his pistol. He croaked quietly and then he let go of the bag of food, as he crumpled to the floor.

"Calm yo' fuck-ass down," Yogi told him.

"Get your ass up," Ice spat and then he kicked him in the face.

Rebel grunted and rolled onto his back, then took a heel in the gut from Ice. The stomp knocked the wind out of him. But a second kick to the face sent him close to unconsciousness.

Yogi reached over and grabbed Rebel by the front of his shirt. He then pulled him up from off the floor and punched him in the gut. "Where the fuck is she?" He asked bluntly.

Rebel was dazed and bloodied. With fear-filled eyes, he looked from one face to the next. "Wha-wha-what's up, man?" He stuttered, as blood leaked from his mouth. "Why are you nig-AAHHH!" He cringed and yelped in pain, when Ice punched him hard in the lower back.

"Where is she?" Ice pressed the 9mm, up against his temple and asked.

Crying, Rebel looked at Ice and begged, "Don't sh-shoot me, man. Please."

Ice drilled the muzzle of the 9mm into his temple. "Where the fuck is she?" He asked again.

Rebel grimaced and then he pissed on himself.

Yogi slapped him across the face. "Answer the fucking question?" He barked.

"Sh-she's in Tip's apartment."

"With who?"

Rebel turned his bloody face and looked at the gun in Ice's hand. He gazed at it for a swift moment, and then started to sob. "She's wi-with Rev," he muttered, as tears tumbled down his cheeks.

"Rev and who?" Ice asked, jamming the 9mm into his ribs.

Rebel yowled and cringed. "Rev is the only one there," he said, and then he started to weep uncontrollably.

Yogi narrowed his eyes on Rebel and then smirked wryly.

"Just look at his fuck-ass," he said to Ice. "I told you that this niggah was a straight up bitch." Yogi shoved Rebel ahead.

"Lead the way, fool," he ordered aggressively.

Rebel dropped his head and then he continued sobbing. He then led the way out of the lobby, and then down the corridor that led to Tip's apartment.

They walked by a much older man. He looked away and then hurried along quickly about his business, when he saw Rebel's bloodied face and the gun in Yogi's hand. When they got to Tip's apartment door, Yogi knocked and then he pressed a thumb over the peep-hole.

"Who?" Rev asked loudly, from inside.

Rebel hesitated. But when Ice jammed him in the back with the 9mm, he yelped, "Open the door, man!"

Rev cracked the door open just enough to peep out.

"Bullshit!" He then snapped loudly, and tried to close and lock the door, when he saw Rebel's bloodied face.

Only before he got the door locked, Yogi raised a foot of his size fourteen Timberland boots and kicked it in. The door swung back like a turnstile and slammed against the wall with a loud 'Blam!' Ice and Yogi then charged inside.
Rev already had his gun drawn and cocked. He bolted towards the back door. But as he ran, he raised his Desert Eagle and squeezed off a couple of wild rounds.
Ice ducked and took aim. He then fired back at Rev, but missed him by a mile. Yogi did the same, but Rev was already out through the back door and sprinting away wildly. Yogi started after him — but he dove for cover, when bullets from Rev's Desert Eagle slammed into the wall above his head. He waited a few beats, before getting up and sprinting towards the back door. But as soon as he got there, he was greeted by another slew of bullets. He fired back at Rev, before taking cover behind the wall by the door—then he charged outside when the gunfire ended.
Ice started after them, but stopped when he saw Rebel laid out on his back in the doorway. He was heaving and gasping heavily, with a bloody hand on his stomach and the other across his eyes. A bullet from Rev's Desert Eagle had slammed into his gut and left him desperately clinging onto life.
Ice shook his head at him pitifully. "Better you than me," he said, before turning away and going in search of Kyla. He found her in the bedroom, tied across the bed with a piece of duct tape across her mouth, and tears streaming down the sides of her face. Her eyes got wide, when she saw him. But just as he ripped the tape away from her mouth, he heard the blaring echoes of police sirens.
He started to untie her wrists. "Kyla, I've got to get outta here," he said, just as Yogi appeared in the doorway, breathless.
"We've got to go," Yogi panted. "The police are on their way."

"I hear them," Ice said, as he untied Kyla's other wrist. He looked her dead in the eyes, when he was through. "The police are coming. You gonna be okay, you hear me?"

Kyla was too shocked to speak, but she nodded her head frantically.

Ice grabbed her by the shoulder. "We were never here," he said to her. "No matter what happens, Kyla. Yogi and I were never here."

She nodded again.

"Come on brah!" Yogi pressed.

Ice gave Kyla a benign look, before he turned away. "What happened to Rev?" He asked Yogi, as they both ran to the back door.

Yogi shook his head and said, as he ran, "The niggah got away, yow. He was too fucking fast."

CH-29

Amelia flung her cell phone down on the bed. Then she ran out of the bedroom and into her mother's living room. "Kyla's okay!" She screamed blissfully. "Kyla is with the police and she's on her way home."

"Thank you, good Lord Jesus," Miranda uttered, as she put away her knitting needles and got up from the couch, smiling.

Danielle let go of Dane's hand and she hurried over to her best friend. "I told you that she'd be okay," she said, as they embraced.

"Who found her? Was it the police?" Aisha asked from around the table across the room, where she was doing her homework.

"No, it wasn't the police," Amelia replied happily. "She wouldn't say who it was that found her, but I'm almost sure that it was Trav'."

"I'm so glad that she's okay," Danielle said, with a toothy smile across her face.

"Me too," Amelia responded, with a hand at her chest. She then took a deep settling breath. "I was so worried for her. Only God knows how I would've taken it, if they had killed her."

"The good Lord wouldn't have allowed that to happen," Miranda assured. "He may allow us to go through a lot, at times. But he'll never let us go through too much."

"Amen to that," Danielle agreed laughing, and getting everybody to join her.

There was a feeling of extreme happiness, floating around inside of Miranda's living room. The news of Kyla being found and was safely on her way home, had enlightened everyone's heart and put their minds at ease.

"So what is gonna happen now?" Aisha turned in her chair and asked. "Is Mike Simms going to prison?"

"He sure is," Amelia cocked her head and said confidently. "After putting us through so much, only God can save his ass now."

"And I'm gonna pray that he doesn't," Miranda sassed, with her face scrunched up.

After a very long time of saying nothing, Dane said, "His ass deserves to be in prison."

"Him and all of those people that he had working for him," Danielle added, as she snuggled up to her man.

"His ass is going to prison. Y'all better believe that!" Amelia said, just as the doorbell rang. "I'll get it," she announced, and then she turned away quickly.

When she got to the door, she looked into the peephole and her face lit up. She yanked the door open and flung herself at him. "Hey you," she said, as she embraced him tightly.

A bit surprised by her open affection, Ice slowly wrapped his arms around her. "What's this about?" He asked, with a bashful smile on his face. He was feeling flushed, because of how everyone inside of the room was looking at him.

"I missed you," Amelia cooed, as she pulled away. She looked up into his face adoringly, before taking his hand and dragging him inside. "Come here, I want for you to meet my mother."

With her widest smile ever, Amelia led Ice into her mother's living room. Then she introduced him to everyone except for Danielle, who he had already met before. The introductions seemed to take forever.

When they were finally over, Ice looked at Miranda and said, "I've heard so much about you and Aisha. It feels as if I've met you guys before."

Miranda wrapped an arm around Aisha, who had taken a seat on the couch next to her. She narrowed her eyes at Ice. She was almost certain, that she had heard his voice and looked into his eyes before.

"This probably ain't your first time meeting us," she smiled, with her eyes still narrowed and her head slightly tilted.

Ice felt his stomach churn. The way that Miranda was looking at him, had him thinking that she knew who he is. He swallowed the lump in his throat. "I don't think that we've ever met," he replied a bit nervously. "But if we have, then it will come back to me. It's not in me to ever forget a beautiful face."

Miranda flashed him a warm smile.

Aisha moved around on the couch, with her eyes fixed steadily on Ice's face and her lips curled into a knowing smile. "Your voice sounds so familiar," she said. "You sound just like the guy who—"

"Would you like something to drink?" Miranda asked, cutting off Aisha. She knew exactly what Aisha was about to say, and she didn't want her to say it in front of Amelia.

"I'm good, but thanks." Ice answered, giving Miranda a thankful stare.

"Well, in that case," Miranda said, getting up and pulling Aisha up with her. "We're gonna leave you two alone. It was nice meeting you, Travis. Don't be a stranger."

"I won't," Ice replied, as Miranda and Aisha walked out of the room.

Danielle got up from her seat, next to Dane. "I'm outta here too," she said, reaching for her handbag and sweater.

"You're leaving?" Amelia asked.

"Hmm-mmm. Dane is taking me out to the movies."

"Don't you two ever get tired of going out?"

"Nope . . . we can never get tired of having fun," Danielle chuckled, as she and Dane made their way towards the front door.

As soon as they stepped out, Amelia moved towards Ice. She wrapped her arms around his neck and then she pulled him into a kiss. They kissed slow and passionately, taking their time to explore each other's mouth and to bask in the warmth of their bodies.

After only kissing for a minute that felt like a very long hour; Amelia put a hand against Ice's chest and then she pushed him away. "Where were you?" She asked, breathing unevenly.

Ice looked at her for a moment, and then he turned away. "I was on the road with Yogi," he said, taking a seat on the couch.

"Doing what?"

He looked up at her and smirked. "What is this? Am I being interrogated?"

"Yes," Amelia answered, taking a seat across his lap. She wrapped her arms around his neck. "Were you the one who saved Kyla? I know it's you Trav', so don't lie to me."

"They found Kyla?" He asked, acting all surprised. "Is she okay? Where is she now?"

Amelia framed his face and then she looked him dead in the eyes. She then threw her head back and laughed, when he looked away. "You're such a bad liar," she said, getting up.

"What makes you think that I'm lying? Did Kyla say that I'm the one who saved her?"

Amelia waved him off. "Whatever Trav', I know it's you," she giggled, as she walked away.

He got up and started after her. "Where are you going?" He asked, with a coy grin etched across his face.

She glanced over her shoulder at him. "I'm going to put a few things together," she explained. "I'm spending the night at your place. And I don't feel like driving all the way back over here, before going to work in the morning."

$$$$$$$$$$$$$$$$$$$$$$$

Rebel looked as if he was seconds away from dying. His features were corpse-like and his skin pale. He had an intravenous line and a couple of wires attached to his body, and his breathing was labored because of the cannula in his nose.

He was laid out on a gurney, inside of a small curtained off room. His left wrist was cuffed to the metal bracket above his head, and his feet slightly elevated and shackled.

Rebel knew that he was on his way to prison, and the thought of being there had him holding back tears. He had already been questioned by the police and briefed on all of the shit that he was in. But when the curtains across from him parted, and Albert Barrett stepped through, followed by police captain, Joe Martinez, he just knew that things were about to get a whole lot worse.

"Mr. Mark Simms, or should I just call you Rebel?" The police captain greeted Rebel, with a wide smile.

Joe Martinez was a stout, dark-skinned Hispanic, with salt and pepper hair and a pot belly. He pulled his badge and showed it to Rebel. "I'm Police Captain Martinez," he introduced himself. "And this gentleman here is my good friend, State Attorney Albert Barrett." He signaled with a shift of his head. "I hope you don't mind, but we'd like to ask you a few questions."

"I've already been questioned, like ten different times," Rebel croaked.

"We know that," Barrett smiled, as he stepped closer. "But the questions that we are here to ask will help you out."

"I don't need your help. I'm gonna hire a lawyer."

Barrett looked over at Martinez and they busted out laughing.

"What's so fucking funny?" Rebel asked, with his face bent up. He was clearly stressing, but he was trying his best not to show it.

Barrett pulled a handkerchief from his back pocket and then he wiped his face. "Do you really think that a lawyer can help you?" He asked, still cackling. "We've got too much on you, son. And Kyla Williams is willing to testify against you in court. Just your kidnapping charge alone, is enough to put you away for life."

"Not to mention attempted murder, assault and battery, conspiracy, sexual molestation, rape—"

"I didn't rape nobody!" Rebel bawled at the captain, then grimaced in pain. He put a hand over his gunshot wound. Then he wiped the side of his teary face, on his shoulder. "I didn't rape anybody," he repeated dolefully.

"We know you didn't," Martinez said. "But your friend tried and he's dead, so somebody has to take the fall."

Rebel looked fearfully at the captain. "You can't do that," he said, with tears falling down his cheeks.

"We sure can," Barrett chipped in. "You may beat that rape charge in trial, but it will still leave a blemish on your name. And you'll still do life for the other charges." Barrett slid his hands inside of his pockets. "Do you have any idea, what they do to rapists in prison?"

Rebel's eyes widened, as he released a gush of tears. "I didn't rape nobody," he started to sob, with his shoulders jumping.

"It's over for you, Rebel," Martinez pressed. "You're going to prison, for a very long time. You'll probably end up killing yourself in there."

"Not if he helps us out," Barrett interjected. He then stepped closer to Rebel and held onto the bedrail. "We know that you're not the one calling the shots, Rebel. We know it's your brother."

"So if you know this, then why are you fucking with me?"

"Because we need for you to tell us."

"Tell you what?" Rebel raised his face and asked.

"Tell us everything," Barrett said coolly. "Give us the names of all the cops and prosecutors that your brother has working for him."

"I don't know their names—"

"You're a fucking liar!" Martinez sneered.

Rebel dropped his head. "I swear to God. I don't know their names," he cried, with snot leaking from his nose. "I know that he's got a lot of them working for him. Only he never, ever tells me their names."

"What about his drugs?" Martinez asked. "How is he getting them? Who is sending the supply to him?"

Rebel raised his head and he stared fearfully at Martinez. He stared for what seemed like hours. Then when the thought of him doing a lengthy bid came back to him, he whimpered, "He gets his drugs from Pedrazza. He gets a hundred keys every month, through a shipping agency.

"You know the name of the shipping agency?"

Rebel nodded.

"Who was it that helped you to kidnap Kyla?" Barrett asked, keeping his voice even. "She said that it was two of you."

Rebel hesitated before saying, "It was me and Rev."

"Who is Rev, and where is he?"

"Rev works for my brother, but I don't know where he's at. He's probably hiding out at his girlfriend's house in Pompano."

"You know where this girlfriend lives?"

Rebel nodded.

Barrett looked over at Martinez and smiled. He then pulled a tape recorder from his pocket and showed it to Rebel. "We've got some more questions for you, Rebel. But I wanna record your answers, is that cool with you?"

With his eyes bloodshot red, Rebel looked from Martinez to Barrett. "Am I going to prison?" He sniffled.

Barrett glanced down at the tape recorder inside of his hand, and then he gave Rebel a far-fetched look. "You're going to prison, whether you help us out or not. But if you do help us, then we'll help you with a far less prison sentence. We'll also make sure that you're protected, while you're there."

Rebel dropped his head sadly. He then waited for a long while, before whimpering, "What is it that you wanna know?"

CH-30

Amelia turned away from the dresser, looking stunning in her black Ralph Lauren skirt suit and high Gucci stilettos. The pleasant smile on her face was more than enough, to tell the world that her night with Ice was well spent.

As he always did, Ice had brought her to multiple orgasms and left her swooning and tingling all over. They had made love to Dru Hill's, *Enter the Dru* album. Amelia could still clearly remember how Ice had quietly hummed inside her ear; the words of each song, as he carried her through a climactic abyss.

With her bribery issues cleared up and Kyla safely back home, Amelia was now anxiously ready to put Blood away for life. She had never been more eager to get to work. Her soaring confidence had her beaming, like a lighthouse on a deserted island.

After spraying on a light mist of the Coco Chanel perfume, which Ice had bought her when they first met; Amelia strutted over to the king-sized bed and gave Ice a long, hard kiss on his cheek.

"Baby, I'm leaving," she said lightly. "I'll call you, just as soon as I get out of court."

Ice stirred, rolled over and then got up. "What time is it?" He asked groggily.

"It's close to seven thirty."

Ice dry washed his face. He ripped the sheets away, and then flung his legs over the side of the bed. "Gimme a minute, I'll follow you down to your car," he said, as he got up.

She wrapped her arms around his naked torso and then placed her head against his shoulder. "You don't have to. Go back to sleep. I'll be okay."

"Not with Rev still out there, trying to get to you," Ice thought. He then dry washed his face for a second time and said, "I'm not letting you walk out of here alone. I won't be seeing you for the majority of the day. So I wanna get every bit of you, while you're here."

She looked up into his face. Then she turned away, shaking her head. "You've got five minutes," she cooed, as she walked over to the dresser.

$$$$$$$$$$$$$$$$$$$$$$$$

It was exactly seven thirty, when Rev stepped out of his girlfriend's apartment. He had a gray duffel bag stuffed with clothes in one hand, and $150,000 amongst other things inside of the back pack over his shoulder.

He was on his way out of Florida. He knew once the police questioned Kyla, that it wouldn't be long before a warrant was issued for his arrest. His girlfriend's apartment would've been the perfect spot for him to hide out, since only Blood and Rebel knew about her. However, he didn't want to stay there because of her inquisitive, loud-mouth stepmother.

Many thoughts flooded Rev's mind, as he walked down the driveway towards his girlfriend's BMW — thoughts of killing Ice, Yogi, and Amelia before leaving town, were some of them.

The bleak morning was still and lifeless, so it didn't take him long to catch sight of the black dodge charger that was cruising down the street towards him. For a brief moment, he took nothing of it. But when he saw the blue minivan across the street, with the two white men inside, he immediately figured out what time it was.

"Oh shit," Rev muttered quietly, as he let go of the duffel bag. Then just as he started to turn to make his way back inside of the house, the loud acceleration of the dodge charger's powerful v8 engine, sent the still, lifeless morning into a chaotic frenzy.

Out of nowhere, an army of police officers appeared. The majority of who were decked out in full black riot gear. "Freeze! Police!" They all screamed simultaneously. But Rev had no plans of doing what they wanted, so he pulled his Beretta PX4 from his hip and he took off running.

"He's running! He's running!" A chorus of voices yelled. "He has a gun! He's got a gun!" Followed loudly.

With his head down and his Beretta aimed steadily behind him, Rev squeezed off a couple of rounds as he ran. He didn't hit a damn thing. Neither did he get inside of the house, before a wave of slugs slammed into his body, pitching him over face first into the concrete.

$$$$$$$$$$$$$$$$$$$$$$$$

Less than five minutes after Rev was killed over in Pompano, Ice and Amelia stepped off the elevator inside of Ice's apartment building and made their way through the lobby. A bright and beautiful day greeted them, when they stepped outside. But just as they started across the parking lot, Shanequa stepped out of a white Nissan Altima, with her face tight and her eyes blazing with jealousy.

"Ice, can I talk to you for a minute?" Shanequa asked saucily. She then walked up to Ice and Amelia, with mischief written all across her face.

Ice clenched his jaw and then his nose began to flare. "I ain't got nothing to say to you, Shanequa, and how in the fuck did you get through the gate anyway?"

"You're worried about the wrong damn thing," Shanequa propped a hand on her hip and said. "You should be worried about what I have to say. And I'm sure that you don't want me to say it in front of your little girlfriend."

Amelia sucked her teeth and then she cut her eyes at Shanequa. She then turned to Ice with her face made up. "Trav', I ain't got time for all of this. I can't be late for work," she sneered, with a whole lot of attitude.

Ice kissed her on the forehead and then he looped an arm around her waist. "Come on, let's go. I don't know what she's on, but I ain't on it," he muttered, as they started off.

"So Ice, it's like that?" Shanequa asked, now trailing behind them. "I'm talking to you and you're just gonna take off?"

"We ain't got nothing to talk about."

"You sure about that?" Shanequa stopped and asked. Annoyed, she put a foot forward and folded her arms below her breasts. "When was the last time that you spoke to Blood, Ice? Did you even tell him that you're out here fucking the prosecutor, who's trying to send him to prison?"

Ice's knees buckled and cold sweat sprung from his pores instantly. He stopped, because Amelia had slowed to a stop.

"So you're not gonna answer me?" Shanequa pressed deliberately, when she saw Ice's panicky reaction and the confused look on Amelia's face. "Or is it that you don't want your little girlfriend to know that you work for Blood?"

Amelia stiffened, as dizziness came down on her. She pressed a hand against her churning gut and then she looked at Ice through blurred eyes. "Trav', what is she saying?" She asked faintly.

Ice stood frozen, not knowing what to say, as he stared at Shanequa with pure hatred. He could feel Amelia's eyes on him, burning holes into his face as she gazed at him in disbelief.

"Tra-Trav'…" Amelia whimpered.

Ice kept his eyes on Shanequa, as his anger swelled.

Shanequa twisted her mouth to the side and then she continued with her mischief. "So, you didn't know that the guy who tried to rape you was his best friend?" She looked at Amelia with her eyes burning with devilry. "Sheee-iit," she continued. "They even went to school together."

Amelia's eyes were moist and huge. "Trav'… Is all of this true?" She whimpered timidly, unable to stop the lone tear that was tumbling down her cheek.

Ice turned his head and looked at her. The pain that he saw in her eyes sent his pulse into a frenzied gallop. He reached out to her. "Amelia I—"

"Don't," she said and then she stepped back away from him. "Just tell me if what she's saying is true."

"Go ahead Ice. Tell her. Tell her that you work fo' Blood," Shanequa jeered, with her arms folded and her lips curled spitefully.

Ice shot her a black look and then he pointed a finger in her face. "You need to stay the fuck out of a niggah's business, Shanequa. All you do is go around and create conflict," he spat with venom. "You think this is gonna make us get back together?! Bitch, I don't want your triflin' ass."

"Niggah please," Shanequa cocked her head and spieled. "I don't want you either," she said, with her face scrunched up and a hand at her hip. "I spilled your little secret just to get even with your fuck-ass. Besides, Rev is now getting all of this." She patted her front, not knowing that Rev was dead.

Flooded with rage, Ice stepped towards her with his teeth gritted and a fisted arm up and back. Shanequa clamped her eyes shut—cocked her head—and then she flung her hands up over her face.

But Ice didn't punch her in the face, as the voice in his head was telling him to. Instead, he slammed his fist into his palm and raged loud and furiously, "Get the fuck away from me, Shanequa! I've just about had enough of you!"

Shanequa was stunned and shaken by Ice's explosive outburst. She had never seen it before. It had her petrified, and not wanting to move because of fear. But when Ice made another step towards her, with his fist still balled up and rage burning inside of his eyes; she yelped and spun around. Then she darted off, towards the Altima.

Ice didn't wait for the Altima to move away. He turned to Amelia, just as soon as Shanequa was inside. "Amelia, please let me explain," he begged, as his disposition changed from blinding rage to timorous.

The pain in his eyes had no effect on Amelia. She herself was in too much pain to even show him any sympathy.

"So, it's all true?" She asked tediously, staring into his face with her eyes brimming with tears.

"'Melia, if you just gimme a minute to explain, I'll — "
"I don't want you to explain shit to me." She cut him off
calmly, with a raised hand. She then used the back of her hand
to wipe away a streaking tear. "All I wanna know is if all that
I've heard is true."
Ice dropped his head.
"Mothafucka, answer me!" Amelia finally exploded, with her
face twisted with rage. As soon as he raised his head she
asked, "Is it all true?!"
Ice stood silently, staring at her. Knowing that he couldn't lie,
he nodded.
With a quick swing, she slapped him hard across the face and
then she stormed away. "Stay the fuck away from me, Travis!
And lose my fucking number!" She sobbed, as she ran
towards the Lexus.

$$$$$$$$$$$$$$$$$$$$$$$$

Blood was inside of his cell, smoking weed and waiting to be
taken to court. He was in front of the mirror above the sink,
staring at his obscured reflection, and wondering what should
be his first move, when he was allowed back into the free
world.
An image of him and Amelia having sex popped inside of his
head. He smiled at the thought. Then he took a hard drag
from the joint and blew the smoke at his reflection.
"Yow, Simms! You've got a visit!"
Blood turned away from the mirror and saw C.O Jackson,
standing at his cell door. "Visit?" He spat scornfully. "I don't
want no fucking visit, I'm on my way outta this shit."
"It's Batch and your attorney; they wanna holler at you, before
you go in to court."
Blood sucked his teeth and then he dropped the remaining
joint into the toilet.
"They better not be coming at me, with no bullshit," he said,
as he stepped out of the cell.

A couple of minutes later, Blood stepped off the elevator behind Jackson, and followed him through the visiting area. When they got to visiting room D4, Jackson stepped up to the door and he knocked.

"Come in," Batch answered from inside.

Jackson pushed the door open and then he stepped aside. "I'll wait out here," he said, to no one in particular.

Blood stepped inside the room and shot a hard stare at Bill Ferentz, who was seated behind the small metal table. He then looked over at Batch, who was standing next to the lawyer. "This shit couldn't wait, 'til I'm out?" He asked hotly.

"Believe me, if it could, then we wouldn't be here," Batch replied timidly.

"Mr. Simms, please have a seat," Ferentz implored shakily.

Blood looked over at him. "Fuck sitting down. I wanna know why you mothafuckas dragged me down here, when it's almost time for me to go to court."

Ferentz sighed heavily and then he pinched the bridge of his nose. "Mr. Simms, before we get into why we're here—"

"Before nothing, crack'r! You mothafuckas had better tell me why the fuck I'm down here!"

"Blood, we've got a big problem."

Blood looked over at the corrupted cop. "Problem? What kind of fucking problem?"

"Miss Clarke is back on your case," Ferentz said, in a low fearful tone.

Blood snapped his head around and stared at the lawyer. "What the fuck happened to the other prosecutor? Didn't you give him the money that he asked for?"

Ferentz started to blink repeatedly. He then wiped away beads of perspiration from his forehead and said, "He did get the money, but he was pulled off the case."

Blood's nose flared.

"That's not all," Batch pitched in, while staring down at the floor. "Rev is dead, and your brother got shot and is now in the hospital, under police watch."

Blood's hands formed into tight balls, at his sides. He glared angrily at Batch, with his lips twisted. "Is this a fucking joke?" He growled, in a gravelly tone.

Batch swallowed hard and then he took a small step back. "I know better than to joke around with you, Blood," he said, with worry lines across his forehead. "If it wasn't true, then I wouldn't have said it. And then to make matters worse, Rebel is talking. He's snitching. He's yapping about everything that you had going on, and all that you told him to do to get you outta jail."

"They're filing new charges against you," Ferentz added. "And kidnapping is one of them. I know that you may not wanna hear the truth. But the truth is, I don't see any way out for you."

"Rebel fucked up, Blood. I know that he's your little brother, but he bitched out."

Blood stared lividly at Batch. "If you hadn't of fucked up, then he wouldn't have!"

"How did I fuck up?" Batch asked sheepishly. "Rick was the one who fucked up, by losing your case file."

Blood didn't reply, he just continued staring at Batch with murder in his eyes, and rage seeping from his pores like steam.

"Your brother just shot down your only chance at freedom," Ferentz muttered. "With him giving evidence against you, there's no way for us to win a trial against Miss Clarke. If we go to trial, she will eat us alive. And I'm certain that she'd ask for the death penalty, when we lose." Ferentz pulled away at his collar. Then he swallowed the lump inside of his throat when he saw the cold, insane look inside of Blood's eyes. "I think that we should accept Miss Clarke's offer."

"You're telling me to take a plea of a fucking life sentence?!" Blood exploded. "What the fuck do I look like, crack'r?!"

"Mr. Simms, we can't win."

"You can't win!" Blood roared lividly. "I ain't spending the rest of my fucking life in prison!"

"Blood, they've got your prints on the machete that you used to kill Bam," Batch said. "And now they've got your own brother on tape, saying that he was there when you did it."

"Fuck that!" Blood barked. "I ain't spending the rest of my fucking life in prison!" He repeated.

"It's either prison or death," Ferentz said, as he wiped his mouth with the back of his hand. "With all of the charges that they will now pile against you, I just don't see how you'll get any less than life."

"Blood, take Miss Clarkes offer," Batch urged. "You never know, you'll probably get it overturned, a couple of years down the road."

Blood rushed across the room and then he grabbed Batch by the front of his shirt. "Don't tell me what the fuck to do!" He barked in his face.

"But there's no way around it," Batch muttered shakily.

Blood shoved him up against the wall, and then he punched him hard in the gut. "You wanna fucking bet?" He growled, as Batch doubled over in pain. Blood then turned away from the corrupted cop and spat a nasty wad of saliva in Ferentz's face. "Crack'r you're fucking fired," he said, as he turned and marched out of the room.

CH-31

Because of her blinding tears, Amelia could barely see the road ahead. She sobbed as she drove; unable to stop the tears that flooded her face and burnt their way down her cheeks, like salt inside of a fresh wound.

Despite her excruciating heartbreak, she was still on her way to work. She wasn't gonna let despair and distress stop her from sending Blood to prison. Not when all that was happening to and around her, were all the repercussions of his cruelty.

It was going on seventeen years, since Amelia cried because of heartbreak. When her first ever boyfriend broke up with her, she had vowed never to love another man as much as she loved him. Only Ice caused her to break that vow, without her even knowing it.

She had no idea that she was so deeply in love with him. If it wasn't for her finding out the truth, she wouldn't have realized that he had consumed her body. He was like drugs that left her retching, like a junkie dying for a fix.

Despite their small age gap, Amelia was really looking forward to settling down and starting a life with Ice. From the first time that she had laid eyes on him, inside of the mall; the barrier that she had placed around her heart for men of his kind, slowly fell away.

She was now mad at herself for letting her guard down, and then giving her heart to someone that she thought she knew but didn't.

She now felt as if Ice had planned all of his moves. She concluded that when they met at the mall, that he deliberately kept her there, so that his friends could tear apart her apartment. She even figured out that he was there when her mother almost got raped.

She now knew for sure that he was the one who helped Aisha to get away, then hindered Tip from shooting her mother. But what she didn't want to believe — and what her heart was telling her, was that the part he played in her calamity was his planned way to protect her. She just didn't want to believe her broken heart. All she wanted to believe was that she hated him.

Lost in her painful thoughts, Amelia ran through a red light and almost crashed into a dodge caravan, which sped by in front of her. The near fatal collision dragged her back to reality, but it didn't mend her broken heart. So she continued on her way to work, as if she didn't care that she almost lost her life.

"How could I have been so fucking blind?!" Amelia yelled at herself, and then pounded a fist onto the steering wheel. She then wiped her tear-filled eyes, as anger took over. "You made me love you, Travis. You made me fucking love you," she ranted, as she continued to drive like a road hog.

"All you had to do was tell me the truth," she thought, while gunning the Lexus by a slower moving Jaguar.

The shrill ring of her cell phone jarred her eyes away from the road ahead, and almost sent her crashing into the back of a Lincoln Navigator. But she retrieved her cell phone and set her eyes back on the road, just in time to swerve away from the black SUV.

When she looked at the phone and saw Ice's number on the screen, her anger raised a notch. But she still accepted the call and brought the phone up to her lips and then screamed, "Stop calling my fucking phone!"

$$$$$$$$$$$$$$$$$$$$$

Ice slammed his cell phone down on the bed. Then he dropped his face into his hands. Amelia didn't give him a chance to say a word, before she screamed at him and hung up. This left him in more pain than ever before. He was clearly hurting and devastated by what had happened.

His once comfortable bedroom, no longer had that homely feel that he liked so much. He now felt as if he was in a prison cell, with no window, no air condition, and no ventilation whatsoever. He felt hot and humid, as if something was clamped around his throat and stopping him from breathing.

Even though he was seated on his king-sized bed, he felt as if his legs were about to give way. He had told himself that he wouldn't break down and cry, but his eyes were glossy and his breathing was uneven.

Something had shattered inside of him, when Amelia walked out of his life. He didn't know what it was, but it left him grieving. It also left him with a hole in his heart as big as the Atlantic.

How could he have grown to love her so much, in such a short period of time? He had no idea, but he knew that he loved her. He loved her so much, that he wasn't sure if he could live without her.

Now that she was gone, he realized that what he was feeling for her was far more than sexual. There was a connection between them and only God himself could come down from heaven and tell him that she wasn't feeling it too.

All his adult life, he had craved for a woman like Amelia. She was classy, elegant and she was sophisticated. But when they were inside of the bedroom, she was a beast, a freak, and a sexual goddess, who knew exactly how to please her man.

She was a whole lot of fun to be around. And not only was she smart and intelligent, she also had her life figured out and her goals set.

Rubbing his aching temples, Ice pondered over what he could do to get her to forgive him.

"All I was trying to do was protect you!" He shouted, and then got up and started to pace. "I love you, Amelia," he announced unexpectedly. "I love you more than I have ever loved any other woman."

After pacing for about ten minutes and realizing that it wasn't doing him much good, Ice took a seat back on the bed. His mind was a blurred mess, and his heart was beating as heavy as he was breathing. His bedroom reeked of Amelia. And no matter how hard that he tried, he just couldn't accept that she was gone — and couldn't bear to know that she could end up in the arms of another man.

Fighting with the urge to break something, Ice reached for his phone and made a call to the one person that he knew could help him.

"Hello," she answered, after three rings.

Ice took a deep breath before saying, "Good morning. This is Travis."

"Oh, hi Travis. How are you?"

Ice sighed heavily. "Not so good," he replied.

"You sound terrible."

"I feel terrible." Ice said, getting up.

He then went back to pacing.

"You wanna talk about it?"

"Yeah, I do," he answered dolefully. "But I don't wanna talk over the phone. If you have the time, can we talk about it over breakfast?"

"Sure. Just tell me where and I'll be there."

Ice checked the time on his wrist. "Can we meet up at the IHOP, down the street from your house?"

"We could do that. How long will it take you to get there?"

"About twenty minutes," Ice said, while hurrying towards his closet.

$$$$$$$$$$$$$$$$$$$$$

Amelia turned away from her truck, and then she made slow, lethargic steps across the parking lot and towards the courthouse. She had a depressed look on her face and her eyes were still a bit glossed over. She was still aching over what had happened earlier. But she had a job to do and she was at the courthouse to do it.

She sucked in a deep breath and bit into her lip, when she saw her boss waiting by the door of the courthouse.

"Mr. Barrett, what are you doing here?" She asked, as she climbed up the few levels of steps.

Albert Barrett pulled his hands from his pockets and he narrowed his eyes at her, when she got close. "You okay?" He asked suspiciously. "You look like shit."

Amelia sighed heavily. "I feel like shit, but I'll get over it," she replied.

"Hmmmm . . . . Well, I've got some good news and it should put a smile on your face."

"I doubt it," Amelia mumbled, as she glanced at her watch. When she saw that it was 8:45, she stepped by her boss and pushed the courthouse door open. "Mind if we walk and talk. I've only got about fifteen minutes to spare."

"Fifteen minutes is more time than I'll need," Barrett smiled, as he stepped inside of the courthouse.

$$$$$$$$$$$$$$$$$$$$$$$$

Miranda was nowhere in sight, when Ice got to the IHOP. But as soon as he settled for a secluded table and took a seat, she stepped in through the front door. When she saw Ice, she smiled, waved and then she hurried over.

"Sorry, if I had you waiting," she said, as she slid into the booth across from him.

"I just got here," Ice told her, while looking around inside of the restaurant for a waitress. "Would you like to order something to eat?" He asked her.

Miranda shook her head. "The food can wait. Let's talk."

Ice sighed heavily. "I don't know where to start," he said, in a doleful tone. "I've got so much to say."

"Then start by telling me how you ended up at my house, the night that I almost got raped and killed. I know you didn't want to be there. But honestly, I'm grateful that you were."

Ice raised his head and looked at her. "How did you figure out that it was me?"

"I don't think that I could ever forget the voice of the person, who saved my life."

"I wish that I could look at it the way that you do. As much as I'm glad that I was there that night, to intervene with what was planned; I'm still having a hard time forgiving myself, for being a part of it."

"You eventually will. The Lord God sent you there, for a reason. And I really believe that you didn't disappoint him." Miranda reached across the table and gave Ice's hand a light squeeze. "So how did you end up there?" She asked interestedly.

Ice fell back in his seat and said, "For you to get a full understanding of everything, I would have to start on how Blood ended up in jail."

"I've got time," Miranda said, with a warm smile.

Ice ran a hand down over his face and then he licked his dry lips. He gazed down at the table top, wondering how much he could tell Miranda. He wanted to tell her everything; wanted to open up and tell her why he did what he had to, and why he wanted out.

It took him a few seconds to decide that he would tell her as much as she would listen to. But just as he was about to get started, a teenage waitress walked up to the table. They both ordered pink lemonade. Then as soon as the waitress flounced away, Ice took a deep breath and said, "I was there the day that Blood killed Bam. Bam and I weren't close, but standing there and seeing him getting chopped to death, made me realize that I had to get out of the drug game, and away from the people that I had as friends. . ."

Ice paused and took a deep settling breath, and then he went on to tell Miranda, of what led up to him meeting and falling in love with Amelia.

He left nothing out. He told her about his involvement with Blood and what they had going on, before he decided to step away. He then explained how he ended up at Amelia's house and how he saw her for the first time; along with how he had to trick his friends into leaving there, without harming her. Hearing the underlying pain in his voice had Miranda saddened. But she didn't interrupt him. She just sat back and allowed him to say, all that he wanted.

Twenty minutes and a glass of lemonade later, Miranda had heard enough from Ice to convince her that he was deeply in love with her daughter. Her respect for him went up a notch, when he explained how he had to step away from his friends to protect Amelia. But when Miranda heard how he went about saving Kyla, she had to blink away moisture from her eyes.

"… and now because of Shanequa and her vindictiveness, Amelia won't talk to me," Ice was saying. He exhaled loudly and then he looked Miranda in the eyes. "I swear to you Miss Miranda, all that I was trying to do was protect her."

"I believe you, Travis," Miranda replied. "But what I believe won't make things any better between you and Amelia. It's up to you to find a way to fix things between you and her."

"I wish that I knew how," Ice muttered. He dropped his head and gazed at his empty lemonade glass. "I really wanted to tell her everything, but I just didn't know how. I really didn't want to tell her the truth, only to chase her off."

"It's never a bad thing, to tell the truth," Miranda advised. She looked steadily at Ice. "So what are you gonna do now?" She asked him.

Ice shrugged. "I don't know. I'm not trying to hurt her anymore, than I already have. But at the same time, it's killing me that she won't talk to me."

"Give it time. She will," Miranda said, with a smile. "I know my daughter very well. She's not good at bottling up her feelings. If she doesn't like you, then she won't talk to you. But if she's in love with you, then she won't stay away from you for too long."

"But, I don't know if she loves me."

"Believe me, she loves you," Miranda said, with her customary friendly smile. She reached over and touched Ice on the back of his hand and then asked, "So what is it about my daughter that has you liking her so much?"

"What is there not to like?" Ice replied.

Miranda smiled and nodded. "So, did you two ever talk about settling down together?"

"No." Ice shook his head and said, "We were too busy having fun."

"I see," Miranda chirped, behind a quiet chortle. "Well . . . that's the main reason why I know that you two will get back together. From my past experiences, it's not hard finding someone to be with. But believe me, it's not easy finding someone to keep you happy."

$$$$$$$$$$$$$$$$$$$$$$

Amelia's Gucci heels were tapping loudly on the gray ceramic tile, as she ran down the corridor towards Judge Silverman's courtroom. She wasn't all smiles. However, she was feeling a whole lot better after hearing Rev was killed and that Rebel was in police custody; singing like a bird.

She was now eager to get inside of the courtroom; eager to see the look on Blood's face, once she reveals that his own brother has offered to testify against him, if he takes his case to trial.

The courtroom was dead quiet, when Amelia stepped inside. Only a few seats were occupied, and everyone seemed to be impatiently waiting for Blood's hearing to get underway. Amelia looked over at the defendant's table, expecting to see Blood and his entourage of high paid lawyers. Only to her surprise, the table was empty. She made a quick look around inside of the courtroom, but she didn't see Blood, or any of his attorneys.

"Miss Clarke, do you mind telling me what's going on here?"Judge Silverman greeted Amelia, as soon as she got to the prosecutor's table. "You're just about late, and the defendant and his attorney are still not here."

"Please forgive me, your honor," Amelia apologized. "I got here minutes ago, but I was outside conferring with my boss."

"And what about the defendant?"

"I have no idea," Amelia shrugged, as she took another look around the courtroom.

"This is bullshit," the Judge muttered, as he looked over at the clerk. "Get a hold of Mr. Ferentz. Tell him if he's not here within the next five minutes, that he's gonna have hell to pay."

The clerk walked away. But just as she was reaching for the telephone, the courtroom door flew open, and Scott Rosenberg walked in followed by Blood, along with the two C.O's who were escorting him.

Amelia got up from her seat. "What is this?" She asked abruptly. "What happened to Mr. Ferentz?"

"I fired him," Blood replied, as he shuffled along in his cuffs and shackles.

Amelia snapped her head around, to face the Judge. "Your honor, this is absurd. I wasn't informed of the defendant's change of counsel."

Judge Silverman leaned into his mic, with his eyes on Rosenberg. "Mr. Rosenberg, what's going on?" He asked. The small bodied Jew looked over at Blood and got a slow, reluctant nod. He then looked up at the Judge and said, "Your honor, if you'll allow me, my client and Miss Clarke to approach the bench, then I'll explain."

The Judge leaned back in his seat and then he signaled the trio up to his bench.

"This shit had better be good," Amelia muttered to herself, as she made her way up to the front of the courtroom. As soon as she got up to the Judge's bench, she asked, "Mr. Rosenberg, what is this about?"

Rosenberg pulled off his glasses. "My client would like to make a deal with you," he answered.

Amelia turned her eyes on Blood. He didn't have the same hostile look that he usually walked around with. Instead, he was looking like a man who knew that he was on his way to prison—possibly death row.

"A deal?" Amelia replied, as if she wasn't interested. "I already made my offer. So it's either that, or we're going to trial."

"All I'm asking for is a deal better than life," Blood said calmly.

Amelia cocked her head and then she raised her brows. "Are you fo' real?" She asked. "Do you have any idea, how much of a bind that you're in? Your own brother is willing to testify against you, just to save his own ass. And he's already given detailed information on all that you've done, ordered, and whatever else that you've got going on."

"Mr. Simms is quite aware of his brother's doings," Rosenberg announced. "That is why he's willing to settle; that is, if you'll offer him a better deal."

"I'm not interested in negotiating," Amelia replied, looking Blood dead in the eyes.

Blood frowned and dropped his head, and then he muttered, "What if I was to give you the names of all the cops and prosecutors that I've got working fo' me? Could I get a better deal then?"

Amelia glanced up at the Judge. Then she looked over at Rosenberg. "Is he serious?" She asked, acting as if she hadn't expected him to roll over and snitch.

"He is," Rosenberg answered. "Make us a manageable deal and he'll make you a list, right here, right now."

Amelia looked up at the Judge.

"Don't look at me," the Judge said. "This is all on you. But if it was on me, then I wouldn't hesitate to make him a better offer."

A few seconds of silence went by before Amelia turned to Blood and asked, "You're actually willing to snitch on all of those who worked fo' you?"

"For a better deal than life, fuck yeah."

Amelia sighed heavily. All of this was a part of the plan that she and her boss had put together.

"So, what about Pedrazza? We need Pedrazza," she pressed. Blood looked at her stunned. He was wondering how she knew about his California based cocaine supplier.

"Your brother told us about him," Amelia revealed, knowing what he was thinking. "Give us Pedrazza and the names of all the cops and prosecutors who worked fo' you. Then, we'll work something out."

Blood waited for a thoughtful moment. Then he looked at Amelia and stated humbly, "If that's what it will take, then I'll do that."

Amelia smirked, as she turned away. "Let me go and get my boss," she sang cheerfully as she hurried down the aisle. "I think it's best, if he's here fo' this."

"Take your time," Blood replied. "'Cause I've got quite a few names fo' you."

REPERCUSSIONS
EPILOGUE...

SIX WEEKS LATER

Amelia sat at the table inside of the busy Chinese restaurant with her head down, and her unblinking eyes glued to her plate of white rice and kung pao shrimp. The loud clinking and clattering of all the eating utensils around her was loud and disturbing, but she wasn't bothered by them. Neither was she bothered by the other four dozen customers that were inside of the restaurant, or by her mother's and Danielle's loud laughter around the table.

They were at the restaurant having lunch. But Amelia's mind wasn't on the food in front of her—it was on Ice and how badly she missed him. It was going on six full weeks, since Blood snitched his way into a twenty five years plea deal. Amelia had really wanted for him to spend the rest of his life in prison. But after he offered assistance in setting up Pedrazza, and giving the names of five of her co-workers—Rick and Frank Hibbert included—along with eight police officers, including Batch and Morris; she backed down and offered him the twenty five years that he accepted.

She was a bit surprised that Blood rolled over and snitched, the way that he did. She just didn't expect it. Because the aggression and fearlessness that he had shown, was like nothing that she had ever seen. He was hands down, the most callous and intractable criminal that she had ever faced in court. Yet he turned out to be no different than the others, because he too, cracked under pressure.

Frank Hibbert, Morris, and six others were arrested, less than two hours after Blood signed his plea deal. But there was no word on Batch. It was as if he fell off the globe the minute the warrant was issued for his arrest.

As for Ice, Amelia hadn't seen him since she slapped him and left him standing in the parking lot of his apartment building. He had called her multiple of times after that day, but she purposely ignored his calls. It was something that she now wished she hadn't done, because it was now going on four weeks, since she last heard from him; and it was now starting to take a visible toll on her.

She had thrown herself into work, trying to get him off of her mind. Yet nothing that she did, seemed to ease the torment that she was going through missing him. Her stomach still fluttered, whenever he popped up in her mind. And whenever she reminisced about their lovemaking, her entire body throbbed and pulsated.

"Amelia," Danielle interrupted Amelia's thoughts. "Are you even listening to me?"

"Huh?" Amelia raised her head, startled.

Danielle twisted her lips exasperatedly. "What damn planet were you on?" Danielle asked.

Amelia sighed. "Sorry D, my mind was somewhere else."

"Hmm-mmm," Miranda chimed in. "We all know where your mind was. And one of these days, it's not gonna come back."

"Mom, what are you talking about?" Amelia asked, reaching for her glass of water.

"You know exactly what I'm talking about, so stop playing dumb."

"I wasn't thinking about Trav'.

"Yeah, right," Danielle drawled, with her eyes rolling and her lips twisting. "I don't know why you keep on punishing yourself, like this. You've been stressing over him for over a month now, yet you refuse to pick up the phone and call him."

"I'm not gonna call him," Amelia said, while sipping on her water.

Miranda gave her a pitiful look. "You're not hurting anybody but yourself. Just look at you. Ever since you broke things off with Travis, you've been walking around with a sad face. You don't even go out anymore."

"Go out?" Danielle chipped in animatedly. "I can't even get her to go to the damn gym."

"I told you that I don't have the time. I've got a lot going on at work."

Miranda rolled her eyes, unbelievingly. "How much longer are you gonna keep going on, like this?" She asked. "Are you gonna wait until you're on your deathbed, to call Travis and tell him that you miss him?"

"Mom, I'm not gonna call him."

"Do you want me to call him fo' yo—"

"No!" Amelia snapped quickly. She took another sip of water, and then she put the glass away. "I'm the one who told him that we can't be together, so I guess I have to deal with the repercussions."

"You were so wrong, for doing that," Danielle said, with her head over her shredded pork with Peking sauce. "Ice went through a lot to protect you, and you repaid him with a loud fuck you. You my girl 'Melia, but you were wrong fo' doing that."

Amelia fixed her eyes on Danielle. "So he wasn't wrong, for doing what he did?" She asked.

"What did he do, other than risk his life to protect us all?" Miranda quipped. "If it wasn't for him, then I probably would've been raped and killed. And only God knows what would've happened to Aisha, if he wasn't the one who found her that night."

"Kyla would've been dead fo' sure," Danielle added.

Brows furrowed, Amelia bit into her lip before saying, "Ya'll make it sound, as if he wasn't wrong fo' lying to me."

"What was the lie that he told you?" Miranda asked.

Amelia looked at her mother for a long moment, before saying, "He could've told me that he knew Mike Simms."

"And would you have given him a chance, if he had?"

Amelia looked on thoughtfully.

"You wouldn't have," Miranda determined, as she reached out and swiped a lock of hair from in front of Amelia's face.

"Baby girl, listen to me," Miranda continued in a soft, caring tone. "We all know that you love Travis. And there's no doubt in my mind that he's crazy about you. I don't know why God chose to put you two together, the way that he did. But he did it. And honestly, I would love to see you and Travis back together. I see how he keeps you happy. And believe me, a genuinely happy relationship is not that easy to find... Why do you think that I'm still alone, after so many years?"

They all giggled quietly.

"Do you love him?" Miranda asked, after a while.

"Mom, you know that I do."

"Then call him."

"But what if he moved on?"

"There's only one way to find out... Call him."

$$\$$$

Somewhere in Orlando, Batch looked out through the peephole of his motel room door and smiled when he saw Champagne on the other side. He had been at the small, secluded town ever since Blood took his plea deal and snitched.

He hadn't had any contact with anyone in Broward County. And the only time that he left his motel room was when he had to shop for food, at the nearby corner store, or get his freak on, at a hole in the wall strip joint a few miles away. He had met Champagne at the strip joint. She was the one who approached him and told him that for a hundred dollars, he could take her home and have her to do whatever. Batch immediately jumped on the offer. He gave her the address of where he was staying, and told her to meet him there.

"Hey there handsome," Champagne smiled at Batch, after he had opened the door to let her in.

Batch stepped out of the way, with his eyes all over her bulging cleavage. "What took you so long?" He asked her.

"Car trouble," Champagne replied, as she stepped into the room. She was dressed in a skimpy jean skirt, a snug fitting sleeveless blouse, and a pair of black knee high boots. "I hope you didn't start without me," she flirted, as she walked over to the dingy sofa in the middle of the room.

Batch closed and locked the door, before stepping after her. "I wouldn't dare deprive you, of all that you're getting paid for," he chortled, as he reclaimed his spot on the sofa.

Champagne dropped her bag and then she positioned herself in front of him. "So what you wanna do?" She asked, while putting her hands on his shoulders and then setting her legs over his.

"You're the professional," Batch murmured, as she slid a hand down inside the back of his t-shirt.

"Do you want me to dance fo' you, before we get started?"

"You can, if you want to."

"Well, I want to," Champagne stated, as she started to sway her hips and grind steadily against his crotch.

After about a full minute, Batch was fully hard and throbbing. He took a deep breath before closing his eyes. "Oh baby, you're worth every damn dime," he moaned, as she started to thrust against him.

He held onto her thighs and started to feel his way, up underneath her skirt. But just as he was about to go in between her legs, there was a loud "THUD! BLAM!" of the front door being knocked in — then within a split second, a dozen police officers were charging into the room and screaming loudly, "Police! Police! Don't move! Don't fuckin' move!"

Batch shoved Champagne off of his lap and then he dove for his gun, which was on the armoire. But before he got to it, Champagne dove on top of him and she shoved his face down into the tiled floor.

"Not so fast detective Batchelor," she told him, as her partners with assault rifles aimed, formed a circle around them.

Champagne got up from on top of Batch, scowling angrily. "What the fuck took y'all so long?" She snapped, at no one in particular.

"We were giving you enough time to get your freak on," one of the officers joked.

"Freak this!" Champagne stuck both of her middle fingers up at him.

They all laughed.

Realizing that he was the main target of a raid, Batch sat up and looked around at all the unfamiliar faces, above the guns that were pointed at his chest. "What is this about, fellahs?" He asked, getting up.

"You don't know?" A tall white officer asked. "You're being arrested, mothafucka. And we're gonna tie your ass up like a pig and drag you back to Broward County."

Batch turned his head and then he looked at Champagne. "You fucking bitch, you set me up?" He snarled at her.

"My name is not fucking bitch!" Champagne snapped. Then she kicked him hard, in between the legs. "It's undercover agent, Natalie Summers. And just so you never forget, here's a reminder."

She kicked him between the legs a second time, and then walked out of the room, as he was being roughed up and cuffed.

$$$$$$$$$$$$$$$$$$$$$$$$

Decked out in a navy blue Armani suit and black glossy wing tips, Ice stood at the window of his second floor office with his hands inside of his pockets, and his eyes on all that was going on downstairs at his car lots.

No longer sporting long flowing braids, he was looking smooth with his low brush hair cut. A whole lot had changed for him since he opened up his car dealership three weeks ago. He felt good about all of the money that he was making, and he was gladly accepting his role as a successful business man. He had cars going off the lot, faster than he could replace them. And his twenty eight employees all seemed happy to be working for him.

But despite his sudden leap to success, Ice wasn't happy. He was still heartbroken, and still not wanting to move on with his life, without Amelia. There wasn't a day that he didn't think about her and how badly he missed her. He was convinced that he would never find another woman like her, so he wasn't looking. He wasn't even taking notice of all the women, who were trying to get with him; after his sudden leap to success.

With Amelia out of his life, Ice wasn't doing too much of anything. He spent the majority of his days inside of his office, trying to come up with ways to upgrade his car dealership. Then he spent his nights at home watching Sports center or BET.

He refused to believe that Amelia was out of his life for good. Nor did he want to believe that she wasn't somewhere out there, missing him. On more than a dozen occasions, he had picked up the phone to call her. But he always put it back down, after a few minutes of indecision.

After watching three pleased customers leave the dealership in their new rides, Ice turned away from the window and he walked over to his desk. He eased down inside his wing-back executive leather chair. Then he reached for the car and driver magazine that he was reading earlier. He pulled the magazine open. But just as he was about to get into it, there was a light knock on his office door that stopped him.

"Yeah, what's up?" He asked sitting up.

The door eased open, and Kym stuck her head inside of the office.

Kym was Ice's cousin, Yogi's younger sister and the managing director of the car dealership.

"You've got someone out here, looking fo' you," she said, behind a pleasant smile.   "Who is it?"

"Someone that I think you should see."

"This someone doesn't have a name?"

Kym rolled her eyes. "You wanna see this person, or not?" She asked impatiently. "I'm trying to get back to work, you know."

"You are at work," Ice smirked at her.

"Well you don't pay me to screen those who ask to see you," she replied, while pulling her head out of the office. "I'll send her in," she shouted from the hallway.

Not in the mood to be bothered by anyone, Ice went back to the magazine. He was only a few words in, when he heard the light tap on the door.

"Come in," he said, without even taking his eyes away from the magazine. He heard when the door was pushed open. He also heard when the person stepped inside of the office, but he still didn't raise his head to see who it was.

"Did I come at a bad time?"

Ice froze. The voice sent his pulse into a frenzied gallop and had his blood curdling. He took a deep breath. "Amelia?" He then muttered quietly, as he raised his head.

"Hey," she smiled a bashful smile at him. "Did I come at a bad time?" She asked again.

He sat, staring at her. Stunned, he didn't know what to say. She dropped her head and then she started playing with her fingers. "Hey, if you want me to leave then I'll leave," she said dolefully. "I just wanted to see how you were doing."

Still a bit stunned, Ice eased up out of his seat. "Please don't leave," he said, walking up to her. "It's just that I can't believe that you're actually here."

She raised her head and found him less than a yard away. Just his near presence caused her to shudder and tingle all over.

"So, how have you been?" He asked, still inching closer.

She studied him for several beats, and then she looked away. "Not as good as you," she said, admiring his lavish office. She paused for a moment and then said, "You really did good for yourself. I've been hearing and reading a lot about your dealership."

"It's doing okay, but I'm not."

She squared her shoulders and looked at him. "Why is that?" She asked quietly, warming all over, as he continued to inch closer to her.

He held her eyes with his. "I missed you, Amelia. I missed you a lot." He placed a hand on her arm and she shuddered. "I wish that I could change what happened, but I can't. And believe me, all I was trying to do was protect—"

She put a finger to his lips and then she made a small step into him. "I don't wanna talk about the past," she said, and then she ran a hand over his thick shiny waves. "Why did you cut your hair?"

He stared at her. "I wanted to step away completely from the old me. What? You don't like it?"

She smiled for the first time. "I do," She admitted. Her voice came out soft and silky smooth. "I think that it fits the new you." She dropped her head on his shoulder. "I missed you too, Trav'. I miss the times that we used to spend together."

Taking a deep breath, he hesitantly wrapped both arms around her. "Is it too late?" He asked nervously. "Is it too late, for us to work things out and get back together?"

She raised her head and then she looked him, dead in the eyes and asked, "Is that what you want?"

"More than anything," was his answer.

"That's what I want too," she revealed, still holding his eyes with hers. She wrapped her arms around his neck and brought her lips close to his. "Trav'," she hummed in a sexy, seductive way. "Could you do me a favor?"

"Anything," he whimpered against her lips.

She closed her eyes and then raised her chin. "Could you please kiss me, before I—"

He stopped her, by pressing his mouth against hers. Then just as how he had been planning to for the past six weeks, he kissed her hard, long, and passionately.

THE END

REPERCUSSIONS by SHAWN STARR

Made in the USA
Lexington, KY
14 June 2015